Praise for

The Neurodivergent Learner

"With the latest science, personal experience, and engaging narrative, Dr. Emily lights a path not just to understanding neurodivergent learners, not just to helping them function, but also to positioning them for success as students and beyond. Dr. Emily shows how to go beyond just completing school and schoolwork to benefiting from it as much as or more than any other student."

—Holden Thorp, PhD, editor in chief of *Science*

"Dr. Emily's book is the one I wish I'd had when my kids were younger. It's deeply practical, with helpful scripts and email templates, while grounding everything in how neurodivergent children's nervous systems, sensory worlds, and learning styles actually work."

—Megan Anna Neff, PsyD, AuDHD clinical psychologist, founder of Neurodivergent Insights, and author of *Self-Care for Autistic People*

"Neurodivergence is like a snowflake—no two cases are alike—so how did Dr. Emily write a book that can help *everyone*? Her approach is full of 'scripts' that will help you facilitate vital conversations with teachers, administrators, and your incredibly awesome kid. With this book, you will have everything you need to connect with your child and with the people who support them."

—Penn Holderness, *New York Times* bestselling coauthor of *ADHD Is Awesome*

"*The Neurodivergent Learner* is the resource so many families need at the very start of this journey, with the potential to help an entire generation of neurodivergent kids move through school without the trauma so many of us know all too well."

—Deborah Reber, Founder & CEO of Tilt Parenting, author of *Differently Wired*

"Instead of 'How do I help my child fit in at school?,' Dr. Emily teaches us to ask, 'How do I help the people around my child understand who they already are?' This book provides an affirming framework paired with real, usable tools and exactly what parents have been missing."

—Emily Kircher-Morris, LPC, coauthor of *Neurodiversity-Affirming Schools* and host of *The Neurodiversity Podcast*

"Expertly balancing professional and lived experience, Dr. Emily weaves a compelling narrative of actionable, interesting, and realistic interventions to help any school or family better understand and meet the needs of their child. If you work with and/or love complex kids, this book is a *must*."

—Matt Zakreski, PsyD, author of *Neurodiversity Playbook*

"This book is equally essential and brilliant—a must-read for all parents of neurodivergent children. Dr. Emily offers concrete tools and important education, often kept only in therapy offices, making them accessible and easy for parents to understand and implement."

—Jessica VanderWier, psychotherapist and founder of Nurtured First

"*The Neurodivergent Learner* is filled with tangible, principled tips for families that want to empower their autistic and ADHD children in their unique learning journey. This book asserts that all neurodivergent children deserve to lead fulfilling lives that align with how their brains and bodies actually work and helps parents figure out how to get them there."

—Devon Price, PhD, author of *Unmasking Autism*

THE
Neurodivergent Learner

THE Neurodivergent Learner

A New Approach to Your Child's Success in the Classroom and Beyond

EMILY W. KING, PhD

TEN SPEED PRESS
California | New York

TEN SPEED PRESS
An imprint of the Crown Publishing Group
A division of Penguin Random House LLC
1745 Broadway
New York, NY 10019
tenspeed.com
penguinrandomhouse.com

Library of Congress Cataloging-in-Publication Data
Names: King, Emily W., 1979– (author)
Title: The neurodivergent learner: a new approach to your child's success in the classroom and beyond / Emily W. King, PhD.
Identifiers: LCCN 2026011164 (print) | LCCN 2026011165 (ebook)
ISBN 9780593838709 hardcover | ISBN 9780593838723 trade paperback
ISBN 9780593838716 ebook
Subjects: LCSH: Neurodivergent children—Education | Students with disabilities
Home and school | Education—Parent participation
Classification: LCC LC4015 .K45 2026 (print) | LCC LC4015 (ebook)
LC record available at https://lccn.loc.gov/2026011164
LC ebook record available at https://lccn.loc.gov/2026011165

Hardcover ISBN 9780593838709
Ebook ISBN 9780593838716

Editor: Thea Diklich-Newell | Production editor: Liana Faughnan
Designer: Amani Shakrah | Production: Dan Myers | Copy editor: Janet Biehl
Proofreaders: Jane Hardick, Andrea Peabbles, Miriam Taveras, Sibylle Kazeroid, and Chris Fortunato | Indexer: J S Editorial, LLC | Publicist: David Hawk
Marketer: Brianne Sperber

Manufactured in the United States of America

1st Printing

First Edition

The authorized representative in the EU for product safety and compliance is Penguin Random House Ireland, Morrison Chambers, 32 Nassau Street, Dublin D02 YH68, Ireland, https://eu-contact.penguin.ie.

To my boys, who make my life exponentially better

Nurturing neurodivergent children isn't about changing them—it's about changing us.

Emily W. King, PhD

Contents

PART II
Supporting Your Learner

PART III
Empowering Your Learner

Introduction

Connect First, Then Teach

I had been a mother for only two years when I started noticing differences in my son's development. As I watched my friends' kids gain skills and waited for him to hit the same milestones, I felt anxious and left out. Sometimes I wondered if I was imagining it all, until his preschool teachers asked for a conference. They saw it, too. This was really happening.

As a child psychologist specializing in developmental delays, I knew what I needed to do. I scheduled evaluations, enrolled him in a specialized preschool, and found the best therapists to help him gain as many skills as possible before he entered elementary school. But my professional knowledge didn't protect me from the emotional journey of accepting that my son was on a different path than I had expected.

Becoming a parent requires us to surrender to the unknown, but as an anxiety-prone young mother, the unknown was not my jam. I thrived on making plans and sticking to them. This child had his own plan incongruent to the expectations around him. The misalignment between our expectations and his reality caused all of us such distress that I quickly realized my approach to parenting needed to change. Instead of following plans not designed for him, we had to let his needs be our guide.

Letting go of what we think our child should be and embracing the unknown is a gift. Letting go freed me from the anxiety that had been driving me to try to fit my unique child into a standardized hole. Fast-forward to today, my two neurodivergent teenage sons—who could not be more different from each other—have taught me lessons I could never have learned in graduate school. It's this unique blend of clinical expertise and lived experience that has allowed me to do the work I do with so much passion and has led me to write this book.

Over the past twenty years, I have also learned from the neurodivergent children, families, and educators I've partnered with in schools and in my psychology practice. They taught me to connect first, then teach; to take care of myself first, because our children can feel our calm; and to listen when a child is telling—or showing—us what they need. I've learned from classroom teachers who have adapted curricula and incorporated accommodations to make learning accessible for everyone. I've learned from parents who have created solutions I can then share with other families. But I've learned the most from the neurodivergent children themselves, who have become my best teachers by helping me learn what feels safe and engaging to their nervous system, so they have the capacity to learn both inside and outside the classroom. My hope is that this book will help you nurture your unique child, who is growing up learning in a world that wasn't built for them.

If your child was recently diagnosed, you may have found this book because you are desperate for resources to help you understand your child better. Or you may have come to this book in the middle of your journey, already armed with some tools and knowledge but wanting to know what else you can do to help your child. Wherever you are on your path, welcome. You will work with many professionals along the way, but this book was written to empower you to be the best advocate for your child's learning at school, at home, and in the community. You will learn how to choose the best school for your child, how to collaborate with teachers, and how to extend your child's learning beyond the classroom. I will share stories about parents on similar journeys, and you will hear the perspectives of neurodivergent children. My hope is that you will feel ready to connect with, advocate for, and walk alongside your child as they grow into their authentic, joyful self.

Connection Matters

As a child psychologist with a doctorate in school psychology, my early training focused on evaluating children for developmental delays and learning disabilities to determine whether they needed early intervention or special education services. If a child presented with a skill weakness, I would identify a diagnosis based on testing data and recommend a therapeutic intervention. This system of evaluation and recommendation was modeled after the medical system; however, if the medical system is a round hole, then child development is most certainly a square peg, with no two pegs alike. School psychologists use testing to gather the most accurate information about a child's skills in order to get them access to the support they need, but beyond the diagnostic feedback session, there is so much more we can do to help neurodivergent children.

After working in public schools in North Carolina as a school psychology practicum student, I completed my school psychology internship and postdoctoral training in a large public school district in Houston, Texas. I loved my school-based work in Houston. I served a different school every day of the week and worked with preschool through high school students who were struggling for one reason or another. While some students had a hard time learning because of ADHD or a learning disability, most of the kids and teens I served had complex emotional and behavioral concerns that interfered with learning. Many were significantly impacted by emotional dysregulation that stemmed from trauma, neurodivergence, or both. It was during my time as a school psychologist that I developed the holistic mindset I have today when thinking about nurturing the whole child, their family, and their teachers. Together we have to help kids feel safely connected to the people around them, which builds trust and leads to learning.

After I returned to North Carolina following the birth of our first son, I knew I wanted to help children beyond testing and diagnosing. I wanted to find out what was getting in the way in order to help neurodivergent learners feel more motivated, confident, and capable. They had so many untapped skills to share! I soon discovered that many of the autistic children I worked with could learn skills within the context of my office and their relationship with me, but these skills did not transfer to their home or classroom. I found cognitive behavioral therapy to be limiting for some neurodivergent clients because they struggled with the insight and attention needed to reflect on their behavior and implement strategies outside the therapy session. I began adapting games and incorporating my clients' interests so that therapy, in contrast to the world outside, was a safe place where they could feel joy and connection. I often used visuals, such as Venn diagrams, rating scales, and flow charts, to help children communicate what was going on in their brains and to scaffold our conversations. I've included some of these visual strategies in this book.

For younger neurodivergent clients, I sought additional training in the DIR/Floortime therapeutic approach, which opened my eyes to the connection between our autonomic nervous system and learning. Through play, using the DIR/Floortime approach, I was able to teach children to identify where they felt sensations in their body, learn words to match those sensations, and practice communicating their feelings to others. I helped parents and teachers connect with kids by using the same vocabulary to support the child's communication of emotions and desire for help. While I was able to help children identify and express their feelings through therapy and consultation, the stress of school still remained a constant barrier.

Learning is hard for many neurodivergent students who are overwhelmed at school. I have come to understand that neurodivergent learners need the following variables, in this order, to learn effectively: sensory safety → relational safety → pace alignment → incorporated interests → executive functioning strategies → autonomy. These are the stepping stones to empower a neurodivergent learner and thus are the framework for this book.

How to Use This Book as a Resource

I organized this book in three parts to parallel your journey as a parent: preparing your child to enter school, supporting your child through elementary school, and empowering your child outside the classroom. Part I begins with finding the best school fit for your child because they must feel safe in the space around them in order to learn. In Chapter 2, we'll discuss the importance of relationships with adults at school because children must feel safe within these interactions in order to build trust with teachers. Once children feel safe in a space and with others, their learning can begin. However, for most neurodivergent learners, we have to be mindful of their stamina to learn throughout a school day, as they manage their sensory experience and demands being placed on them, so in Chapter 3 I walk you through how to manage your child's energy. We round out Part I with Chapter 4 to help you understand how to motivate your child by incorporating their interests, being mindful of their learning pace, and expanding their frustration tolerance.

Part II focuses on supporting your child, and we begin in Chapter 5 with what so many parents dread: homework. Homework is often incongruent with neurodivergent learners' executive functioning abilities, and I offer strategies that help. In Chapter 6, I walk you through understanding test anxiety and memory skills and review accommodations that help. Beyond academics, neurodivergent learners also need support developing friendships, so Chapter 7 includes strategies for collaborating with teachers to help your child find social satisfaction. And Chapter 8 includes the most relatable experience for parents of neurodivergent children—getting a call from the school—as we discuss how anxiety impacts behavior.

Our kids are always learning, even outside the classroom, so in Part III I walk you through empowering your child to find their thing, to embrace how they learn best, and to grow in their autonomy. In Chapter 9, you'll discover ways to learn that also regulate your child's nervous system through nature, animals, movement, and music. One of the hardest learning curves for neurodivergent kids can be taking care of their bodies and their belongings, so in Chapter 10 we discuss how sensory sensitivities and executive functioning weaknesses impact self-care, and I offer strategies to support your child in these moments. As you begin thinking about building a village for your child, Chapter 11 discusses finding allies who will enrich your child's life. And in Chapter 12 we end with helping your child build self-awareness and gain as much autonomy as possible.

As you know, raising neurodivergent children is not a linear path, so while I wrote this book to be read straight through, you will also likely find it helpful to reread the chapter you need at any given moment. Feel free to jump to Chapter 5 on homework, Chapter 7 on friendships, or Chapter 8 when the school calls. Each chapter shares a story with real-life examples, science to help you understand your child, and strategies for you to implement. My goal is to leave you feeling seen, informed, and capable of walking with your child on this journey.

As you wait for your child's milestones to emerge, you may find yourself pushing too much because you don't want them to miss out. Or you may feel afraid you will upset your child, so you don't push at all. There is a sweet spot somewhere in the middle that feels like a dance between overwhelming them and enabling them. You won't always get it right, and every day will not be like the last or the next, but what I hope this book will help you do is to see the benefit of slowing down. Pause. Breathe. Observe your child. You won't know how to help until you step back to see what your child is already doing on their own.

Defining Neurodivergence

Our abilities as humans are naturally diverse, including our intelligence, sensory experience, communication, motor coordination, attention, and learning. While we are neurodiverse as a population, some of us are neurodivergent. The term *neurodiversity* first emerged in the mid-1990s among autistic adults communicating inside an online forum and was popularized by the Australian sociologist Judy Singer.[1] In 2000, the American activist Kassiane A. Asasumasu coined the term *neurodivergent* to indicate a mind that significantly diverges from our "dominant societal standards of 'normal.'"[2] In contrast, anyone whose neurocognitive abilities are considered within our dominant societal standards is considered *neurotypical.*[3] These terms paved the way for the neurodiversity movement, where we don't see every problem as a medical one to be fixed but rather a constellation of traits that warrants the acceptance of differences and the collaboration of medical, mental health, and education professionals to help neurodivergent learners thrive.

Neurodivergent individuals experience consistent struggles that often require a diagnosis in order to access support at school or in the community. For the purposes of this book, I will be focusing on types of neurodivergence related to development and learning. I have chosen to share stories, research, and strategies for children who are diagnosed with autism, attention deficit hyperactivity disorder (ADHD), a learning disability, or are identified as twice-exceptional (i.e., as intellectually gifted and also as autistic or as having ADHD or a learning disability), because they make up the largest group of neurodivergent learners receiving special education services in American classrooms. Specifically, in 2023 the National Center for Education Statistics reported that of the 15 percent of children in American public schools who have an individual education plan (IEP), the most common eligibility for services is specific learning disability (32 percent) followed by speech and language impairment (19 percent), other health impairment (used for ADHD) (15 percent), and autism (13 percent).[4] Some argue that intellectual giftedness and intellectual disability are not part of neurodivergence; however, by definition, having cognitive abilities significantly discrepant from the norm puts learners at risk of not receiving the instruction they need. No matter what your child's diagnosis, most neurodivergent learners struggle with attention, motivation, emotional regulation, and socialization, which makes learning harder for them.

Language and Lived Experience Matter

Historically, person-first language (e.g., *child with dyslexia*) has been considered more respectful than identity-first language (e.g., *dyslexic child*); however, some communities prefer identity-first language because they experience their brain wiring as a part of who they are rather than as something they have. For instance, according to the National Institutes of Health, the autistic and deaf communities most often prefer identity-first language.[5] However, preferences can vary by location, with both types of language being used in the United Kingdom and Australia, while autistic adults surveyed in the United States strongly preferred identity-first language.[6] An international survey of 875 individuals with neurodevelopmental disabilities, not just autistic individuals, indicated that 42 percent preferred identity-first language, 34 percent preferred person-first language, and 23 percent felt the terms could be used interchangeably.[7] Many parents continue to feel that identity-first language is stigmatizing, as we grew up in a generation where calling someone "autistic" was an insult, so we cannot imagine referring to our child in the same way. As a child psychologist, I defer to how the neurodivergent individual, or their caregiver (if the child does not yet understand their neurodivergence), would like to be identified.

Because most neurodivergent individuals prefer it, throughout this book I use identity-first language (e.g., *autistic child*) as opposed to person-first language (e.g., *child with autism*).

The stories you will read in this book are a mix of real experiences and stories inspired by families and educators I have worked with over the years. All names and some details have been changed to protect the privacy of those who have trusted me to walk beside them on this journey, unless they preferred to use their real names. I share quotes from real neurodivergent kids, their parents, and their teachers, as well as from neurodivergent adults who graciously described their lived experience. My goal in sharing stories from my experience as a parent and a psychologist as well as neurodivergent voices is to remind you that you are already a part of a larger community that "gets it."

You Matter

I believe I have written the book that I needed when my son was first diagnosed. It's also the kind of resource that I have wanted to give every parent I've worked with for over twenty years. I hope this book helps you gain confidence in partnering with your child to show them that learning doesn't just happen in one place and isn't limited to childhood. Instead, learning happens anywhere and anytime our abilities and motivations collide, sparking the curiosity that propels us to grow. While this book focuses on how your child learns, my hope is you will keep learning from the lived experience of neurodivergent adults, other parents on this journey, and the teachers who are ready to collaborate with you along the way. Above all, I want you to know that you are far from alone. There will be hard days, and because of those hard days, you will have moments of joy that you will come to treasure.

A long time ago I started living life one school year at a time. Somehow those school years added up to an education for my son. You don't have to have all the answers right now, and you're not supposed to. Your child will teach you to be patient, open-minded, and curious as you figure out the next best step. One day you will look back and realize that your child has learned so much more than you ever thought possible. And so have you.

Part I

Preparing Your Learner

Chapter 1

School Readiness and Fit

"My school feels good to me."

As a child psychologist working with neurodivergent children, my goal is never to make a child more neurotypical. I don't believe that ADHD is something to be fixed or that autism is something to be cured. As human beings, we are meant to be biologically diverse, and that includes our brains. Yet we have been led to believe that there is one way for children to be successful: through academic achievement. In order to successfully achieve, we have to pay attention, follow directions, complete assignments, and make good grades—all tasks that neurodivergent learners struggle with because they involve emotional regulation and executive functioning skills.

Over the last twenty years in my work with neurodivergent leaners, rather than "fixing" neurodivergence, I have focused on helping these uniquely complex children recover from the anxiety and sadness they experience growing up in a world that wasn't built for them. There are countless ways they've redefined and found success, and I'll share many of those in this book. However, I always come back to the external stressor that I can't control from inside the therapy room, and an area where I know so many parents of neurodivergent children need extra help: school. School is hard for neurodivergent learners, not because they aren't trying hard enough—quite the opposite. These kids are often expending most of their energy to remain still and pay attention amid the pace, noise, seatwork, testing, and socialization that comes with learning in a classroom. As parents, we want our children to feel happy, included, and confident in the classroom, but many aspects of the general education classroom are misaligned with how our kids learn. If we respond by teaching them strategies to manage their anxiety about school but not by changing the underlying cause of why school is hard for them in the first place, neurodivergent learners will continue to struggle. I believe we can change the system from the inside out by staying curious and collaborative with teachers, following our kids' interests, and celebrating their individualized successes along the way.

Our first assignment as parents of neurodivergent kids is to find the best learning environment we can for them. Let's start with the story of Micah and his mom, Laura, who called me because she was perplexed by her son's distress about school.

Micah's Story

I first met Laura in the waiting room of my therapy office after we had spoken on the phone about Micah, who had recently started kindergarten. Laura was at a loss as to why her son seemed to do fine once he got into school but had melted down at home every morning and afternoon since the school year began. "He never did this in preschool," she explained. "We were in a great routine, and he never resisted leaving me at drop-off."

As I thumbed through Laura's intake paperwork, I saw that Micah had attended a half-day preschool, so he had some prior school experience. When I asked Laura to picture the morning and the school day from Micah's perspective and describe the differences she noticed between preschool and kindergarten, her words described two very different learning environments. Preschool had been a four-hour school day housed in a cozy church full of familiar people, multiple recess opportunities, and hands-on learning. Kindergarten consisted of several classrooms in a much larger building, new people, frequent transitions, and more noise.

I could see the realization unfold on Laura's face as she explained the difference in environments: Kindergarten was more of a sensory processing load for Micah, who had always struggled with sensory demands. We dug into Micah's developmental history of not sleeping through the night until he was a year old, having trouble tolerating abrupt noises as a toddler, experiencing tactile sensitivity to clothing, and struggling with independent toileting. Micah was likely overwhelmed and exhausted by the end of the school day and anxious the next morning about what was to come. The good news was that once Micah was in the classroom, he did well, but his stress before and after school indicated that his efforts during the school day left him little energy for anything else. While he had settled into a rhythm at his preschool by four years old, the transition to an elementary school building was proving more difficult. After school, he needed time to recover with his mom at home, where he felt safest.

I wondered if Micah was struggling because he was not developmentally ready for the demands of the environment around him, while Laura felt he needed to start school because he was academically bored in preschool. Herein lies a common dilemma for parents raising neurodivergent children with uneven skills: They are ready to learn, but not always within the overwhelming environment of a traditional school building. Many neurodivergent learners are not yet able to identify or communicate what feels overwhelming to them. And most general education teachers don't have the training to identify the sensory overwhelm and anxiety that can be mistaken for oppositional behavior. Laura and I began discussing what support would help Micah not feel so overwhelmed at school, because before he could effectively learn, he would need to feel relaxed in his body and safe with the people around him.

Accessing Support in Public Versus Private School

In public school, your child may qualify to receive support through a 504 plan or an individualized education plan (IEP). Students identified with a disability who qualify for a 504 plan may receive accommodations like extended time on tests, taking tests in a separate setting, or preferential seating. Students who need a higher level of support, such as specialized instruction with a special education teacher or flexibility on the part of the general education teacher to modify the curriculum, may qualify for an IEP. These decisions are made by school-based teams in public schools, which you are a part of as the parent.

Private schools may offer learning support plans, but they are not required by law to educate everyone regardless of ability, and it is not guaranteed they will have staff trained to meet your child's needs. That means that private schools can ask your child to leave if they don't feel they can support them. The exception here is private schools that specialize in educating neurodivergent learners. These schools, however, are not required by law to educate everyone, and they may have limits for supporting a child who is physically aggressive, for instance. But most specialized private schools have smaller classes and teachers trained to understand autism, ADHD, or learning disabilities.

Laura's story is similar to my own. My son had been successful in preschool programs with minimal support. We knew that kindergarten would ask more of him, yet even with all the accommodations we had in place, the sensory demands of the elementary school building overwhelmed him, and he was often in a state of fight-or-flight. Through many IEP meetings, additional evaluations, teacher conferences, and therapist consultations, we were able to find the best learning environment for him in a smaller classroom within our public school district.

As you will discover throughout this book, in order to effectively access the skills needed to learn, a child must feel safe in their environment, in their relationship with their teachers, and within their own body. When parents of neurodivergent kids talk about a school, activity, or person being a good "fit," what they mean is that their child's skills and strengths are aligned with the setting and the relationships around them. This goodness of fit is important because neurodivergent children often have more sensitive nervous systems and are corrected more often than their neurotypical peers, which can lead to feelings of hypervigilance or frequently believing they are in trouble. Our primary goal for children, but especially our neurodivergent learners, is to help them feel safe, connected, and trusting of those teaching them so they are more available to learn. That's why we need their school to *feel* good, and safe, to them.

Lived Experience

"The extremely bright fluorescent lighting in the hallways and classrooms during the early morning hours creates a significant challenge for me in terms of maintaining focus and concentration." —Nolan, age nine

"I think the fire alarm is one of my least favorite things about school. Unexpected fire drills can make me agitated and always impact the rest of the day. At lunchtime there is also the problem of the many smells; the different foods all mixed together make me feel overwhelmed and sick. It can often upset me for hours after." —Alicia, age eleven

What the Science Says About Sensory Safety

Over the years I have noticed parallels in how neurodivergent learners and students with a history of trauma experience school. One early example of working with students with trauma has always stuck with me: When I was a psychology intern in Houston, I saw an elementary student being physically restrained. This child had become physically aggressive toward staff, and while he wasn't (to my knowledge) neurodivergent, his behavior was similar to many of the reactions I'd seen from neurodivergent children in classroom environments that felt unsafe to them. I'm sure the school administrator felt she was keeping everyone safe; however, looking back on this, I doubt the student himself felt safe. His trust in the adults around him was deteriorating before my eyes. There had to be a better way.

In my work with autistic children, specifically, I continued noticing that their nervous system responses were similar to those of students with trauma. No matter if their upset came from a loud, unexpected noise or from a teacher asking them to get out a pencil in a rushed tone, both seemed closer to emotional dysregulation than their neurotypical peers. Both neurodivergent students and those with trauma histories were hypervigilant in their own way; they were busy surviving. These observations set me on a journey as a school psychologist—trained to evaluate, identify, and plan support for students—to discover how stress and anxiety impacted learning. As adults, we know that stress interferes with our attention and productivity, but children often don't yet have the insight to understand where their upset is coming from. To truly understand the intersection of stress and learning so we can help neurodivergent learners adapt, we have to get to know our nervous system.

Autonomic Nervous System

Our autonomic nervous system is responsible for regulating bodily functions that we don't even think about, like our breathing, heart rate, and digestion. When our nervous system is in a parasympathetic state of resting and digesting, we are considered to be inside our "window of tolerance," feeling calm, balanced, and engaged. However, when our autonomic nervous system perceives a threat, it switches into a sympathetic or hyperaroused state, leading to a fight-or-flight response. This process, called neuroception, signals a reaction in our body to protect us before we have time to even think about it. If the threat of danger persists despite our fight-or-flight reaction, our autonomic nervous system shifts into a hypoaroused state of shutdown or freeze. (See figure on page 20.)

Now, think about what Micah's body and brain were experiencing during the transition into school every morning. He must have been feeling overwhelmed by something he recalled from the day before and was not yet feeling sufficiently safe or capable of transitioning with ease. His sympathetic nervous system had taken over, signaling threat of overwhelm and making routine tasks feel daunting. In order to help this transition feel less threatening, Laura and I needed to brainstorm how to help him expand his capacity to tolerate emotions, as well as collaborate with his teacher to help him feel safer at school drop-off.

Window of Tolerance

We all have a unique capacity for emotional regulation based on our brain wiring and lived experience. The psychiatrist and researcher

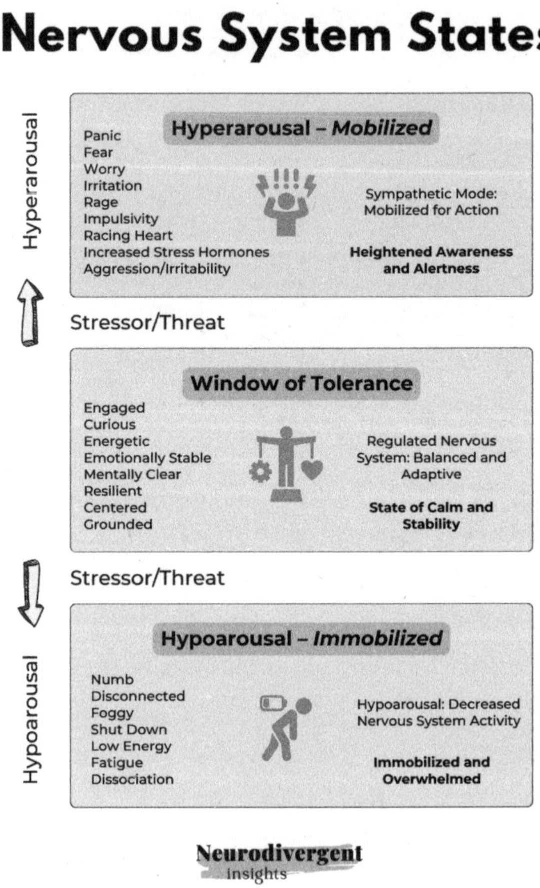

Megan Anna Neff, PsyD

Daniel J. Siegel described this optimal zone of emotional regulation as the window of tolerance. For some people, the window of tolerance is wide, which leads to flexibility, while other people have a narrow window, which makes them more prone to stress that pushes them outside their comfort zone more easily and more often.

Inside the window of tolerance, our emotions are well integrated, creating room for us to access curiosity, problem-solving, and collaboration. However, as stress increases and we are pushed outside the window, our thinking can become rigid or chaotic, making learning, problem-solving, and communicating more difficult. As Siegel suggests, outside this emotionally integrated window, "the 'higher' cognitive functions of abstract thinking and self-reflection are shut down. The prefrontal circuits linking these cortical processes with the highly discharged limbic centers are functionally blocked, and rational thought becomes impossible."[1] In other words, when a person is pushed outside their window of tolerance, their nervous system has gone into a state of fight-or-flight, and they are not able to access the part of their brain needed to reason with information and make decisions. In this moment it doesn't matter how intelligent a child is; if they cannot access their executive functioning, communication, or problem-solving skills, information is not getting in or out.

Siegel's window-of-tolerance framework offers an alternative perspective on the "noncompliant" neurodivergent child because it shows us that the child may not be choosing negative behavior but is having an unconscious response in order to protect themself from something that feels overwhelmingly difficult. Due to their sensory sensitivities, their difficulty making predictions about—or waiting for—what comes next, and their challenges with emotional regulation, neurodivergent individuals appear to have a narrower window of tolerance, more easily getting pushed into fight, flight, or shutdown.[2] This explains why the autistic students I worked with seemed to react in ways so similar to those who had experienced trauma—they were experiencing trauma, too, but to them the threat was a busy, crowded classroom. Their nervous systems were doing what they were evolutionarily wired to do to feel safe; it's just that their perceptions of danger differed from those of a neurotypical brain. For these reasons, it's important to notice our child's pattern of triggers so we can create sensory-safe environments for them, which will help expand their window of tolerance.

Understanding Sensory Safety

I recently took one of my sons to a college basketball game. He loves sports, seeing the players up close, and relishes the fanfare.

However, once we were at the game, he developed a stomachache that would come and go. He was tired from a recent sleepover, and his patience with the referees was growing short. I couldn't figure out the cause for his stomachache, and I certainly couldn't control the refs, but I did have earplugs. He hadn't complained about the noise, but I wondered what would happen if we took one sensory experience down a notch. It worked. With the sound dampened from the earplugs, he locked into watching the game and seemed to forget about his stomachache.

Sensory processing refers to our ability to register, regulate, and organize incoming sensory information for the purpose of responding to the stimuli in our environment.[3] Our capacity to handle environmental sensory input ebbs and flows depending on a number of factors. Our window of tolerance tends to shrink when we are tired, sick, overwhelmed, or uncomfortable and to expand when we are rested, well, confident, and safe. As adults, we can recognize our sensory needs, problem-solve, and adapt to or avoid overwhelming environments. However, when children are overwhelmed, adults have to help them feel sensory safe, whether that sensitivity is happening internally, as with a stomachache, or coming from an external factor, like a basketball arena or a classroom.

Sensory processing differences are often associated with behaviors that reduce a child's engagement in school and overall well-being.[4] While sensory processing differences affect 13 to 16 percent of neurotypical children,[5] 93 to 96 percent of autistic individuals have sensory differences, and individuals with ADHD experience significantly higher sensory sensitivity, avoidance, and seeking behaviors, compared to those without ADHD.[6] It's clear to see how each neurodivergent learner comes to school with a unique nervous system influenced by individualized sensory differences, previous experiences, and their own window of tolerance.

How to Determine School Fit and Readiness

Once we sorted through what Laura felt was overwhelming Micah, we problem-solved how she could collaborate with Micah's teacher to reduce demands at school and increase support at home. Laura and the teacher came up with a carpool transition plan based on Micah's love of math. Each morning, while they put on his shoes and got into the car, Laura was able to distract him by asking him to solve addition problems. Then Micah's teacher met him every day at carpool with a notecard containing a new math equation. The distraction of this preferred task kept Micah comfortably inside his window of tolerance and proved to him that he was safe with his teacher because she was showing up with something he loved as he transitioned into school. Approaching this from both Laura and the teacher's perspectives helped reduce Micah's anxiety during school drop-off. Below you will find ideas for determining the best school fit for your child, for promoting sensory safety, and for best preparing them for the transition into school.

Think About the School Environment

Imagine Your Child in the Space

The most important thing you can do is think about the school environment with your child's sensory sensitivities, activity level, and interests in mind. While trusting relationships are crucial for your child's sense of safety at school, before they meet their teacher and classmates, the building has to feel good to them. If you are concerned that the space and sounds of the building will be overwhelming or if you think your child will not get enough movement throughout the day, work with school staff to incorporate movement, music, time outside, and engaging with their interests into their school day. These all promote emotional regulation and widen a child's window of tolerance. Remember, no school is the best school, and no school is perfect. There are only schools that are the best fit for *your child.*

Ask the School Staff Your Questions

If you get to choose your child's school, talk with school staff to determine the best learning environment for your child. Here are several questions to ask:

- How many students and teaching assistants are in each class?
- What are the nonacademic options for student learning throughout the day (e.g., art, music, theater, physical education, dance)?
- How many recess opportunities per day do you offer?
- How many transitions are there throughout the day?
- Is there a calming sensory space students can use for a break?
- How much homework is assigned each night?
- How do you support students who need help completing their work?

Notice How Your Child Feels About School

When your child is in the best learning environment *for them,* they won't resist going to school. They may have some anxiety in the beginning, but once they are settled in, you will be able to tell if their school feels good to them simply by observing their mood in the morning. In addition to school drop-off, notice your child's mood when they get into the car or off the bus at the end of the day. Are they irritable more days than not? This could indicate a problem you want to ask their teacher about. If your child has communication differences, you will need to establish direct communication with the teacher from the beginning.

Ideas That Promote Sensory Safety

When you visit your child's school, think about the lighting, noise, crowdedness, and smells as well as what they might need when one of those senses is overwhelmed. Here are some ideas:

- If fluorescent lighting bothers your child, ask if the lights can be lowered and lamps be used during certain times of day to promote calm.
- To concentrate, to enter loud spaces, or for fire drills, use noise-canceling headphones or earplugs. It's even better if these are available for everyone to normalize sensory accommodations.
- If the smells or noise of the cafeteria are overwhelming to your child, ask if they have the option to eat in a teacher's classroom, or if the school counselor hosts a social group during lunchtime.
- Request flexible seating, where a child can sit on a bean bag, stand, or lie down on the floor while working with a clipboard or reading.
- If your child is a sensory-seeker and needs additional movement, ask if they can run errands to get extra energy out before seatwork.
- Make sure sensory rooms are being used not as a consequence but as a preventive strategy for when your child feels their overwhelm building.

Preparing Your Child Before School Begins

If you feel your child's learning environment is already the best fit, but they need additional support during the transition of starting school, here are ways to best prepare them.

Get Your Child Used to the Space

Think about how your child processes new information. If your child needs to *see* a space without simultaneously *feeling* a space, use photos to introduce the school building and staff. Some kids love maps and numbers, so you can use that strength to explain the room numbers, or get a map of the building from the school to help them establish a picture in their mind. Once you feel your child understands what the school looks like, visit the school before the first day so they can get used to the physical space without classmates. That way, on the first day, they will be used to the building layout and will just need to process the people. Experiencing all the newness at once can be overwhelming, so breaking it down into smaller steps is a helpful approach.

Help Your Child "Meet" the People Before Meeting the People

When our kids first meet people, they are processing many things. *Am I familiar with this person? How do they know my name? Do they seem nice? How much will I see them at school? What do I say? Am I supposed to look at them, or is looking away okay?* An autistic child might not be able to communicate the sensory and social effort it takes when meeting new people, but they are likely feeling it. An ADHD child may need to use their energy for learning rules rather than faces. In order to help your child process new faces and the roles of each person, without the sensory and social load of meeting them at the same time, gather digital photos of the adults your child will meet so they can scroll through them to increase familiarity. Identify which teachers will help with what topics and which rooms and people match the routine your child is building in their mind. Some children benefit from a video call with their new teacher and a recorded video tour of the classroom so they can get to know them and the space without leaving the comfort of home. That way, when they meet their teacher in person, they will already look familiar, and your child will likely have an easier time processing the sensory and social demands of the experience.

Make Things as Predictable as Possible

If you are raising an autistic child, you already know your child thrives when routines are predictable. Children with ADHD or processing weaknesses also rely on routines so they don't have as much to keep up with. While all kids benefit from structure, a lack of structure can be emotionally overwhelming to the neurodivergent learner. Simply telling them the plan is not enough to prepare them for what's coming. Autistic children often process information much faster visually than auditorily, and ADHD brains rely on visuals to support working memory weaknesses. Creating visual lists, routines, and schedules is the most effective way to help them understand a new routine. Use this visual schedule as consistently as possible; you'll soon be able to step back as your child learns how to use the list independently. They may even memorize it!

It's helpful to begin using a morning routine a few days before the first day of school so you can see how your child responds to it. Involve them in creating the visual plan, especially if they have opinions about the order of the routine, so they can feel ownership in the process. For children who are not yet reading, a visual plan can include drawings or photographs of familiar items, like their shoes, toothbrush, or backpack. For a child who is reading, this visual can simply be a checklist on a whiteboard in the kitchen. There are three different levels of visuals you might find helpful: (1) family calendars (when), (2) checklists (what), and (3) step-by-step of a task (how).

Practice Student Skills at Home

Practice Asking for Help

One of the best ways to prepare children for school is to have them practice asking for help and waiting for an answer. Young neurodivergent learners may not be able to identify when they are frustrated, much less communicate their needs, but these are two very important skills to work on over time. During their school journey, things will feel too hard, too much, and too lengthy, so create a goal for your child to be able to identify this feeling and ask for help, even if they communicate it nonverbally. If your child cannot yet say, "I need help" when they are frustrated, identify a gesture or word that indicates "help." (Raising a hand works!) Practice noticing your child's overwhelm and prompt them to use their "help" signal. This way, if your child struggles to ask for help, but you have come up with a plan that works at home, you can tell your child's teacher about their "help" signal so they can use it during the school day.

Practice Movement Breaks While Sharing Space with Others

In many cases, movement breaks are problem-solved along the way, as teachers notice that a child needs to move more often than scheduled break times allow. If you have already found a strategy that's helpful, coach your child on standing or moving their body but staying in their space. For instance, you may have a strategy at home during dinner that works, such as allowing your child to stand or pace while eating or telling a story. Or you may not have a strategy and worry that your child will need to move more than allowed. Talk with your child's teacher about how they can access movement breaks, and share ideas that have worked before, such as running errands, doing wall push-ups, or being allowed to stand or sit on the floor while working.

Teaching Your Child to Wait

When learning in a group, there is waiting time. Your child's teacher will not always be able to begin when your child is ready or be able to answer your child's question right away. Think about how your child waits at home, and share this reality with their teacher. By design, classrooms are more structured and predictable than our homes, so your child may very well adapt to the natural structure of taking turns in school, but if they need help waiting, classroom jobs are my favorite strategy. To reduce idle time in the morning, brainstorm with your child's teacher to make sure your child has a job to start their day. This gives an active child an intentional way to move their body, such as handing out pencils or running an errand, and a sense of accomplishment as a part of the classroom community, all of which lead to feelings of connection and competence before the learning begins.

Give Teachers a Crash Course on Your Kid

Teachers Helping Teachers

Teachers are busy people and usually operate with a no-news-is-good-news mindset. If you think it would be beneficial for your child's new teacher to talk to your child's previous teacher, connect them! For instance, talk with your child's preschool teacher about strategies that have worked during circle/carpet time, and relay this information or give permission for teachers to speak directly. Teachers love to share ideas that prepare their colleagues to help a student, and while they likely don't have time to connect with every single teacher of all their students, neurodivergent learners need this extra step.

All About Me, Neurodivergent Style

On the first day of school, many teachers will have a child complete an "All About Me" worksheet to share their favorite color, favorite animal, who they live with at home, and what they did this summer. However, these details don't tell us anything about a child's skills, emotional regulation, or executive functioning needs. I recommend that parents of neurodivergent learners create an "All About My Child" one-pager for their child's teacher. (For an example, visit learnwithdremily.com/downloads.) Introducing the teacher to your child based on their skills and regulation needs in addition to their interests gives them a head start in creating a safe learning space for them. For instance, if talking to your child when they are emotionally dysregulated causes more upset, your teacher needs to know this up front so they can give them time and space before offering a solution. This kind of front-loading strategy will help save the teacher time and prevent stress for your child, which will benefit everyone.

Predict What Your Child Will Need Help With

You already know which skills your child has not yet mastered. If your child is not yet able to identify their emotions and ask for help due to emotional regulation and communication differences, it's helpful to let your child's teacher know that they will need support with this from the get-go. You may feel that other skills are emerging, as in, your child can sometimes do these things independently but only when they are rested or the house is quiet. Share circumstances that make your child successful, so their teacher can encourage the growth of these skills through scaffolding. Scaffolding may look like assigning a peer helper to demonstrate, using a visual checklist, or practicing independent tasks outside of chaotic transition times. If there is a skill that your child is independent with, share that with their teacher, too! Teachers always want to know what your child is capable of; it's one less thing for them to problem-solve. Also, know that it's possible your child will become more independent at school than at home due to the structure and routine of the classroom. Don't take this personally—independence anywhere is a success! Stay in communication with your child's teacher about what they are capable of so you don't fall into the trap of helping them with skills at home that they can actually do on their own.

Share What Boredom Looks Like for Your Child

Neurodivergent learners are at more risk for boredom than their peers often due to their short attention spans or their tendency to find their own thoughts more interesting. Explain to your child's teacher what it looks like when your child gets bored. For example, do they put their head down or start doodling, or do they ask a million questions? Instead of leaving a teacher to figure out why your child is engaging in a certain behavior, let their teacher know if your child has a consistent go-to "I'm bored" behavior, so they won't assume your child is just "being difficult" and so they can support their boredom with a strategy that helps them learn to wait quietly.

Stay Collaborative and Curious for Flexible Solutions

Sometimes your child might be supported in the general education classroom but will also need to meet with a special education or gifted education teacher, or both! Stay open to whatever combination of support your child benefits from. Helping your child understand that their teachers also have different strengths in teaching them will help normalize their own uneven skill development.

Tip: Social Stories

When you visit a new school, either alone or with your child to meet the teacher, take pictures of spaces and people so your child can scroll through the pictures later to get used to the visuals of the space and process this new information. If your child is reading or if you would like to read them a story about their school morning drop-off or school day, you can incorporate these pictures into a social story to help them process the details of the transition, drop-off, or school day before they experience it. A social story, first created by Carol Gray, is written from the child's point of view, at their language level, and creates a moment of connection with a safe caregiver to walk through a new situation. Social stories help lower a child's anxiety by helping them know what's coming next and is well documented in the research for reducing negative behavior.[7]

When to Be Concerned: Leaving a School

There may be times during your child's school journey when you question school fit. Unfortunately, this is common among parents of neurodivergent learners because it can be hard to tell the difference between a tough day and a situation that might make your child hate school for years to come. I am never concerned about a onetime hard situation, but I am concerned about a pattern of hard situations. Keep these ideas in mind to guide you:

- If your child is resisting going to school on a daily basis, or on the first day back from a weekend or break, begin working on a plan to ease their anxiety about the transition into school. However, if their resistance persists for weeks or months, it might not be the best fit.

- If your child needs a higher level of support, talk to teachers about what's available at your child's school. Many neurodivergent learners can stay in the school where they are, or at least in the same school district, but they need a smaller classroom for part of the day, specially trained staff to work with them more closely, or accommodations to reduce their anxiety. However, if the school isn't able to support what you think your child needs, then it might be time to consider another option.
- If you don't have another option outside your local public school, and there are things about the school that you cannot change—like the size of the building, the number of kids in the classroom, or a culture that doesn't feel accepting of your child—talk to the principal, school counselor, or school psychologist about your concerns to see if they have any ideas for flexible solutions.

Teacher Email Script: All About My Child

Dear [Kindergarten Teacher],

Welcome to a new school year! I'm writing to give you a little background on my son's development, share strategies that we've figured out help support his engagement with learning, and tell you more about his interests. [Child] is the youngest of two boys and he was diagnosed with ADHD when he was in preschool. He's very active and moves quickly but is also very joyful and social. He tends to need lots of movement to help him balance classroom expectations to sit and stay in his space.

At home, it's helpful to distract him at times of transition with a "helping job" like unlocking my car or carrying my water bottle to the car. [Child] LOVES to build LEGO sets and can hyperfocus on this at times, but we've also used LEGO bricks in math to help engage him with learning.

[Child] is already reading, so if he seems bored with learning letters, you might see him put his head down. I am happy to send in some of his favorite books that he loves to look at when he has to wait; this is a strategy I've found helpful if he has to wait for his brother to finish getting ready.

I hope this is helpful in giving you a head start connecting with our little guy. We think he's pretty great and look forward to partnering with you this school year!

Thank you for all you do,
[Your name here]

Kid Chat Script: Talking to Your Child About a New School

You can introduce your child to the idea of their new school by pointing out similarities to things they are already familiar with and positive attributes you think will spark their excitement. These conversations might go something like this:

> Introducing the idea of the school: *You know how you love having two recesses at preschool? Well, you will still get to have two recesses in kindergarten, but the playground is even bigger! Let's go visit this weekend to play on the playground, and we can check it out.*

Prepping for meeting teachers: *You know how you love LEGO sets? Well, I've already talked to your kindergarten teacher, and she has LEGO building as a free-time activity! We're going to meet her today, and we'll check out her LEGO collection to see what you think.*

Preparing for the first day of school: *You know how you had a cubby, circle time, playtime, and learning time in preschool? You'll have all that in kindergarten, too, but the people will be new. You've already met your teacher and checked out her LEGO sets and the classroom. Today will be similar but with more kids. If anything feels like too much, you can go to your teacher for help. I'm your helping person at home, and your teacher is your helping person at school. I'll be ready to give you a big hug when I pick you up today!*

Chapter 2

Building a School Family

"My teacher gets me."

From the moment you held your baby, you likely felt the nurture instinct kick in. Your body may have softened, your voice likely dropped to a hush, and you may have rhythmically swayed to help your baby feel safe. We are biologically wired as mammals to share our calm with our infants. This is *coregulation,* or the ability to manage our emotions and behavioral responses with the help of another person. As humans, we are naturally drawn to protect our most vulnerable, and it's in these early interactions that infants and caregivers begin the reciprocal dance of attachment.

John Bowlby and Mary Ainsworth defined the stages of attachment in the mid-1950s,[1] outlining that children initially become attached to their primary caregiver and subsequently learn to trust caregivers beyond this first relationship. Over time Bowlby's ideas received criticism for being narrowly focused on the mother-child relationship, not taking into account relationships formed by fathers and grandparents.[2] Also, some researchers argue that attachment is more fluid than Bowlby and Ainsworth originally proposed and that our attachment style can change throughout life based on our relationships and lived experience.[3]

I believe the latter is especially true for neurodivergent learners who often rely on relationships beyond their primary caregivers, like teachers and therapists, for coregulation away from home. This is the village many parents raising neurodivergent kids talk about, and this community is necessary to support the growth of our complex children. As a parent and professional, the work of the pediatric psychologist Mona Delahooke has always guided me in better understanding how coregulation develops within the primary caregiving relationship and then expands from there. As Delahooke explains, a child enters the first stage of social and emotional development, called regulation and attention, through the first interaction with their primary caregiver.[4]

For instance, when your child cried as an infant, you provided attention by soothing them, and so they learned to trust that you, a more emotionally regulated person, would help them feel better. Trusting another person to help us feel better is at the root of emotional safety and the development of self-regulation. As long as a child feels safe, they will develop more social engagement and connection with the world around them. For example, when a child smiles and coos at their caregiver, over time these interactions evolve into feeling emotionally safe within surrounding relationships.

While the timing of every child's social milestones varies, this reciprocal dance of connected communication often begins before children have even spoken words. For instance, if a child wants an object across the room but is not yet walking, they will use their body to reach or point. As parents learn their child's communication cues, these reciprocal interactions grow in complexity. A parent can hide their face with their hands, use a questioning tone of voice indicating confusion, and then reveal their smiling face to the baby in shared surprise. What a fun game! These playful interactions help keep young children emotionally regulated and connected by allowing their nervous system to practice the feeling of excitement away from their caregiver and return to safety as needed. This dance encourages both the parent and the child to keep coming back for more. This game of peek-a-boo is an example of building what the psychologist and researcher Stephen W. Porges calls the "social engagement system."

As a child's communication expands to include social problem-solving, they will begin expressing what feels wrong in their environment. There will be problems like no more milk, uncomfortable diapers, and broken toys that toddlers and parents solve together through gestures, tone of voice, and single words or phrases. Children begin to feel the power of expressing their opinions, asking questions, and describing their feelings either through spoken words or actions.[5] And throughout these experiences, children begin to understand who they can trust to help them get their needs met, and to discover preferences for interactions that bring them joy.

Now, think back to your own child's first few years of life. Did anything disrupt this dance of social engagement? Was your child hard to soothe? Did they have difficulty communicating? Were they more interested in objects than in people? While it's well known that children with disrupted caregiving due to adoption or living in foster care can struggle to build secure attachments, differences in neurobiology—such as autism, ADHD, and sensory processing differences—can also impact the early parent-child dynamic. If a young child is exceptionally fussy or active, parents are likely exhausted in the first few years. I experienced this when one of my sons was especially hard to feed and the other was not able to sleep through the night for the first year of his life. Even though I'm a trained professional who saw these disruptions in feeding and sleep as early signs of sensory sensitivities, it was still difficult. For new parents, or those without a background in child development, this can be an especially confusing time.

When I first meet with parents of school-age children in my psychology practice to discuss their child's behavior, I always ask a seemingly unrelated but very important question: How easy was your child to soothe as an infant? While I'm looking for a child's history of sensory sensitivities and emotional regulation, I'm also wondering how effortful coregulation has been for the parent. You may have felt you were doing something wrong with your poor sleeper or picky eater, but looking back on your child's ability to be soothed can give you clues about their biological patterns of sensory and emotional regulation to help you understand that you did nothing wrong. The way we coregulate with children evolves as they grow up and is influenced by their ability to self-soothe and their physical size, as well as our stamina to remain emotionally regulated alongside them. In other words, we don't coregulate with a third grader in the same way we would soothe a toddler, but if they're neurodivergent, that might be exactly what they need.

Children are often expected to be able to self-regulate by the time they're of school age. However, children who experience a developmental difference, such as autism, a sensory processing difference, or a high activity level, often require coregulation into the elementary years, and when they don't receive it, it tends to lead to negative behavior. This can be a frustrating time for parents raising neurodivergent children, as they start to notice that school is harder for their child. In this chapter, we're going to look at the importance of building a school family to expand your child's secure, safe, and connected attachments in order to create a wider circle of coregulation to support their learning.

Ethan's Story

When Sarah first brought her ten-year-old son, Ethan, to my therapy office, I could tell he had come against his will. Even though sunlight was streaming into my cheerful waiting room, he sat hunched over on the comfy couch, arms crossed, head down, his face in a scowl. I didn't take one bit of this personally because I knew that he was just having a hard time.

In order to get to know Ethan better, I needed him to trust me. From my previous conversations with Sarah, I knew that he was struggling with transitioning away from screens, doing what his parents asked, and completing homework—basically anything non-preferred was overwhelming for him. Ethan's parents were exhausted from walking on eggshells and felt they couldn't take him anywhere in the community without fear of a rude outburst. Sarah also struggled to believe that anyone else could handle supporting his mood and behavior, so she was having trouble trusting his teachers.

But Ethan had gotten out of the car and walked into my office, so that was our first win. I had coached his parents on explaining to him who I am and what we do here, prior to meeting me, so he could feel comfortable. Results from this strategy vary. Some children are highly anxious and need a parent to join them in the therapy playroom. Some are anxious to separate but are quickly distracted by my extensive collection of fidgets. And some are like Ethan. No matter how many games I have or fidgets I offer, they don't notice them because they are outside their window of tolerance, busy managing their feelings. Ethan was also a tween, defined as ages nine to twelve years old, and I knew that his own opinions were becoming stronger by the day. Most tweens and teens struggle to imagine what a therapist can offer that might be worth their time.

I knew from my conversation with Ethan's parents that he was autistic, intellectually gifted, and dyslexic and that he loved to build things. As a therapist to neurodivergent kids, my only goals for the first session are to (1) discover what catches a child's engagement and (2) build trust. Yes, it's important for me to know that Ethan is autistic, gifted, and dyslexic, but those details only shape the context of our work together; they don't allow me in. I wanted to hear all about his interests because interest sparks engagement, and when kids start communicating about something they love, you can see the anxiety that grips their body slowly releasing its hold. In other words, as trust in the relationship builds, anxiety starts to melt away. This moment is magical to watch.

But Ethan appeared stuck on my waiting room couch. His brain was likely flooded with negative emotions ranging from anger about being at this appointment to anxiety about what he imagined was about to happen. My guess was that somewhere underneath it all he was also sad that everything felt so hard. In his current state, he couldn't verbally communicate any of this to me because he was outside his window of tolerance. He was instinctively using his sense of neuroception, the neural process that evaluates risk in an environment, to determine whether it was safe to engage with me. Despite his gifted intelligence, Ethan's autonomic nervous system wasn't feeling safe enough for his social engagement system to communicate. I knew I couldn't reach him through conversation; his brain, and more specifically his nervous system, was not ready to connect. It's this felt-safety through connection with others that helps us return to our window of tolerance. More specifically, it's within this felt-safety that our social engagement system allows us to trust the people around us so we can engage in play and learning.

I could have approached Ethan with a verbal request to come sit down and get started playing a game. Even though this is not a threatening idea to an emotionally regulated child, his brain was in a stress state, and any demands, even the task of joining a game with a new person, likely felt threatening. So I moved forward with the assumption that he didn't have the energy to "care" about anything I was saying. All his energy was tied up processing his emotions.

I started with a short tour of my office. Once I helped Ethan orient to his new surroundings and showed him how he could get his needs met if he was thirsty or needed to use the bathroom, he was able to see that I was interested in taking care of him before asking anything of him. This was the first step in establishing myself as a safe person. While walking down the hall, Ethan caught a glimpse of my playroom and the Hoberman sphere, an expandable plastic ball that fascinates most engineering-minded kids. He stepped into the playroom to check it out. He slowly expanded and collapsed the ball, looking at it from all angles. Without saying anything, I joined him in the playroom and put out my hands for him to toss the ball to me, which he did. His interest in how the toy worked was leading to a budding trust in me—the infancy of a relationship.

Before a word was spoken, Ethan and I were able to connect. We sat on the floor across from each other, and I showed him how I could put the Hoberman sphere on my head. Without telling him what we were going to do, he got a good idea that I wanted to play. Soon we were throwing the Hoberman sphere back and forth, and Ethan's mood began to lift. He would anticipate my toss of the sphere, which comically expanded and collapsed in midair. He began to smile, even giggle a few times. We were coregulating. Only as Ethan began to feel better could I see his skills emerge. He started asking questions about his surroundings, exploring toy bins, and commenting on familiar items. I started thinking through how I would expand our interaction in therapy based on the skills I was observing and the trust that was emerging within our therapeutic relationship.

Lived Experience

"I can tell my teacher understands me if they give me grace and are kind." —Anonymous, age thirteen

"Most educators genuinely want to help and care deeply about their students, but they're often juggling large caseloads and limited resources. When parents and educators see each other as allies, it creates space for honesty, creativity, and better outcomes for kids."
—Anonymous school psychologist

What the Science Says About Relational Safety

Just as we can feel uncomfortable in a physical environment that is too cold or too loud, relationships can become an "environment" we can *feel*. For instance, you may have to interact with a colleague who criticizes your ideas to the point that you're anxious about openly sharing any. Or have you ever had a boss whom you really didn't like? Maybe your gut tensed up and you had to steady yourself every time you interacted with them. Were you able to access your creativity, share your ideas, or grow in this kind of environment? Probably not. That's because your autonomic nervous system was likely on alert, spending all its energy regulating your emotions during these interactions.

Now imagine that you are a child who has not yet mastered self-regulation, and you feel this way about your teacher. Not only is school hard for you due to the misalignment of the curriculum with your skills, but you don't feel you are able to share your interests because no one else in the third grade seems to be talking about aerospace engineering. When parents talk about a teacher who "gets it," they are most often talking about a teacher who understands that their child has strengths and interests that need to be nurtured, whether the curriculum includes them at that grade level or not. Or it's a teacher who celebrates their child's interest even when they're off topic just because they see the joy on a child's face. We need to support the creativity and curiosity of neurodivergent learners even *more* than their neurotypical peers so we don't miss out on their brilliance.

Polyvagal Theory

We've previously touched on the window of tolerance: When we feel emotionally regulated, our capacity expands, so our mind can open to new learning. Establishing felt-safety for a child is synonymous with helping them return to their window of tolerance—or as seen through the lens of polyvagal theory, with their nervous system being in a state of homeostasis. Porges, the psychologist and researcher who developed Polyvagal Theory, described our autonomic nervous system as a "neural platform for behavior and psychological experiences."[6] When our neural platform is steady, we are able to let down our guard because we trust our environment and the people in it. In other words, think of your child's nervous system as the foundation that supports the weight of sustained attention, social engagement, and new learning.

As an example, I knew from Sarah's descriptions that most of Ethan's negative behaviors were the result of his autonomic nervous system going into a fight response meant to protect him from the perceived threat of his parents setting limits. Even though the request from his parents to pause screen time or begin homework was not life-threatening, Ethan's sensitive nervous system perceived these demands at a level of danger that was activating his defenses and, when that didn't work, shutting him down. In order to support Ethan at these times of transition, we had to help him feel less threatened. As I was getting to know him, I looked for ways that he sought comfort so I could help his parents learn how to support him in these moments.

Coregulating Through Relationships

According to Polyvagal Theory, our autonomic nervous system is best regulated by our social engagement system, but what does that look like? Start by thinking about how we help all children return to their window of tolerance through coregulation. When a child is upset, we sit with them, listen to them, talk it through, hug it out, or do whatever else feels natural. Over time these social connections of coregulation, with a securely attached caregiver, help develop a child's social engagement system. As children grow, they expand their ability to regulate with teachers, coaches, mentors, and peers, which helps them develop their emotional regulation skills to one day be able to solve their own problems.

However, a neurodivergent child may be less accepting of coregulation in moments of distress due to communication and sensory differences. For instance, our words can overwhelm them, and they may recoil at our touch. Multiple studies have indicated that emotional dysregulation occurs more often for autistic individuals compared to nonautistic peers and has been connected with both internalizing symptoms and behavioral challenges.[7] Specifically, 58 percent of two-to-five-year-old autistic children experience heightened emotional reactivity, compared to 15 percent of children without developmental concerns. While children with other developmental diagnoses, including ADHD, also struggle with emotional dysregulation, their challenges are less intense than those of autistic children.[8] Children diagnosed with ADHD often experience emotional impulsivity, which can look like an impulsive burst of emotions causing them to quit, lie, or deny fault before they have even thought about the consequences of their actions.

These emotional explosions are one of the hardest parts of coregulation with neurodivergent learners because they push relationships away just when kids need connection to help them regulate. While a neurotypical child can be calmed quickly by a hug or talking it out, neurodivergent kids often need more time and space before the coregulation can begin. Autistic children, for instance, may regulate themselves at first through repetitive play or objects of interest rather than by having someone sit next to them trying to talk them through a problem situation, especially if the person is not familiar to them or they are using too much language. The quick emotions and behavioral responses of kids with ADHD often put them at risk for getting in trouble before anyone has asked how they are feeling. Instead, it's best to first focus on keeping everyone safe, often by giving a child time and space away from the stressor, then figuring out how to connect with them as they are coming back into their window of tolerance.

However, in addition to time and space, children also need their coregulating adult to share a positive or neutral emotional presence to help them return to an emotionally calm state. In fact, research has shown that more frequent positive and neutral parent-child interactions are linked to helping a child learn to regulate their own emotions.[9] In other words, when we model and teach kids *how* to calm down, they begin trusting us—and themselves—when they are upset. Since neurodivergent learners are often more easily pushed outside their window of tolerance when faced with challenges, they need more repetition with familiar, and emotionally regulated, people who can provide predictable support that builds the trust needed to learn how to self-regulate. These familiar people will become your child's school family.

How to Build a School Family for Your Child

With time, flexibility, and play, I was able to create felt-safety for Ethan in therapy, but this can be harder to do in a classroom. Imagine a child knowing that what they are being asked to do is too hard for them but feeling too scared to ask for help. This would be like standing on a stage about to perform a dance routine you thought you had memorized, but the bright lights, itchy costume, and audience attention make your mind go blank, and you run off the stage. But then your trusted dance teacher is waiting in the wings to help you take a deep breath and remember how well you know the routine. With a newfound emotional calm, you head back out there with confidence. If we just tell kids, "You're fine, get back out there," without offering that experience of felt-safety, their overwhelm couples with loneliness. If this happens repeatedly, a child will begin to associate us with being unhelpful and will no longer seek us out as a source of coregulation.

Building a school family involves establishing felt-safety at school by nurturing predictable and supportive relationships with the people who will help coregulate your child throughout the school day. As the parent of a neurodivergent learner, you will naturally be more involved in your child's schooling than their peers' parents. Teachers need collaboration from parents to help them earn the trust of neurodivergent learners so they feel understood and safe within the relationships at school. I have experienced this firsthand over the years as I've volunteered in my kids' classrooms, donated much-needed supplies, and emailed teachers to give them a heads-up if my kid had a rough night's sleep. What follows are more ways to build a trusted school family for your child.

Help Your Child and Their Teacher Establish Trust

Build Familiarity Through Routines

Even before your child begins school, you will have a sense of how anxious they feel around unfamiliar people, or even familiar people who aren't you. After you help your child become familiar with new faces at school, they will need time to build trust with new people through experiences. These experiences are often routines that build familiarity within the plan of the day. While a neurotypical child might get over the hump of adjusting to school in a few days, an autistic or anxious child might need weeks to settle in. This usually has to do with how long it takes them to feel safe. In my experience, neurodivergent children are more sensitive to how people make them feel. A tone of voice or a demand can feel threatening, while a silly connection or a patient tone can be the spark that leads to a new relationship.

When you are introducing your child to people they will see on a routine basis, like a teacher, teaching assistant, or bus driver, help these adults understand how to connect with your child by sharing ways to make them feel comfortable. The more consistently your child feels safe with adults in their routine, the more easily they will predict that they can trust those around them.

Prepare Teachers for Your Child's Triggers

School buildings are not designed with sensitive nervous systems in mind. Not all children have the same sensitivities or have them to the same degree because every nervous system is unique, so don't leave it to your child's teacher to make assumptions with limited information. Be sure to let the teacher know if your child is sensitive to noise (loud or abrupt), crowds, lights, smells, touch, or certain foods, as well as to internal sensory differences called interoception, which we will discuss in Chapter 3. Share comfort strategies from home, but stay open to progress if your child's teacher says after a week or two that they don't need support after all. Sometimes kids surprise us when they get into the school routine. And if not, teachers will be prepared in case they need to provide your child with some extra coregulation.

Introduce Teachers to Your Child's Interests

While social connection brings most neurotypical kids back into their window of tolerance, giving neurodivergent kids time and space to connect with preferred items and topics of interest tends to bring them closer to an emotionally regulated state in which they can talk through a problem. For teachers, it can feel counterintuitive to allow a child to talk about their favorite topic, like video games or the solar system, as a calming strategy, instead of getting to work, but this might just be what a child needs to return to their window of tolerance, after which they will be able to focus on the task at hand. Many times engaging in an activity that increases connection, as I did with Ethan and the Hoberman sphere, will allow your child to trust that a teacher understands that they need a slower pace, which leads to reduced anxiety, and higher trust. As our children begin to trust the adults around them, a school family begins to emerge.

Help Your Child and Their Teacher Strengthen Connection

Share What Works at Home

High energy, impulsivity, and difficulty transitioning can be challenging for a teacher to manage in a group of learners. As kids grow, we want them to become more independent about getting their energy and movement needs met, but this will take practice across home and school environments. If you know that your child needs high levels of movement or a visual plan to transition more easily, share strategies with their teacher that have worked. You could say, "I'm not sure what this would look like in the classroom, but at home when I have [Child] vacuum or carry laundry baskets, it helps direct his high energy into a productive task." The teacher may then come up with a similar classroom job involving heavy work, like moving chairs or carrying baskets of books, rather than passing out pencils or watering plants. Using their extra energy to be helpful will make a child feel effective and seen, all while regulating their nervous system. And when you and their teacher collaborate on what works, you will begin feeling like teammates.

Share Stories from Life Outside School

One of the best ways to help a teacher feel connected with your child is to allow them to know your child beyond the classroom. Many neurodivergent learners, especially those who are autistic or have speech/language differences, may not be able to explain what they did over the weekend or what they enjoy outside school. Yet these details are crucial to helping a teacher connect with your child over topics of interest beyond what they witness during the school day. When my son was in elementary school, I sent a brief email to his teachers every Sunday night letting them know what he enjoyed over the weekend. His teachers were then able to ask him about his weekend using details like "Tell me about riding the carousel at the park" rather than "What did you do this weekend?" Some children are confused at first that their teacher knows about their life beyond the classroom, so be sure to remind them that you'll be talking to their teacher to help them understand that you are all on their team and communicate behind the scenes.

Share Information That Impacts Your Child's Emotional Regulation

As parents, it's easy to think that home life and school life are two independent worlds, but that is far from the truth when you're raising a neurodivergent child. For example, a rough night of sleep can impact emotional regulation in the classroom, and if teachers know your child might need an extra break during the day, they can plan accordingly. Things might happen at school, like your child falling asleep or having an upset stomach, that you need to know about, especially if your child cannot explain all the details. What follows are some important areas to communicate about with your child's teacher.

Medication

Any medication, from stimulants to SSRIs to even just an antibiotic, could have side effects for your child; it's important their teachers be aware of what your child has been prescribed so they can be on the lookout for any changes in health or behavior. Stimulant medications, most commonly prescribed to support ADHD, are short-acting and wear off the same day kids take them, so communication about peak effectiveness and side effects is paramount. SSRIs, most often prescribed to treat anxiety and emotional dysregulation, need to be taken consistently and should not be started or stopped abruptly, so communicating about benefits and side effects when a child is trialing these medications is important. Sometimes I wish teachers and prescribing doctors had a direct line of communication, but the reality is that you are the go-between. The best system I've found for these communications is to email the teacher for feedback on your child's behavior and then cut and paste their response into your physician's patient portal. If your child takes multiple medications, especially those affecting sleep and digestion, consider having a shared Google Doc with your child's teacher to track progress and side effects.

Sleep

If your child's emotional regulation, attention span, or impulsivity is impacted by differences in sleep, be sure to establish a way to communicate easily with your child's teacher. If they're available to you, school messaging apps are often the best way for you to alert a teacher that your child might need to be "handled with care" that day due to waking up at three a.m., or they might need to stay home to get more sleep. These messaging apps are also a great way for your child's teacher to send you a quick note that all is going well or if your child seems too tired to learn or is more irritable than usual.

Nutrition

Many neurodivergent children have food sensitivities, sometimes diagnosed as ARFID, an eating disorder that impacts their ability to regularly eat a variety of food, which impacts their growth. (We'll cover this in Chapter 10.) Not having enough nourishment, being overwhelmed by smells from the cafeteria, or simply sitting next to a classmate whose food looks gross to them can impact a child's mood at school. Be sure to share your child's eating habits with their teacher so they can be aware of when to support them regarding snacks and lunch in the school building. I will never forget a teaching assistant who worked with my son in third grade to gradually expose him to eating lunch from the school cafeteria. Expanding this experience for him allowed him to practice waiting in line, talking to cafeteria workers, and memorizing his lunch number to check out—all skills that went beyond his newfound love of steamed broccoli. Your child's teacher may not notice the monumental feat of them eating something new unless they know to look for it. Tell them so they can share the good news as these milestones develop.

Mood

A child's mood is a concern to respond to sooner rather than later. Tell your child's teacher what their mood is like at home so you can partner in determining if their mood is any different at school. A child's mood will vary related to time of day, fatigue, medication side effects, the type of work they are being asked to do, sensory overwhelm, or a range of other factors; knowing what their mood is like at home at any given time can help establish a baseline. Remember, your child's teacher will likely be helping them coregulate when they are pushed to the edges of their window of tolerance during the school day. When you are building a school family, there is power in neither you nor your child's teacher feeling like you are the only one seeing a problem.

When to Be Concerned: Your Child's Teacher Is Not Collaborative

Your goal as a parent of a neurodivergent child is to partner with your child's teacher to help communicate their needs until they can advocate for themself. Sometimes you may come across a teacher who is not very collaborative, who feels you are infringing on their territory, or who does not feel your child needs individualized attention. This can feel overwhelming, but before you fire off an email, ask yourself these questions to organize your thoughts.

1. Are you getting conflicting information from your child or multiple teachers? (If so, you might need a teacher conference or a group email to hash out the whole story or to clarify why your child may be excelling in one class and struggling in another.)

2. Are you getting feedback that accommodations cannot be made for your child, and you think they're needed? Examples of modifications might include shortening tasks or reducing homework, while accommodations often include taking tests in a smaller setting or extending time on tests. Access to modifications and accommodations may differ depending on your child's school setting and eligibility for specialized services. (Talk to your child's special education teacher, school counselor, or an administrator.)

3. Do you trust the teacher but think they may be overworked and need support? (In this case, talk to an administrator.)

4. Do you trust the teacher to follow through with what they have said, or have they said one thing and done another in the past? (Emailing an administrator could be helpful.)

If a teacher is not collaborating with you, hopefully the school administrator will. Most school administrators understand that many negative behaviors can be prevented when student learning styles are matched with teaching styles. However, if you feel the school administrator isn't collaborative, asking to talk with the school psychologist or signing consent for them to talk to an outside provider (e.g., your child's therapist) to express the benefit of teacher fit may be helpful. If you continue to have difficulty feeling heard or you are confused about the process, consider hiring a parent advocate to help you navigate these conversations.

Email Scripts: Communicating with Your Child's Teacher

Your goal for every communication with teachers is to help your child feel understood by the adults in the building. *When* you talk to teachers is sometimes just as important as *what* you say to them. No quality conversations can happen in the carpool line, so use school communication apps for quick information swaps like "Didn't sleep well, handle with care" and email for longer details like what your child enjoyed on a recent trip. Here is an email formula to follow and a few examples:

Email formula:

1. What you are observing
2. Your child's perspective
3. What you think is going on
4. Statement of trust in the teacher
5. Offer of support, if needed

Hi, Ms. [Teacher],

Our family has had a fun weekend, but [Child]'s worries about school started last night at bedtime. From his perspective, he feels reading is too easy, and he is complaining of being bored. I'm wondering if the books he is reading are below his level? I just wanted you to be aware in case he's not saying something at school. Let me know if you need me to send in books that he is interested in. I'm happy to donate these to the class.

Thank you for all you do!
[Your name here]

Hi, Mr. [Teacher],

I wanted to reach out to share what I'm hearing at home. [Child] told me at bedtime last night that she felt scared of you yesterday when you asked her to clean up her things so she wouldn't miss recess. I can imagine she was having a hard time staying organized because we see this at home, too. Since recess is her favorite part of the day, this may have panicked her. She is also very sensitive to my stern tone of voice, especially when we are trying to get out the door in the morning. I'm wondering if her struggles with cleaning up, plus feeling rushed, made her feel scared of your tone? I haven't heard her say she feels scared otherwise. I would love your perspective on this interaction so we can help her feel less anxious in these moments of transition. Using a checklist in the morning has really helped her stay on track and cut down on how many times I have had to use my stern voice with her. Let me know if you gather any other details, and I will let you know if I hear of any other examples of her feeling overwhelmed.

Thank you for all you do!
[Your name here]

Kid Chat Script: Questions for Understanding Your Child's Perspective

When checking in with your child about their school relationships, if you ask general questions like "How was your day?" right as they hop in the car, they will likely say "Fine" because that's easier than explaining everything that happened during the day. Asking general questions might also make it hard for you to get a read on whether or not they feel a part of the school family. Start by asking your child one of these questions over a snack or at bedtime, and you may get more details:

- *I thought of you today and wondered if anything made you laugh.*
- *What did the cafeteria serve for lunch?*
- *What did you do at recess?*
- *What was art/music class like today?*
- *Who helped you today?*

Once you have more insight into their day, you can talk through if there is a problem they would like to solve on their own or if they need your help asking an adult.

Chapter 3

Managing Your Child's Energy

"It's too hard! I can't do it."

Have you ever tried paying attention when you were in pain? Or attempted to read with an annoying sound in the background? These are examples of sensory experiences interfering with our ability to remain emotionally regulated enough to access our executive functioning skills, both of which are essential to keeping us within our window of tolerance so we can stay curious and open to new ideas. Regulating our emotions takes energy, so the more we operate on the edges of our window of tolerance, the more at risk we are for being depleted of the energy we need to pay attention and learn. The same is true for our kids.

As new learning happens, we are naturally pushed to the edges of our window of tolerance, because we feel unsure of ourselves. It's in these moments that learning becomes a vulnerable experience: a lack of understanding can be accompanied by feelings of inferiority, lack of confidence, or a sense of weakness. We have to reconcile our worth in the context of this not-knowing. As adults, we have the insight to know that we can't be good at everything and the emotional maturity to recognize that we are no less worthy because of a weakness. However, we sometimes fail to acknowledge that children don't yet possess this insight or maturity, expecting them to simply rise to any occasion.

For instance, we often expect our kids to do things by a certain age simply because we think they should be able to. While there are benefits to age-based goals, like continuing to challenge our kids to gain skills and reach milestones, we must account for flexibility when every brain is unique. When it comes to neurodivergent learners, energy levels are a particularly important part of this equation. If we can better align what we teach our neurodivergent kids with how they learn, we can help prevent their exhaustion by naturally engaging them in learning—and this can have meaningful effects on how we think about teaching all children. I truly believe our neurodivergent learners are showing us a better way to access education: through curiosity.

There is something magical about following a child's curiosity. The questions they ask and what they wonder about are windows into how their mind works. You might even think of it like the flow state many of us access during creative endeavors, or when it feels like output is effortless. If we follow a child's curiosity, their growth potential feels limitless. It's even more rewarding as a parent when we get to witness their curiosity in real time. When my son, who struggles to attend to anything that's not moving as fast as his brain, asked, "Will you read with me?" I tried to play it cool—I didn't want to ruin the moment by being "cringe"—but this was a big deal. My kid felt safe and connected enough to invite me into his learning, which he had most recently described as "too boring." If your child struggles to learn in traditional ways—defined here as sitting in a group and listening to an adult present information—I want to help you figure out how, when, and where your kid wants to learn. Many times this involves noticing more about your child's emotional regulation to ensure they have the energy needed to stay curious about learning. These moments of staying curious are not only helpful glimpses into what grabs our child's attention but also clues about where our kid feels capable of directing their energy.

Throughout Chapters 1 and 2, we discussed kids needing to feel safe in their environment and with the people around them in order to learn, but what about feeling safe in their own body? In this chapter, we will discuss interoception, the sensory system inside our body monitoring the sensations of inner motion.[1] We use interoception every time we register pain or heat intolerance, feel hungry, or sense the urgency to use the bathroom. As our brain works to breathe deeply through pain, get somewhere cooler, find a snack, or hold our bladder tight until we reach the bathroom, we are expending energy to meet our body's needs and usually can't focus on much else at that moment. In other words, when our energy is being directed toward monitoring our bodily functions or regulating our emotions, we don't have much left over to take in new information, so learning is paused.

We all have a unique set of resources, but neurodivergent learners tend to expend more energy trying to stay inside their window of tolerance than neurotypical ones.[2] This may be because their nervous systems are more easily overwhelmed. Or it may be that they are having to work harder to live and learn in a world that wasn't built for them. From my perspective working with neurodivergent children and raising my own, it seems the answer is most likely both, and it depends. Every child's nervous system is different, but so is every family and classroom. We have to begin thinking not just about what we are trying to teach our kids but when, where, and how they are able to show up with the energy needed at any given moment to learn, especially if their energy is more easily depleted by sensory demands, uninteresting topics, or weaknesses in executive functioning.

Savannah's Story

Savannah's parents first brought her to me for play therapy because she often became upset when preschool peers disrupted her play ideas. Other children were trying to play with Savannah, but she seemed overwhelmed to have them in her space. Her parents also described how after preschool she would repetitively play with her dollhouse, lining up the characters and furniture the same way every time. Savannah was so focused on the play that it was hard for her to transition to dinner, causing a huge meltdown. While I worked with Savannah's parents to allow her time to recover with solo play in the afternoons and to add structure through visual schedules to help her transition, I also wondered why Savannah felt so overwhelmed at school and how I might be able to help.

The fact that Savannah was playing alone was not a problem in and of itself. However, her parents explained that when she was rested on the weekends, she was much more flexible and enjoyed having her parents play with her, unlike at school when she would become upset at any peer who entered her play and would push them out of the way. In other words, Savannah was able to stay emotionally regulated in play with her parents, but was unable to stay emotionally regulated when playing with peers. While our long-term therapy goal was to help Savannah tolerate playing with peers at preschool, our short-term goals included helping her learn to feel the upset in her body, express her upset safely, and seek coregulation or access self-regulation so she could safely share space with others. If Savannah could master this formula of emotional regulation, she could follow it for years to come.

The same can be said for learning as for play: Before kids are able to learn in a group, we have to help them build the emotional stamina to manage their energy with learning. We achieve this with a combination of support from adults available for coregulation, visual strategies to scaffold independence, and practice from the child. Only then

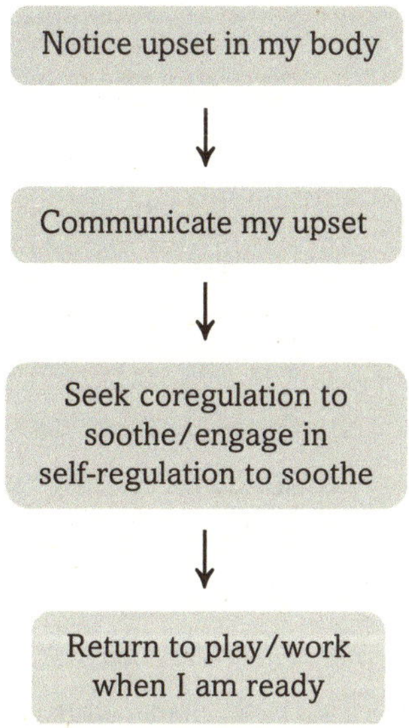

can the neurodivergent child reap the benefits of learning in an inclusive classroom.

Gradually over time in play therapy, I was able to help Savannah trust me as a play partner and show her that she could still have fun even if the play changed from how she expected it to go. In order to achieve this, I couldn't enter her play abruptly, as many of her four-year-old classmates did. Instead, I sat with her but did not intervene, to help her get used to the idea that I was in the room and so she could feel safe playing next to me. I knew from her speech and language evaluation that she struggled to express herself with words, but she understood what others said. My next goal was to help Savannah continue to feel safe while I showed curiosity about her play by commenting and asking questions. Eventually, she felt safe enough to let me into her play and expand her plan by incorporating some of my ideas, but in ways that appealed to her through her sensory preferences, interests, and humor.

Through play therapy, I was able to expand Savannah's window of tolerance while carefully monitoring her emotional stamina. There were some days when Savannah's parents told me she had not slept well, and her play was often more self-directed those days. On days where she seemed more flexible and engaged, her parents and I brainstormed why she was doing well so we could try to replicate her progress.

Savannah's story illustrates that sustaining our energy to learn is not just about academic ability but also about tolerating new information from the people around us. If we are curious, motivated, and have the skills to attend to new ideas, we are not using as much energy as when we are uninterested, unmotivated, and struggling to pay attention. Preschoolers like Savannah show us what they need by how they react behaviorally, even if they're unable to voice those needs. In these moments, the behavior is communicating a child's emotions and likely their need for support. When overwhelmed, Savannah withdrew to solitary play, and when she was rested, she had the bandwidth to allow myself and her parents into her play. I have seen this same pattern time and again with neurodivergent learners. When stressed, they seem to regress and behave like a younger child, and when rested and supported in a way that meets their emotional regulation needs, they are more able to take setbacks in stride and stay curious. In other words, they have more energy to learn.

Lived Experience

"My son is tired every day after school. He can get overwhelmed by large gatherings [school assemblies, events] with lots of people, colors, activity, and louder sounds, so those days can be even more tough." —Anonymous parent of a ten-year-old

"It is hard to concentrate when it is too loud and takes longer to understand a concept. It is noisy when there are too many people. It makes me cover my ears." —Sarah, age nine

The Science Behind Emotional Energy

When we are met with a challenge, our nervous system registers a threat, causing us to put up our defenses for protection. And when we experience safety, we are more receptive to new learning because we are not expending energy protecting ourselves from perceived danger. The pediatric psychologist and author Mona Delahooke writes in her book *Brain-Body Parenting* that feeling safely connected establishes a "sturdy platform" for children and helps them meet expectations by expanding their capacity for flexibility and decision-making, whereas a "vulnerable platform" increases a child's defensiveness, which often shows up as behaviors that adults deem "difficult"—like refusing to do what is asked, lying about what really happened, or fighting with a sibling.[3]

Delahooke explains that a child's negative behavior is not only defensive but also biologically protective, helping to keep them safe from the dangers their nervous system perceives through the process of neuroception, which we discussed in Chapter 2. The intensity of a perceived threat will depend on how sturdy our body feels to absorb it at any given moment. For instance, it's much easier for one of my kids to inadvertently startle me on a day when I haven't slept enough compared to a day when I'm well rested. Our nervous system is wired to keep us safe, but this ongoing threat assessment takes emotional energy that is hard to measure and sometimes hard for us even to feel.

Budgeting Energy

According to Delahooke, "we are never just a 'body' or a 'brain'; we are always both," reacting to a world on a continuum from receptive to defensive. To better understand this, we need to look at the work of Lisa Feldman Barrett, a neuroscience researcher who studies interoception and coined the term *body-budgeting*.[4] Barrett wrote that body-budget regions of the brain "send predictions to the body to control its internal environment: speed up the heart, slow down breathing, release more cortisol, metabolize more glucose, and so on," all things that happen instantaneously when our nervous system is automatically sensing whether we are safe. Barrett explained that our interoception is always functioning, similar to how our blood keeps pumping and our digestive system keeps working, even when we aren't paying attention to our body.

Interoception

Now imagine that you struggle to feel the sensations inside your body, an experience clinicians refer to as "interoceptive hyposensitivity," where it's difficult to notice your internal body cues. Most parents and teachers are aware that many neurodivergent children may experience sensations happening *outside* their body, like noises, lights, or crowded environments. However, research suggests that many autistic and ADHD individuals struggle to accurately identify the interoceptive sensations happening *inside* their body, too.[5] Many can struggle to feel hungry or full, know when they are hot or cold, register when they are in pain, or sense the urge to use the bathroom.

Neurodivergent kids often notice these sensations only when they become imminent, not giving them enough time to ask for what they need—like a snack, a jacket, or a bathroom break—if they can even identify what would help. Struggling to make sense of their internal sensory states also impacts a child's ability to emotionally regulate. In other words, if a child struggles to notice what feels off in their body, it's harder for them to figure out what they need to feel better. These interoceptive differences—often coupled with language differences—make it harder for children to identify and communicate when they need help.

If you've ever been stumped as to why your child is so irritable, only to find them feverish later that night, you have just experienced your child not being able to express their interoceptive sense of feeling sick. As adults, we know how it feels when a cold is coming on, but it's hard for a neurodivergent child to recognize the onset of symptoms, let alone communicate them. Another example is when a child is easily upset and appears to have little stamina for tolerating anything nonpreferred, but then their parent realizes they have been constipated for days and have been using all their energy to manage tension in their gut. The same pattern happens when children are tired, hungry, hot, or in some other physically dysregulated state that may be hard for neurodivergent kids to feel, identify, and communicate. Further complicating this is that autistic children tend to have more gut, sleep, and neurological issues than the general population, so we have to be sure to rule out additional medical complexities before we ask them to work harder.[6] Many neurodivergent kids just don't have a surplus of emotional energy, and if we push them too far, we run the risk of leading them into burnout, where it can be harder for their nervous system to recover.

Building Emotional Awareness

When I talk to parents and teachers about a child who is "noncompliant," I always ask about their energy level and mood. Noticing how a child's avoidance shows up can give us clues: silly, angry, and disengaged energies are all indicative of different types of avoidance. A silly mood likely means a child has lots of energy but needs more structure and guidance on following the steps of the task. An angry or irritable mood could mean high or low energy and indicates that a child is either overwhelmed or annoyed by the task or the person asking. Disengagement is often low energy—sometimes labeled as "lazy"—and can mean a child is either unmotivated or overwhelmed and is feeling incapable of getting started. While a child's mood is most often what we see, it is only the tip of the iceberg when it comes to figuring out what is going on beneath the surface. What lies beneath, inside a child's nervous system, has much more to do with their energy reserves. As the psychologist and author Ross Greene says, "Kids do well if they can."

A parent's concern over a child's mood is often what brings them into therapy, but as a therapist to neurodivergent kids, I'm also wondering if the child is even aware of their mood. Many kids will say they feel "bad" but will not be able to explain it in detail. This is because an additional challenge related to differences in interoception is difficulty identifying emotions, known as alexithymia. The occupational therapist and author Kelly Mahler describes alexithymia as a surface term and suggests we think more deeply about what interoceptive difference might be causing this difficulty.[7] As adults caring for children with weak interoceptive perception and possibly weak communication skills, we can first look to patterns of a child's mood for clues about what might feel overwhelming to them; however, we can't assume they have the emotional awareness to identify their feelings and fix it without support. As the trusted adult in our child's life, we have to help them understand what it feels like to be cranky, angry, or sad by helping them become aware of their emotions.

Over the years, some of the most effective moments in supporting the emotional growth of neurodivergent learners in therapy have included helping them notice how the energy levels in their body connect to their emotions and building a feelings vocabulary to describe them. I once worked with an intellectually gifted child who was not able to describe how he felt when he came to therapy after school. I often got an "I don't know" paired with a shrug. Even when I shared my observation that he looked tired, he was not able to explain if he was too tired to talk, too tired to play a game, or too tired to sit up. I also knew that he was gifted in robotics and fascinated with building circuit boards. So I drew three shapes of a battery on a whiteboard, each with a different level of power. He was immediately able to point to the middle one, which helped me know how much gas he had in the tank for therapy that day. Over time he was able to label these batteries with words describing his emotions (e.g., *annoyed, mad, furious; happy, excited, thrilled; cautious, nervous, scared*) and thus convey the size of those emotions, which helped him connect his energy with his emotions.

Beyond what neurodivergent kids can discover about their emotions in therapy with a mental health professional, many also benefit from working with an occupational therapist to support their interoceptive awareness and with a speech-language pathologist to support their communication of the sensations they feel in their body. Once a child is able to recognize and communicate, whether verbally or nonverbally, when they feel tired, frustrated, or need help, then they are ready to gauge their own ability to take on new learning experiences.

The Learning Circle

For many neurodivergent learners, the unknown can feel scary, and pushing through that feeling takes a lot of effort—and energy. Even when using the approach of growth mindset, which was introduced by the psychologist Carol Dweck and teaches that we are always learning and mistakes are expected, neurodivergent kids are often skeptical and don't see how their effort now is going to be worth it later. This concept of investing in something for future payoff, also known as delayed gratification, is difficult to trust if you live in the moment, as many impulsive kids with short attention spans tend to do. In fact, the psychologist Russell Barkley calls this "nearsightedness to the future," explaining that individuals with ADHD "can only deal with things near in time; now is more compelling."[8]

I started to notice this pattern years ago in my therapy practice related to avoidance around schoolwork or chores—basically anything nonpreferred that took effort. Many of my clients are concrete thinkers who view their skills in two categories: "I'm an expert at this!" or "I can't do it." Being great at certain things without trying, which is common among gifted kids, takes little effort; the decision to avoid things that aren't immediately intuitive feels like an easy one. Many autistic learners struggle with cognitive rigidity and "intolerance of uncertainty," leading to more frequent anxiety and avoidance of new learning.[9] Therefore many neurodivergent learners have little experience with the effort needed to build frustration tolerance, and they miss out on experiencing the long-term payoff that comes from investing energy now to be good at something in the long run.

I needed a way to use my clients' concrete thinking to help them understand that we can't go from not knowing something to knowing it instantly. I wanted to teach them that there is a third category—the gray area—where all the learning happens, and it's uncomfortable in there! This is how the Learning Circle came to be.

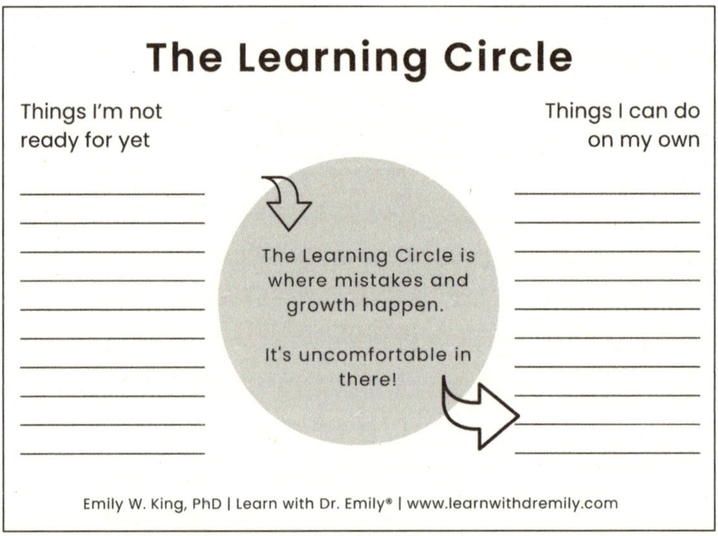

Here's how it works: All kids have a range of skills at any given time, but they break down into three main categories: skills that are (1) not developmentally present yet, (2) emerging, and (3) mastered. Skills that your child is not yet developmentally ready for are the skills that you don't trust your child to do well or safely—like asking your toddler to use the stove. Mastered skills are the skills your kids can do even if they are tired and hungry—as in, they can get themselves dressed to go to the doctor even if they are feeling sick. Emerging skills are all the skills in between that your child can do on some days but not every day, in some settings but not others, and with some people but not everyone.

These emerging skills remain in the Learning Circle until they become consistent, inching their way toward mastery—and autonomy. To begin categorizing your child's skills, look for patterns of emerging skills and increase support until consistency improves. For instance, sit down and tie shoes or practice pouring milk together. The more consistently we help our children practice emerging skills, the more they are able to build stamina for these new experiences, which sets them up for a lifetime of feeling safe when learning. As a child's skill becomes more consistent, we decrease support until that skill is independently mastered. In other words, when your child is not developmentally ready, we do "for"; when the skill is emerging, we do "with"; and when the skill is mastered, they do it themself.

By showing kids that it's supposed to feel hard and effortful when they're working on emerging skills inside the Learning Circle, you're able to help them think about the ways they need to preserve their energy and recover after these tasks or events. For instance, if they spend the morning learning to ride a bike, they will need more time for rest in the afternoon. Or if they are going on a field trip tomorrow, they need rest, nutrition, and routine to support the effort they will expend during this new travel experience.

I have used the Learning Circle in countless situations to help concrete thinkers understand that they have to go through the process of learning to get to mastery. I gently incorporated ideas rooted in exposure therapy to slowly habituate them to the idea of effort. Inside the Learning Circle is where we build frustration tolerance and where we need all our strategies like movement breaks, sensory breaks, deep breathing, slowing down the pace, safe relationships, incorporating our interests, and even rewards for trying again and again until a skill is mastered. (We'll talk more about motivation and rewards in Chapter 4.)

How Change Zaps Energy

Even when all the stars align for our kids in regard to school fit, teacher fit, and schedule fit, unexpected changes will always arise that cause stress and are taxing on neurodivergent learners. Spirit weeks, school assemblies, and fire drills are just some of the changes that not only disrupt the flow of a child's learning but send many neurodivergent learners into states of stress, causing them to expend their energy in processing the change and ensuring they're still safe. Here are a few energy-zapping scenarios to look out for:

- If your child likes to wear the same pair of shorts every day, then it is absolutely okay for them not to dress up for spirit week. Helping your child adjust to seeing their teacher in a costume will be enough to process.
- School assemblies can shorten the schedule for the rest of the day, and while most students don't even notice this, those who love routine certainly will, and the change will likely increase their anxiety. Supporting your child with a visual of the new schedule for that day will be helpful.
- Fire drills are some of the hardest experiences for children with sensory sensitivities. Normalizing the use of noise-canceling headphones and practicing the plan can help many anxious learners.
- Unexpected people—like substitute teachers, volunteers, or new students—can throw off a routine-oriented child. If this is a trigger for your child, let teachers know early in the school year so they can help prepare your child when

they will be absent or a new person will be in the classroom.

My older son, in particular, struggled when anything was different about school. This was partially due to the fact that he has an excellent memory for his schedule (and everyone else's) but also because he became overwhelmed when something unexpected changed. One year changes to the school schedule happened so often, due to hurricanes and snow in North Carolina, that I felt my son needed a category in his brain for these days. We needed a name for them, so I called them wacky days and explained to him, using humor and stories of previous wacky days, that even though the day was all out of order, he was still safe. I used the Dr. Seuss book *Wacky Wednesday,* which he loved, to explain that the people and activities were all out of place, but in the end, he would still come home safely. You could use this same idea of wacky days if another caregiver is picking up, an after-school activity is canceled, or a relative is coming to town to stay with your family. Whatever changes in your child's routine from their perspective, acknowledge it and remind them that they are safe and connected to their people even when things are wacky.

There are many reasons your child might say, "It's too hard! I can't do it!" and most of them have to do with the effort it takes to tolerate frustration when learning something new. When you are met with resistance from your child, remember that low energy can lead to what manifests as "difficult" behavior, so it may be worth considering if anything unexpected happened that day, or if they may need extra time to recover.

How to Manage Your Child's Energy So They're Ready to Learn

Savannah had always felt safer when she was in control, so I wasn't surprised that her parents reached out to me with a new problem a few years later when she was in third grade. Savannah was doing well academically and following all the rules, but as her dad described, she seemed "wound up tight." She was developing rituals that took her more than an hour to move through in the morning, and after school she was retreating to her room to play with her dollhouse, which she hadn't touched since kindergarten.

Her parents felt they were doing something wrong because she was so well behaved at school. I reminded them that she was likely out of energy and that repetitive, solo play in her room was restorative for her, as it had been when she was younger. Her parents had not realized that she was so tired after school, but my comment resonated with them. They had noticed that when Savannah was overwhelmed, she became more rigid and seemed to regress in her play. When she was rested, fed, and with familiar people, she was capable of being more flexible.

What Savannah's parents had been witnessing was emotional exhaustion. Savannah's energy was zapped by having to emotionally regulate herself with classmates in her space, others around her not following the rules, and her teacher asking her to transition before she was finished with her work. After recognizing the triggers that were depleting Savannah's energy during the school day, her parents were able to help her teacher understand how much energy she was expending to hold it together at school. Her teacher was then able to give her sensory breaks and pair her with peers who didn't overwhelm her, which helped. While Savannah needed more support during the school day and rest at home, some neurodivergent children with high energy need more movement before they are asked to sit down to focus on work. Here are more ideas on managing your child's energy in order to prepare them to learn.

When Your Child Fatigues Easily

Notice Your Child's Energy Patterns

Fatigue is sometimes one of the hardest patterns to notice because it is a moving target and your child might struggle to identify and communicate how they feel. But you can look for patterns through sluggish movement, changes in sleep habits, and irritability. Notice when emotional dysregulation shows up: Is it on certain days of the week and times of day, with certain people, or during certain activities? If you can't figure out a pattern, think about what your child might be experiencing internally when they are irritable, such as hunger, anxiety, loneliness, or pain—including gut discomfort like constipation or a food allergy. Many times in my work with parents they have recognized a pattern in retrospect, only after a child eats something or uses the bathroom, for example, and they are no longer cranky. Once you notice your child's patterns, you can begin making changes to help manage their energy throughout the day and the week. For instance, you can add downtime after school to help your child recover from the day or move dinnertime and bedtime earlier to prevent the hunger and fatigue that often lead to emotional overwhelm.

Be an Interoception Detective and Make It Routine

If your child struggles to notice their internal body cues, you have to be a detective who looks for signs indicating their internal discomfort. Think about your child's early developmental patterns such as sleep, fussiness when hungry, pain tolerance, and independent toileting. If your child's awareness of these cues felt delayed, and especially if they are more sensitive than most, that could be an indication that they are spending lots of energy regulating their nervous system, and you will need to help them learn these energy patterns as they grow. We do this by teaching kids to sleep, eat, and use the toilet on a schedule first, until their internal body cues catch up developmentally. This is an example of using external motivation in the form of routines to keep a child rested, fed, and comfortable rather than simply waiting for them to feel tired, hungry, or the urgency to use the bathroom. We'll cover more on supporting self-care in Chapter 10.

Help Your Child Communicate What They Feel

Your child's ability to communicate when they feel tired, hungry, anxious, or sick will of course depend on their language skills. Even if your child communicates with words, their behavior or language may come across as mean or rude when they're fatigued, making it harder to figure out what they need. Don't take their words personally; receive them as a sign that your child's nervous system is outside their window of tolerance, in a "fight" state, which makes communicating politely harder at that moment. Some children may lose their language altogether when they are upset, and it's at these moments when we need to match their language. If your child is no longer talking, it's best to stop asking them questions and giving them instructions, because they are likely not processing your spoken language. Using visuals reminds us to not talk as much, as we can just point to what comes next on a schedule, for instance. Another trick is to teach your child to use their fingers to communicate the size of their overwhelm, where one finger is "I need a minute" and five fingers are "Don't talk to me." This reduction in spoken language when children are out of energy often helps them return to their window of tolerance faster by reducing the sensory, language, and social demands of the moment.

When Your Child Has Too Much Energy

Notice the Pace of Your Child and the Pace of Their Schoolwork

Many children with ADHD tend to move fast and think fast. Some feel that their brain never stops. When my son was young, he had two speeds: fast and asleep. Now imagine you are in a classroom with a pace of instruction set for the masses, but your brain is several steps ahead. No wonder you are bored and distracted! If your child moves at a fast pace, you may have noticed two things: (1) They rush through things, and (2) they give up easily. Kids with ADHD rush through things because they want to be finished as fast as possible. When they think work is too difficult, they often feel it's less embarrassing to not do the work at all than be last or get a low grade, leading them to abandon the task altogether. We have to coach kids who move through life quickly to slow down, which feels like hard work to them. Your child may need to stand or bounce while working, or they may need to know that they are going to work only in ten-minute intervals. Chunking time for an activity can help them practice building their stamina to participate for gradually longer periods of time.

Kids Need Recess—Especially Active Kids

Historically, if a child is not getting their work done, recess is delayed until the work is done. The problem is, however, that recess is essential to a child's development and learning, and withholding it is often detrimental, especially to neurodivergent kids. The American Academy of Pediatrics recommends at least twenty minutes of recess daily for children and adolescents,[10] but research indicates the more movement the better. One study found that physical activity lessened the severity of ADHD symptoms for children,[11] and another found that increasing recess time led to lower chronic stress in fourth graders.[12] If a teacher wants to remove recess for your child, instead discuss what is causing the behavior leading to them not completing their work.

Create Opportunities for Your Active Child to Move Outside School

Children with naturally high energy levels need more movement later into their development than the traditional schooling experience gives them. If your child needs more movement after coming home from school, create those opportunities for them. Walk, scooter, or bike to and from school if you can. Collaborate with teachers about how your child can move their body during the school day. Many families of high-energy kids find they need to swim, jump, and have room to run outside. The balance of sleep, movement, nature, and nutrition will be so helpful for your child. Many children with high energy need wide open spaces like parks and fields to move their bodies enough to match their energy. It makes complete sense to me that the Olympian swimmer Michael Phelps, the Olympian gymnast Simone Biles, and the Olympian figure skater Alysa Lui, who have all talked openly about having ADHD, pursued sports that gave them long stretches of space to move their bodies. If, despite these strategies, you feel your child needs more support with managing their body's energy and emotional regulation, that might be a clue that it's time to talk to their pediatrician about options for medication or consult with an occupational therapist.

Tip: Make Sure to Nurture Your Child's Creativity

One of the ways humans manage energy is through creativity, either by pouring enthusiasm into the learning process or by diving deep into creativity to rest and restore after challenging work. Even if you have found the best school fit for your active child, they may still come home with energy left in the tank. Engaging in creative pursuits, whether that is music, art, or imaginative play, takes energy and enthusiasm that can serve as a protective factor for your child's social and emotional development by helping them get their energy out in a joyful way. A creative outlet is particularly helpful for neurodivergent children because it's often nonlinear, and so is your child's brain. If you feel your child has creative energy that is not being tapped into, follow their interests until you see them light up. This might include taking an improv class, listening to music and dancing together, or going hiking on the weekends so they can experience learning new things in environments that match their energy levels.

Finding a Balance

Help Your Child Find Their Energy Rhythm

Once you have noticed your child's patterns of energy during the day, week, month, and even seasons of the year, you can begin helping them understand the rhythms of their own nervous system. Introduce opportunities to practice activities to see if they help your child either get their energy out or recover from being tired. You can suggest doing something for a week, or just on the weekend, because a trial period is easier to commit to than a new routine for many children who struggle with change. Normalize for them that we all have a different level of energy and validate for them that we all need something different to feel better after doing hard things. When you find something that works, like jumping on a trampoline or napping with the family cat after school, help them connect that those activities can make them feel better because their energy needs are being met.

Support Your Child's Executive Functioning as Needed

Practicing executive functioning skills at home *and* at school will help your child feel that both you and their teacher understand what they are capable of independently, and when they need support. Communicate with your child's teacher about what they can do at school and what they are doing at home. If you find out that your child is cleaning up after themself at school but not at home, get curious about why they aren't doing it at home. Are they out of stamina for the day or are they more capable than you realized? As parents, we sometimes do too much for our kids and can get into patterns of moving them along by doing it for them simply because it's faster. However, when we do this we interfere with their autonomy of building skills. Our challenge is this: Help our kid enough to avoid shutdown, but don't help so much that they never experience frustration that will lead to building emotional stamina for learning.

When to be Concerned: Burnout

It's possible to support your child's energy needs as well as you can, but the natural hustle of daily life and school life combined with the sensitivity of their nervous system sends them into burnout. Most of us are familiar with the term *burnout,* defined here as physical and emotional exhaustion, but we aren't as aware that some children can reach burnout simply from trying to live their life. Autistic children who fatigue easily are the most at risk for burnout, and this usually happens when kids are asked to continue showing up in environments with sensory, social, and academic demands higher than they can process, which can lead to a shutdown response. Burnout may look like school avoidance or work avoidance over an extended period of time, even if they physically attend school. Children in burnout are emotionally shut down, so they may say things like "I don't care" because it's easier not to care than to put forth the effort to try.

Here are some things you can do if you think your child might be experiencing burnout:

- Talk to their occupational therapist or mental health provider about how you can reduce their sensory and emotional overwhelm by reducing demands temporarily so that they have space and time to recover.
- Take a bird's-eye view of their life and see if they are getting enough sleep, nutrition, and joy to fuel the effort they are asked to put forth every day.
- Reduce demands until your child feels more capable of initiating engagement in activities they enjoy.
- As your child is ready, increase opportunities for engagement with interests, especially if this is in trusted relationships with others.
- Focus on the process of learning for your child and not necessarily on academic achievement. Can your child learn a new hobby or art form they are interested in? Can they continue to read for pleasure? This allows them to engage in the process of learning without extra effort.

Teacher Email Script: Checking In on Your Child's Energy at School

Ms. [Teacher],

Thank you for letting me know that [Child] has not been participating in language arts class. Is that class always right before lunch? I'm wondering because [Child] tends to be pretty irritable and avoidant at home when she is hungry, and I'm thinking that she might need a snack for language arts class. Because of her ADHD and dysgraphia, as you know, writing is the hardest subject for her. I imagine that the distraction of hunger can make it hard for her to put forth effort in that class. Let me know if this sounds related to what you see or if you notice any other patterns.

Thank you for all you do!
[Your name here]

Kid Chat Script: Checking In on Your Child's Energy at Home

I'm guessing it feels overwhelming when I leave you a list of chores to do when you get home from school. Is that why you haven't been doing any of them? Are you too tired, or do you not know how to get started with what I'm asking? (If too tired) *Let's make a plan for you to do your chores on Saturday mornings from now on.* (If they don't know how to get started) *I'm going to do the first step with you, and then you can do the rest when you get the hang of it, okay?*

Chapter 4

Motivation to Learn

"I don't care about this."

Assuming that a child's sensory needs are met and they trust the adults around them, the next variable that's essential to learning is motivation. While it's easy to assume that if a child has the skill to complete a task, they should be able to do it, skill alone isn't enough. The child also has to care about learning to propel them forward, especially if learning is challenging for them. Many neurodivergent children are not motivated to meet the demands of those around them just by being told to do something. They *are,* however, motivated by their interests. For some neurodivergent children, interests are soothing because they are familiar and comfortable, while others find interests highly satisfying because the topic feels intensely relevant to them. The YouTuber, musician, and author Penn Holderness describes in his book *ADHD Is Awesome* that sometimes his motivation to write music is so strong that he has to leave meetings, explaining that he won't be able to focus on what anyone is saying until he gets the song written down.

In a classroom, this type of hyperfocus might look like a child tuning out all the noise around them and deeply focusing on reading. Your child's teacher might assume that their ability to focus so intently will translate to other tasks, then become frustrated by your child's unwillingness to participate in something like a transition to cleanup. This can be true in both the classroom and at home. Many parents I talk with say, "I can't get my child to care about chores or homework," and this is often because their motivation for hard or boring tasks pales in comparison to anything else going on around them—especially if it's a screen. In this chapter, you will learn that incorporating your kid's interests into what you need them to do is a motivation game-changer. Love Pokémon? Let's play Pokémon Go at the grocery store! Love 1980s pop music? You get to be the DJ while we clean! Love to talk about climate change? You get to water all the plants in the house! I'll also walk you through the difference between internal and external rewards, making sure the pace of learning is aligned and helping kids build frustration tolerance.

But first, let's see how motivation can play out in a classroom when a student with ADHD just wants to doodle.

Leo's Story

After checking in at the front desk, I made my way down the wide, bright hallway lined with tempera fingerpaint art to Ms. Johnson's second-grade classroom. A single-file line of kindergarteners passed me, and several students waved, noticing that I was a new face. I recalled the receptionist's instructions and turned down the next hallway to find Ms. Johnson's classroom on the left. I quietly entered and caught Ms. Johnson's eyes. "Thank you for coming," she whispered.

"He's the one with the red shoes." I had not met Leo yet, but I had spoken to his dad, Seth, and Ms. Johnson about their concerns. Seth was a single father who had told me he hadn't been concerned until Ms. Johnson asked for more support for Leo.

I had come to observe so I could see what school was like for Leo, who was in fact wearing bright red basketball shoes. I had met with Seth several times in my psychology practice for advice on supporting Leo's high activity level, impulsivity, and distractibility, which was most problematic during writing tasks at school. Seth wasn't seeing the same concerns at home—in part, I thought, because Leo had his dad's full attention as an only child and Seth was used to his son's high activity level. I knew from my conversations with Seth that Leo had always been an active and inquisitive child. Seth had never been concerned about Leo's learning, so he was stumped as to why, ever since the beginning of second grade, Leo would become angry every time he was asked to pick up a pencil. I had already reviewed Leo's psychological evaluation report, and while he did not have a writing disability, testing revealed an uneven profile where his intelligence and reading skills were in the superior, or gifted, range and his writing skills were average compared to others his age. While Leo's writing scores did not indicate he needed writing intervention (the way a child with dysgraphia might), he very likely felt that his writing skills were not as strong as his reading skills and his ability to problem-solve.

Leo was a twice-exceptional, or 2e, learner, which means he was intellectually gifted and also had a diagnosis of ADHD. Accessing needed support can be difficult for 2e learners because they often *look* "just fine" in the classroom, but they *feel* like they are failing. In the classroom, Leo was reading novels above his grade level but struggled to write answers to comprehension questions, leaving him feeling annoyed and defeated. Twice-exceptional students like Leo are at risk for developing negative self-talk despite their strengths, which is what his teacher was beginning to observe. From our phone conversation, I gathered that Ms. Johnson had tried all her tricks, including moving Leo's seat to minimize distractions, offering a reward for completing his work, and having him stay in from recess to get one-on-one help, none of which had worked. The moment I saw Leo's red basketball shoes, I realized why the staying-in-from-recess strategy hadn't worked. If Leo loved playing basketball as much as he loved brightly colored basketball shoes, then missing recess likely pushed him outside his emotional window of tolerance and shut down his learning, whether individualized support was being offered or not.

As I settled into a hard plastic, child-size chair at the back of the room, I first noticed the sensory experience of the classroom. A low buzz of chatter was coming from students working in small groups with math manipulatives. Leo was socially engaged with his group, building and taking apart plastic blocks to demonstrate various quantities. His mood was positive, he cleaned up when asked, and he didn't seem bothered by the fact that a stranger was visiting. I took note of these strengths as social problem-solving, math confidence, fine motor skills with blocks, and flexibility with change. Leo's body moved quickly, and he preferred to stand while working. I recalled from his evaluation that his processing speed was faster than others' his age, and I could almost see the wheels in his brain turning as his body quickly moved through the transition to reading time. When waiting in line for a peer to choose her book, his body became more active, bouncing in place as he tried to control his impulse to pick the book *for* her.

During reading instruction when a classmate was reading aloud to the class, Leo looked frustrated at the slow pace and, rather than following along, flipped pages briskly, appearing to read silently to himself. Because Leo had begun to hyperfocus on reading silently, he missed which chapter had been read aloud and needed a prompt from Ms. Johnson to stop reading and listen to the class discussion. This redirection frustrated Leo; he sighed heavily and whispered under his breath, "I don't care." It was clear to me that Leo's brain was moving faster than the pace of the learning around him. He pulled out a spiral notebook and began doodling. I noted more fine motor strengths, seeing that he had the hand strength to draw, so I wondered what was getting in his way with writing.

When Ms. Johnson asked him to put his notebook away, Leo exploded. He groaned loudly, slammed the notebook closed, and put his head down on his desk. He had clearly been pushed outside his window of tolerance, but it wasn't because he struggled to read—it was because he struggled to slow down. I was starting to form a hypothesis: Even though Leo's writing scores were average compared to his peers, he was likely writing slower than the pace of his thoughts, which caused him frustration similar to what I was observing during the reading lesson. The multiple redirections from his teacher interrupted his deep interest in reading, and he struggled to stay motivated to answer the discussion questions along with the class.

To better understand Leo's learning experience, we have to understand what it takes to cultivate the motivation to learn. In order to maintain motivation to learn:

- Our sensory needs must be met.
- We must feel safe in our relationships.
- Our interests must be incorporated.
- The pace of learning must be maintained.
- Our executive functioning must be supported.

Without one or more of these variables, our motivation begins to crumble and we lose the ability to care.

Building Blocks of Learning

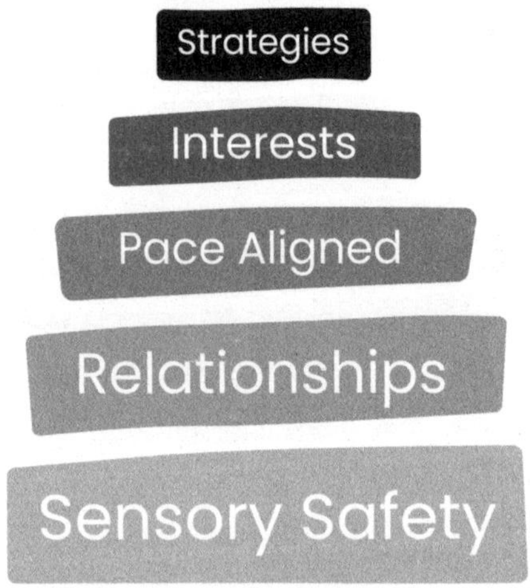

Emily W. King, PhD ~ Learn with Dr. Emily®

However, when the building blocks of learning are aligned and stacked in favor of the child, the more easily they will be able to engage in meaningful learning.

Lived Experience

"When I'm not in school, I learn by going outside and reading in nature." —Grayson, age nine

"I have to see a need or necessity to be engaged in the learning." —Isabel, age forty-three

"I love learning. I am researching a topic or a few topics all the time." —Adrienne, age forty-two

What the Science Says About Motivation for Neurodivergent Learners

Scientifically speaking, there are two types of motivation: approach motivation and avoidance motivation. Approach motivation happens when our brain releases a neurochemical indicating that something enjoyable is about to happen, while avoidance motivation occurs when our brain releases hormones to trigger a sympathetic nervous system response, or fight-or-flight, which moves us away from a threatening or unpleasurable experience.[1]

How Motivation Develops

In order for a child to develop a healthy system of motivation, they need to experience a "combination of internal (intrinsic) drivers supported by positive feedback."[2] We develop both approach and avoidance motivation in childhood by interacting with intrinsic and extrinsic feedback in our body and environment. In other words, when something feels good, we want more of it, and when something feels bad, we want to avoid it. Assuming a child is rested, fed, and comfortable, they are intrinsically motivated by the joy of play and the satisfaction of learning. This pleasurable feeling of accomplishment then leads to becoming more engaged with learning because it *feels* satisfying. However, what drives us to do what we do varies from person to person and is influenced by our internal physiological states, the current environmental conditions, and our past history and experiences.[3]

As we discussed in Chapter 2, infants learn about pleasurable interactions within the safety of their attachment with caregivers. As children grow and experience things that may activate their avoidance motivation, like a fire drill or another child taking their toy, they must rely on a trusted caregiver to remind them they are safe despite feeling startled. This process of perceiving potential danger and checking in with a trusted caregiver for reassurance creates resilience in young children as they grow. However, imagine how this developmental process could get disrupted if a child with ADHD is reprimanded for using doodling as a strategy when bored. This is just one scenario where a neurodivergent child may notice that their effort leads to negative feedback, which might weaken their motivation for using a helpful strategy that isn't hurting anyone. So when putting motivation in the context of a neurodivergent learner, we need to understand not only their sensitive nervous systems but also individual differences in what feels motivating to them, as it can vary widely from what we assume is motivating simply based on their age or gender.

External Versus Internal Motivation

In recent years there has been much debate around rewards, sticker charts, and point systems, all otherwise known as extrinsic motivation. On one hand, if we always reward children with stickers and points, they will learn to work for the carrot and not an internal feeling of accomplishment. On the other hand, if we never put structure around a child, they may never get started and do only the next thing that feels good to them. While external motivation, like praise and stickers, immediately reinforces a child's behavior, it's how children feel on the inside, or their intrinsic motivation, that is considered to have the strongest and most lasting impact for young children.[4]

In my experience with neurodivergent learners over the years, I have landed somewhere between the sticker chart and free-range parenting. While we do need to give our kids freedom so they can grow in confidence, we also need to supportively place structure around them so they can reach their potential. What this might look like in practice is incentivizing a child with a point system (if that's motivating to them) to establish a new morning routine that then leads to smoother transitions into the school day. At first, the points are exciting and engaging, but as soon as the morning routine has become a habit, the points turn into checkmarks, and the intrinsic feeling of accomplishment for a smoother, happier morning takes over as the rewarding experience. If we think of extrinsic rewards like jumper cables to a new routine, we are likely not going to overuse them. There is a time and a place for extrinsic motivation in the short term, but intrinsic motivation should always be the goal in the long term.

External Motivation at School

If your child attends public school, you will likely become familiar with a program called Positive Behavior Interventions and Supports (PBIS). PBIS is a school-wide approach where expectations are communicated to the entire school and students earn tickets for positive behaviors like kindness, respect, and effort. However, Emily Kircher-Morris and Amanda Morin make a great point in their book, *Neurodiversity-Affirming Schools,* when they ask, "Who is deciding what behavior is 'unwanted' and what behavior is 'appropriate'?"[5] Private schools also use school-wide systems to motivate positive student behavior, but each school has a different name for these programs.

The primary barrier to school-wide positive behavior programs working for neurodivergent learners is that behavioral expectations can be too high for students who need to move their bodies, work at a slower pace, or struggle to follow directions. If a teacher is not well versed in understanding sensory needs, impulse control difficulties, and emotional regulation differences, they may assume your child is actively choosing noncompliance rather than struggling to follow directions. Neurodivergent learners can still be externally motivated, but the expectation has to be attainable for them and within the context of their abilities. When you meet with your child's teacher, you may need to revise the expectation and individualize the motivator. For instance, your child may not be capable of completing the same amount of work to earn a ticket as the rest of the class, but they can complete an appropriate amount of work for their skill set in order to earn a ticket. Your child may not care about a paper ticket but may be highly motivated to talk about their cat with the school counselor over lunch. If your child is being reprimanded for not meeting schoolwide expectations that you don't think they have the skills to meet, collaborate with their teacher to get to the bottom of what they are capable of and what will motivate them to succeed.

Internal Motivation Through Interests and Pacing

While we can set up external rewards for our kids, we ultimately want them to become internally motivated to learn. Once a neurodivergent child's sensory and relational needs are met, to increase their motivation, we must incorporate their interests. While most neurotypical learners can often push through learning about topics they aren't interested in to get to a delayed reward, like a fun activity on Friday or a grade on a report card, neurodivergent learners need to know how learning is relevant to them.

Engaging learning through interests is the ultimate example of intrinsic motivation. In fact, most neurodivergent learners struggle to pay attention without their interests being involved. One study found that 96.2 percent of autistic adults believed their specific interests positively impacted their lives and should be encouraged in children.[6] Some adults are concerned that allowing autistic learners to engage in focused interests will interfere with learning; however, researchers have found that incorporating interests often enhances a child's participation and promotes skill development.[7] In fact, if neurodivergent learners are not motivated to engage with what is going on around them, many will hyperfocus on their own thoughts and shut the world out. For autistic learners, specifically, this internal world can feel safer and more entertaining. You may see your child "zone out" when in fact they may be "zoned in" to what I call "their happy place" inside their mind, trying to escape something uninteresting or overwhelming around them.

These are the children who might receive a consequence for not following directions, which pushes them out of their window of tolerance and leads to an emotional shutdown, when they actually just aren't engaged or motivated appropriately. In order to increase a neurodivergent learner's engagement, we have to join them in their interest and see how we can marry that interest to what is going on around them rather than just asking them to step it up. For instance, if a child is deeply focused on their thoughts, but you need for them to join you at the dinner table, you could join them quietly and ask what they are thinking about and then invite them to keep telling you about their interests while you set the table for dinner together. Once you join your child in their interest, think about how you can pair that interest with what you need them to do next.

It's important to always pair an interest with a skill that is challenging for your child, because uninterested plus difficult usually equates to avoidance. Some sample pairings include:

- If reading or writing is difficult, pair with a topic of interest.
- If math is difficult, pair with a motor or visual strength (e.g., cooking, sports, building).
- If group work is difficult, pair with someone with similar interests so they have something to talk about.
- If a child can't get started, pair the task with a visual work plan checklist featuring their favorite fictional character.

Once kids feel safe, connected, and engaged with interests, then we can extend their internal motivation by aligning the pace of learning with their brain. As discussed in Chapter 3, when neurodivergent learners have been working hard to engage with something they are not intrinsically interested in, this effort can zap their energy. That doesn't mean they can't learn new things, it just means we have to be mindful of the timing of new opportunities. For many, how fast or slow the learning is coming at them impacts their emotional regulation and, therefore, their motivation to continue putting forth effort.

For most children, the pace of their learning can be observed in how fast they move their body, process your directions, or tell a story. But as we saw in Leo's story, the pace of a child's learning is not always aligned with what is going on around them. How many times have we as parents gotten frustrated with our child because they need to hurry up? Let's get curious rather than frustrated. It's important to step back and think: Is my child not able to put on their shoes, or are they just not able to put on their shoes quickly? There is a big difference. Many neurodivergent learners can do so many things, but in their own time. When the pace of learning is out of alignment, motivation to remain engaged decreases. We optimize motivation for learning when we are inside our window of tolerance, where we can be curious, compassionate, and creative.

When problem-solving a misalignment with pace of learning, we have to think about what has pushed a child out of alignment and adjust or support accordingly. For instance, many neurodivergent learners are not available for learning every moment of the school day, and when they struggle, we need to ask ourselves: Are they struggling to learn this skill, or are they struggling to learn this skill as quickly as their peers? In Leo's case, was he struggling to read, or was he struggling to wait for his classmates to finish reading? As we discussed in Chapter 3, a child's pace may be impacted by fatigue, sickness, or hunger. We need to look for a pattern, such as a child working well in the morning but struggling in the afternoon. Collaborating with teachers about patterns we notice with academic subjects is helpful, too. For instance, does the child always finish math quickly but struggle to complete writing assignments, and is this seen at home and school? These are the patterns that are helpful to notice and collaborate with teachers about so we can put strategies in place to help.

Motivating a Child Who Is Demand Avoidant

I first heard the term *pathological demand avoidance* (PDA) from a parent in my psychology practice. This parent had researched a constellation of characteristics her autistic child was struggling with and discovered a profile of autism identified by a British psychologist, Elizabeth Newson, who first published research about demand avoidance in 2003. As Newson described it, children presenting with a demand avoidant profile were a subset of autistic children with "avoidance strategies including apparently strategic use of distraction or socially shocking behaviour, and obsessive need for control, reflected in domineering behaviour to peers and adults."[8] As I read more about this profile, which some also call *pervasive drive for autonomy,* I realized that I had been working with these kids all along but didn't have a name for it. Often these children were intelligent, highly verbal, and extremely anxious, which led to verbal or physical aggression when a demand was placed on them. Their avoidance of demands clinically felt like they were protecting themselves from a perceived threat, and even though their reactive behavior helped them feel safe, it was incredibly challenging, and sometimes dangerous, for their parents and teachers.

When learning to motivate children who present as demand avoidant, I have found that giving them autonomy as soon as possible is important. When not in control, which happens often in a parent-child dynamic, these children feel highly anxious about the outcome. When given more autonomy about what will happen next, they are better able to follow a plan. Because of this dynamic, I often recommend that families with a demand avoidant child operate more like teammates with mutual respect for each other than like parents "in charge" and children complying.

Parenting approaches that are structured in a hierarchical way where the adult tells the child what to do and expects the child to follow along are difficult for a neurodivergent child who isn't socially motivated to please. For instance, I've worked with kids who feel their parents are equals and struggle, being younger and less experienced in life. Treating your parents like an equal is considered disrespectful in many cultures, but some kids who are concrete thinkers see everyone as a human being regardless of age. While adults have more knowledge gathered over more years of living, in certain subjects many autistic and gifted kids can be more knowledgeable than some adults. So you may fall into power struggles with your neurodivergent learner when it comes to trying to motivate them. In some instances, it's better to let go of our ego and embrace mutual respect.

Many times families work as a team to get things done around the house and around town but also when researching things and problem-solving. There are times when one teammate has skills the other one does not, and normalizing this may help your child accept when you suggest giving something a try. A trial approach is also sometimes effective. You can say, "let's do the morning routine this way for a week and check in on Saturday about how it's going for everyone." You may feel uncomfortable initially, addressing your young child as though they're older, but many kids will rise to the occasion when treated as an equal. The exception here, of course, is if a child's behavior is emotionally or physically unsafe, in which case you will need to work with a mental health professional who understands your child and family dynamics.

How to Increase Your Child's Motivation to Learn

I wondered if Leo was struggling to write answers to questions because he was so annoyed at waiting for his classmates to finish. But I also saw that students were earning tickets for completing their questions, and I wondered if this was causing Leo to give up on trying as he seemed more motivated to read on his own than he was to earn a ticket. I first suggested that Ms. Johnson allow Leo to doodle while waiting or listening in class. Many students with ADHD need to engage in two things at once in order to attend, so taking away doodling as a strategy was likely making it harder for him to focus. Ms. Johnson and I then defined times in the day where Leo could read on his own without it being connected to written work. When his reading was connected to written work, I suggested written prompts rather than verbal ones, so Leo could work ahead if he wanted to, which increased his motivation to complete his work without waiting. This way he was able to earn tickets for completing his work in his own time and not at the same pace as his classmates. The consistency of this system helped Leo become more motivated to complete his work and helped Ms. Johnson step away from him more often. There is no one way to motivate a neurodivergent learner, but here are more ideas.

Help Your Child Build Frustration Tolerance

Teach Them That Boring Isn't Harmful

Many neurodivergent learners lack the experience needed to persevere when frustrated—which is key to maintaining motivation—largely because they are quick to avoid effortful situations. One way we can help them get used to the feeling of doing hard things is by talking through the idea that boring cannot harm them; it's only momentary discomfort. If your child has a short attention span or is easily anxious, they will need more practice believing that boring tasks won't last forever and are safe. Joining our kids in boring tasks like brushing teeth side by side or cleaning up together can help them feel less alone when doing boring things. We can also teach our kids that being bored is an opportunity for creativity. If your neurodivergent learner has trouble coming up with ideas to occupy themself when they are bored, you might have to help them with a plan. Create an "activity list" with your child to guide them on things to do while waiting for others to be available. At school this might look like a list of quiet activities like reading, doodling, or building with LEGO bricks while waiting for classmates to finish their work. At home it might be watching a thirty-minute show, putting together a puzzle, or playing with Play-Doh.

Teach Them to Notice When They Are Overwhelmed

In order to help them build frustration tolerance, you can also teach your child to notice their patterns of overwhelm. Kids do all kinds of things when they are stressed. Some are physically aggressive, some argue and call us names, some go quiet and hide—every child has a different flavor of expressed overwhelm, and it might vary throughout their development. In my experience, the trajectory of overwhelm progresses from physical aggression to verbal aggression, followed by practice controlling verbal aggression—to not say everything they are thinking.

Some autistic children struggle with the social reciprocity needed to think of a situation from the other person's perspective, which is necessary to be able to reflect on hurting others. Often children with ADHD have difficulty with emotional regulation and impulse control a few years beyond when their non-ADHD peers gain these skills. However, as kids develop and become more aware of their own emotions and their impact on others, we can help them emotionally regulate by offering our calmness through coregulation. This might look like responding to your upset child with validation saying, "I know this is hard. I'll stay until you feel better and then we will figure out what to do next." The goal of working on frustration tolerance is to help your child continue showing up so that their emotional dysregulation doesn't become a barrier to their motivation to keep trying.

When to Use External Rewards

Strengthen Boring Routines with External Motivation

We've touched on how external rewards shouldn't be the only source of motivation, but there is absolutely a place for them in parenting kids with short attention spans. Kids can be motivated only as far as their attention span can take them. If your child has an attention span of minutes, then waiting until Saturday for a reward is not likely to motivate them. They will also likely resist anything that is not fast and fun, so chores are a hard sell. However, they will likely be motivated by external rewards like money, extra playtime minutes, or points that add up to accessing a fun activity. Building in a routine of boring tasks that lead to fun is how we build stamina in kids with short attention spans. Once they get into the routine of taking care of their things and enjoy being able to find their stuff (warning: this may take years), then they will be internally motivated to use strategies to find their things, like a "drop spot" where everything has a home.

Using Technology for Good

Technology is a hot topic in both parenting and education circles because there is a fine line between it being a tool for learning and a distraction that interferes with learning. In the context of supporting neurodivergent learners, technology can be used in helpful ways to support writing tasks and executive functioning skills. For instance, children with fine motor weaknesses can type rather than write, or children with reading disabilities can listen to a story while following along. Technology can also be used as an external reward for task completion. Whether this is watching a show together or looking up pictures of their favorite animals to share with you, we can use technology (with supervision) as a structured external reward when work is complete. Technology can also be used to increase motivation to begin working through visual lists, reminders, and timers. However, it can also quickly become a source of distraction for some neurodivergent leaners so, just like with fidgets, we have to teach them how it's meant to be used.

Teach Them the Difference Between a Tool and a Toy

Ever since the fidget spinner came on the scene, every adult I know has questioned if fidgets are helping kids stay motivated or causing more distraction. Well, it depends. While fidget spinners are usually toys, many other fidgets can help kids stay engaged by keeping their hands busy so their mind can focus, similar to how doodling helped Leo listen. A teacher once told me that she asks her students to self-reflect when they appear distracted by a fidget by asking themselves, "Is it a tool or a toy?" This excellent question causes kids to pause and think about what they are doing and to make a decision about what's helping them learn. If we simply take the fidget away, kids miss the opportunity to decide for themselves. Instead, we can help kids decide if the fidget should be a reward they can play with when they are finished with their work or if it's a tool that is allowing them to stay motivated with their work. The same is true of technology in learning environments. How are they using the internet, a calculator, or an iPad? If they don't yet have the impulse control to use technology as a tool, then we need to talk with teachers about setting up limits to help them stay focused in the presence of technology—or go back to using paper until their brain develops more impulse control.

Nurturing Your Child's Internal Motivation

Help Them Understand When Interests Are Soothing

While interests are motivating, our interests are also soothing for most of us. Many times repetitive engagement in an interest is comforting to an autistic brain, and repetition can be helpful for the ADHD learner to remember things. Just as it's important for autistic learners to understand what soothes them, it's equally essential for us to notice if they are more deeply engaged in their interests than usual, as it may be a sign that they're overwhelmed by life. If you notice this, take a step back and see if you can reduce demands, or if you can allow this repetitive interest to help your child recover from the school day, for instance. Your child may not realize that they need a break to engage with interests or that interests could increase their motivation. Once you make these connections for them, help them understand how they can use interests as a strategy. What's important is that we see engaging with an interest as a tool that can help emotionally regulate a child, bringing them back into their window of tolerance where learning happens. When we recognize this over time and help them learn how to use their interests to not only motivate themselves but recover when overwhelmed, then they will be better able to self-regulate in the future.

Help Them Trust the Process of Delayed Gratification by Enjoying Themselves

If your child has a short attention span, then motivating them with delayed gratification—a reward that comes later for hard work now—is challenging. Delayed gratification is especially difficult for kids with ADHD. For instance, to practice the piano, a child with a short attention span would truly have to like playing the piano or else they won't stick with it. This is why it's so important for kids with short attention spans to enjoy what they are doing. They are likely not going to stick with something in the long term unless they are experiencing intrinsic motivation, otherwise known as having fun, in the short term. Some ideas I've used with my own kids include having a playlist that we listen to only at bath time, playing laundry basketball to get clothes off the floor, and having a dance party after school on Mondays because Mondays are hard! Eventually, bath time, getting laundry into the basket, and Mondays won't be as hard because of all this practice, but to get started, our kids often have to be intrinsically motivated by looking forward to the fun.

When to Be Concerned: Limited Interests

If you are noticing that, more days than not, your child is not motivated by school or has very limited interests, it's time to reach out to a professional for help. Mental health therapists and occupational therapists can investigate your child's interests through play to help you know how to motivate your child in activities at home and school. Also, if your child's mood is irritable when it comes time to do anything nonpreferred, causing you or your family to walk on eggshells, then it's time for more individualized support. The same goes with a limited interest in technology. If you are concerned that your child is exclusively motivated by technology to the extent that you are not able to transition them away from screen time without them becoming emotionally upset, it's time to reach out to a mental health provider.

Teacher Email Script: Sharing Your Perspective from Home

The most helpful thing you can do for your child's teacher is to get your child ready to learn every day. This may begin with consistent morning and bedtime routines, maximizing sleep when possible, and communicating their skills and interests. As a parent, you know what motivates—and what doesn't motivate—your child. Here's a message you could send a teacher if you are curious as to whether they are seeing what you are seeing:

Dear Ms. [Teacher],

I noticed last night when [Child] was doing his math homework that he really struggled to show his work, preferring to do it in his head and writing just the answer. Are you also seeing this at school? I'm guessing it would be helpful for you to see how he got to his answer. At home, he is rushing through his math work to get to playtime, so I'm just checking in about the need to help him learn to slow down during these tasks. Let me know if you have any ideas about how I can motivate him to show his work for you.

Thank you for all you do!
[Your name here]

Kid Chat Script: Helping Your Child Problem-Solve

In order for our kids to build the frustration tolerance needed to persevere with tasks that are not intrinsically motivating, we have to give them time and space. It's hard to see your child about to make a mistake, but when you step back, you can figure out what motivates them independently. Begin with asking your child this question:

> *Is this [tool/tech] helping you get started, or is it getting in the way of your learning? If it's helping, great. Show me how it's helping* [and if it's not, you may have to explain why it's not]. *If it's getting in the way of your learning, let's talk about what you need instead to stay motivated. If being on a Chromebook to type up your work is too distracting because YouTube is just a click away, let's talk to your teacher about how you could do this work on paper.*

Or

> *I know you're having a hard time staying motivated in social studies class because you don't really care about the history of the Roman Empire. It usually helps you stay motivated when we can watch some videos about what you are reading about. Let's write your teacher an email together. Let her know that you're having a hard time staying motivated, and ask if she has any video suggestions. I bet she does.*

Part II

Supporting Your Learner

Chapter 5

Rethinking Homework

"Homework is wrecking our relationship!"

I have had countless conversations with parents sitting in defeat on my therapy couch, trying to find some balance between helping their child complete homework and throwing up their hands at it all. Parents' emotions are often a complex mix of watching their child struggle and remembering their own homework experiences. Plus, homework stress doesn't begin just when our kids pull out their homework folder. Many of us begin dreading the process while driving home from work because we know that when we walk through the door, we will be met with resistance. So we rally our energy to remain as emotionally regulated as possible at the end of our workday. I know this feeling well. In fact, I recently found something I had written on this topic when my kids were younger. See if you can relate.

A Day in the Life with My Neurodivergent Learner

I wake up in the morning ready to implement my well-crafted morning routine that includes the most efficient way to get my kid clothed, fed, packed up, and out the door with the fewest moments of frustration, tears, or conflict. Because school is hard for him, making it through the morning routine and into the school building is our first triumph of the day. During school, he faces challenging tasks. There will be spoken language to process, pencils to grip, a body to keep still, transitions to initiate, social interactions to understand, and nonpreferred academic work to complete. My child is exhausted when I get to him at pick-up. He just "left it all on the field." He needs time to recover, to engage in preferred play, and to rest and reconnect with family. But before he can rest, some days he has therapy to work on emotional regulation, language skills, motor skills, or sensory differences. Some days he will have academic tutoring to reteach concepts one on one. Other days he will have an activity of high interest to engage in something that brings him joy. We won't get home until dinnertime, but this feels worth it. As hard as this is, I also know it's a privilege that our family can pay for this support and that my job is flexible enough that I can go with him to these appointments. But what happens when we get home? There is homework. My child does not yet work independently, so I am now the teacher, except I'm not a teacher. Not only do I not know how to teach my exhausted child, I also need to cook dinner, check on my other child, and return a work call because I left work early to be home after school. It's all too much.

Teachers want us to speak up. Once I explained what our afternoons looked like to my son's teacher, she told me that she absolutely did not want to be causing him or our family more distress. So we collaborated on a better plan. Initially, this plan was for him to do no homework at all, preserving his energy for therapy, engaging with his interests outside school, and relaxing with family in the evening. Over time, as he gained more executive functioning skills, more independent homework completion has followed.

My client Sydney needed a similar plan.

Sydney's Story

Jen sat on my therapy couch with her fingers pressed into her forehead as if she had a migraine. "It's like pulling teeth, and we're all just so exhausted," she said. She had scheduled an appointment with me to talk through the after-school stress she was experiencing with her daughter Sydney nearly every day since the fourth grade began. Because I worked with Sydney in therapy, I was well acquainted with her feelings around learning and could easily see how the homework schedule and expectations Jen described were beyond Sydney's skill set and stamina for that time of day. But I didn't mention this yet.

Jen went on: "If we're lucky enough for her to remember to bring her homework home, we have a chance of getting it done. But even then it's a fight to start it and to get her to stick with it. All this conflict is wrecking our relationship. She clearly doesn't want to be doing more work after struggling at school. I have no idea what to do about it since we have to get this homework done."

After allowing Jen space to vent about the overwhelm she was feeling, I challenged her last statement by asking, "Do you *really* have to get all the homework done?" She looked at me as if I had three heads. She had never considered this; she was simply trying to help Sydney do what the teacher expected. However, I knew that Sydney was dyslexic and had ADHD, so the experience of the school day was already hard for her. She likely didn't get all her work done during class because she worked more slowly than her classmates, only to have more to do after school. No wonder she was resisting it. We need to make sure we are not pushing neurodivergent kids to learn in ways, and at times of day, that are misaligned with how their brain works. To date, general education classrooms have been designed for neurotypical learners, but sometimes, as the computer programming pioneer Grace Hopper said, "the most dangerous phrase in the language is, 'We've always done it this way.'"

I said to Jen: "Sydney is likely not learning anything when she is so upset, and in that moment, your relationship is more important than reading comprehension. Let's talk about what the purpose of the homework is and what skills Sydney has to complete it. Then let's collaborate with her teacher to find a better way."

Jen looked at me with a mix of relief and confusion and said, "We can do that?" She went on to explain that she felt she needed to push Sydney harder, but she had not considered that she was pushing Sydney outside her window of tolerance, causing her to shut down even more. Jen had been reacting out of fear that her daughter would fall behind, but Sydney's distress was diminishing any effort she had to keep up.

Breaking Our Homework Habit

As parents, we often make assumptions about our kids' homework based on our own school experience. Most of our parents were hands-off, and if we didn't get the work done, we were accused of not trying hard enough. For those of us who were high-achieving rule-followers, myself included, it can be hard to imagine that educators are trending toward flexibility with homework in elementary school, but they are. One third-grade teacher I talked to explained that when one of her students is struggling with homework, she first considers if it's the content or the act of doing it at home that is overwhelming. "Home for some kids is such a sacred place that when you bring school into that environment, it stresses them out." She went on to say that homework "is something that should enhance a child's skills that they have already learned at school, and it should never be something that stresses them out, because if it's stressing them out, is it really worth it?" Just because we were held to a certain standard with our homework twenty-five years ago does not mean the same is true for our child.

Neurodivergent children with anxiety due to a learning disability, attention difficulties, or sensory overload are already in need of recovery when they come home from school. When homework is assigned in a specific quantity that is the same for everyone, we ignore the individuality of each child's capacity. Because neurodivergent learners are more prone to burnout, their distress demands a more flexible plan. Our children's emotional overwhelm shows up in their behavior, so if a child is fighting and resisting homework, there is a reason. Any parent reading this book knows that their child's optimal time for focusing is not after four p.m. Plus, when we ask kids to keep working after school despite a low internal battery, we risk damaging their love for learning. But when we pay attention to the patterns of their stress, we can figure out the cost and benefit of academic work after school. We can then collaborate with teachers on a plan for nurturing the skill of independent learning outside the classroom.

There can also be benefits to homework as long as we determine each child's unique readiness for independent learning beyond the classroom and make a clear plan to support them. But first we need to understand what the research says about the effectiveness of taking work home so we can break our habit of expecting the same outcome with homework across neurodiverse groups of learners.

Lived Experience

"Homework is unpaid overtime! After seven-plus hours of school, why do we have to come home, do extracurricular activities, eat dinner, and then do more schoolwork?" —Anonymous, age eleven

"I hate homework! I hate the fact that after I come home from a day of working, I have to work again at home. I just want to relax when I come home and do things that regulate me after a long tiring day of school! The only thing homework does for me is annoy me and stress me out." —Alicia, age eleven

What the Science Says About Homework

In 1989, the researcher Harris Cooper at the University of Missouri analyzed more than one hundred homework studies and, for middle and high school students, found a direct correlation between academic achievement and one to two hours per night of homework completion.[1] However, "for elementary-school students, the effect of homework on achievement is trivial, if it exists at all." This research also found that middle and high school students who completed more than two hours of homework per night showed no additional improvements in academic achievement. Cooper's later work in 2006 and 2008 reinforced his earlier findings: Kids need connection and joy in their lives.[2] At a time when we are finally valuing the mental health of our children throughout their development, it's time to find moderation with homework.

Learning to work independently is a life skill. But we don't get our kids there by asking them to engage in independent tasks before they are ready. We also don't get them there if they never practice working independently. We have to find a balance. As a child psychologist, I define homework as practice away from the classroom. We all need practice with any kind of skill we want to master, and there is only so much time in a day to learn from teachers. Most activities are set up this way, including sports practice and music lessons. But what distinguishes homework from extracurriculars is that we feel it's mandatory. When we are required to do something that we don't feel capable of, it breeds resentment. We feel trapped, and we begin to resist. So I like to think of homework in terms of these two steps:

1. The learner understands the concept or skill.
2. The learner is motivated to improve their skill.

The trouble with homework is that neurodivergent kids are often asked to practice things that they don't understand or enjoy. Or gifted learners are asked to complete homework based on concepts they have mastered, resulting in "busy work."

If the purpose of homework is to practice a skill independently, then let's help children learn how to do that first. Neurodivergent learners need a way to attempt independent learning without feeling defeat, shame, or blame. You can collaborate with your child's teacher to determine what they are capable of doing independently at home and at school and create plans to scaffold independence. In this process of evaluating what's working and what's not with homework and other kinds of independent tasks, we have to look deeper into the science of executive functioning skills.

Understanding Executive Functioning

As parents, we have a sense of when we can step away from our child and see what they can do on their own and when we need to help them. This opportunity to promote independence is afforded to us by our child's executive functioning skills. While our child's nervous system must be emotionally regulated to remain open to learning, it's their executive functioning skills that usher them through the tasks. The weaker the executive functioning skills, the more adult support a child will need to remain on task. Our executive functioning skills allow us to organize our thoughts, initiate a task, attend to that task, see the task through to completion, and reflect on our performance. Children use these skills not only for homework but in daily care tasks and chores at home as well. Any time a child is following multistep directions, transitioning, sequencing tasks, controlling their impulses, or problem-solving, they are using their executive functioning skills.

We are not born with the skills that help us control our impulses, make plans, and stay focused; rather, these skills evolve throughout our infancy, childhood, and adolescence.[3] While genetics provide a foundation for our capabilities, it's our exposure to routines, tasks, rules, games, and impulse control that develop our executive functioning. In other words, if you did everything for your child, they would never learn to do it for themself.

As a parent, you might be thinking that the preschool years and the teen years are fraught with extra needs for emotional support, and you would be right. A child's skills change most rapidly between the ages of three and five years old and again in adolescence. These are the years when our kids need the most structure around them to help them grow through challenges and reach the next level of independence. Our prefrontal cortex, which is the site of executive functioning in the brain, does not fully develop until our mid-twenties—long after most of us have finished school. And for neurodivergent learners, specifically those diagnosed with autism and ADHD, the prefrontal cortex has been found to have structural differences and delays, respectively, that impact not only tasks like doing homework but also decision-making, impulse control, and social problem-solving.[4]

Every part of learning involves our executive functioning. Some experts compare executive functioning to an air traffic controller in the brain, in charge of managing multiple pathways of information and constantly deciding which ones need our attention at any given moment. Our executive functioning skills help us focus on the task at hand, monitor our mistakes, make decisions, revise or pivot our plans, and control our impulses if we become overwhelmed. In the case of homework, such as a math worksheet, the following steps are needed to successfully execute the task from start to finish:

1. Pay attention when the teacher says there is homework.
2. Write down or remember the homework assignment.
3. Put the homework assignment in your folder.
4. Put the folder in your backpack.

5. Take your backpack home.
6. Take the folder out of your backpack.
7. Sit down and take out the homework.
8. Read the directions for the homework assignment.
9. Find a pencil.
10. Start the homework.
11. Ask for help if you get stuck.
12. Stay focused until the homework is complete.
13. Put the homework back in the folder.
14. Put the folder back in your backpack.
15. Take your backpack to school.
16. Take the folder out of your backpack.
17. Take the homework out of the folder and put it in the homework bin.

For children who have difficulty paying attention, initiating tasks, and staying organized, you can see why you might be pulling crumpled papers out of the bottom of their backpack.

If you are reading this book, your child's executive functioning challenges have likely interfered with their task completion at some point along the way. Most often their prefrontal cortex is to blame, and the best course of action is to provide a predictable environment as well as a sense of security. Supporting executive functioning skills is like smoothing the runway to learning.[5]

Neurodivergent learners often need support with homework into the middle school years because their executive functioning skills emerge later for them than for their neurotypical peers. In a study comparing the attention, hyperactivity, and impulsivity of children with ADHD to their non-ADHD peers, researchers found that children with ADHD lagged one to three years behind.[6] I'm often asked by parents if they should be concerned that their child with ADHD acts younger than their chronological age. While I'm not concerned, as this is expected, I remind parents to slow things down and plan to support them on independent tasks like homework longer than they may think. However, don't assume your child won't achieve great things. Your neurodivergent child will make progress; it's just difficult to predict what that looks like or when it will happen. If you stay focused on helping them feel safe, build relationships, seek out interests, ask for help, and try again, their own version of success will begin to emerge.

How to Improve the Process of Homework for Your Child

While it was possible that Sydney didn't have the skills to complete her homework, we needed to determine what she was capable of or, rather, her "just right" zone for learning at that time of day. Jen communicated to Sydney's teacher what their afternoons and evenings looked like and asked for individualized homework to trial a shorter amount of work. It turned out that Sydney's teacher had had no idea how much difficulty she was having at home, because her homework always came back completed. Her teacher wasn't seeing the same struggle during the school day, but she did observe that Sydney's attention span shortened after lunch. Through this collaboration, Jen and Sydney's teacher determined that Sydney ran out of steam for challenging academic work around one p.m. every day. They decided to send home only the work that Sydney was interested in at first and to refrain from sending math home until her teacher observed mastery of these concepts at school. They also added a home/school checklist to Sydney's folder so that Sydney, her teacher, and her mom could communicate every day about whether there was homework. Sydney's teacher was grateful that Jen spoke up and assured her that with this new plan in place, she believed Sydney could improve her homework skills before middle school.

Finding the "Just Right" Zone of Learning

The concept of finding a child's "just right" learning zone is not new. The zone of proximal development (ZPD), a theory of learning developed in the late 1920s by psychologist Lev Vygotsky, has always resonated with me when working with children of all ability levels. Vygotsky defined ZPD as "the distance between the actual developmental level as determined by independent problem-solving and the level of potential development as determined through problem-solving under adult guidance or in collaboration with a more capable peer." In other words, we hit a ceiling of understanding if we are learning alone. When someone with slightly deeper knowledge or greater skill shows us how to level up, we are more capable of learning. The caveat is that the new thing we are learning cannot be too far outside the zone, or we will feel defeated and give up.

The zone of learning is relevant not only for learning academic content but also for building executive functioning skills. Imagine you are a nine-year-old with ADHD who goes to school every day to work hard, but many times you forget to bring home your homework folder, which leaves you feeling defeated. You may internalize these experiences with an "I must be dumb" mentality. In reality, you are very good at writing stories and creating art, but being organized for homework after school is outside your "just right" zone of learning. Your struggles with homework have nothing to do with your intelligence and everything to do with your executive functioning weaknesses. You need a strategy! A defeated child is not motivated to work harder, but an empowered child, who feels capable with visual checklists and reminders, will likely stay motivated to become more independent.

During the elementary years, children have short attention spans and limited stamina, so they are more interested in play than in seatwork. Many parents will need to sit with their elementary-age children to help them attend to their homework. Most children shift from needing parental help with their homework to completing it independently sometime between third and fifth grade. However, neurodivergent children may not be able to work independently for several more years. The tricky part is that there is no road map for neurodivergent learners other than following your child's unique developmental path, which may not parallel the academic curriculum. For some children, having a parent nearby is all they need to maintain attention to homework, but for others it feels like a forced, emotionally charged conflict void of any quality learning. If the latter is your experience, share what you are seeing at home with your child's teacher and ask them about your child's independent work habits at school.

Neurodivergent children, who are emotionally spent at the end of the day, challenge us to reassess our understanding of homework and find a balance that makes the process worth it. Because homework correlates to higher achievement scores in the middle and high school years, there is a benefit to preparing kids for more independent work toward the end of elementary school. However, we need to advocate for a balance of independent work after school that adds practice for skills already understood, not forced completion of work that is too difficult. The goal is to find the zone of learning that works best for them, and to rethink your definition of success when it comes to your child's progress. Keep reading for strategies to support your neurodivergent learner at homework time.

Set Your Child Up for Independent Success

Begin with What Your Child Can Do Independently and Adjust from There

Can she play independently for ten minutes? Often, the first thing children can do independently is something of interest because they are internally motivated. However, if you know your child can play with Play-Doh (preferred) for ten minutes independently, it does not mean that she can also complete homework independently for ten minutes. Account for the fact that homework is nonpreferred, and make an adjustment. See if she can do homework independently for five minutes, or see how long she can attend to homework when you sit with her. For supporting unpreferred tasks, set a visual timer (I like the Time Timer) to help your child see how long they will try attending to the work until taking a break. Instead of saying, "You need to get the work done by the time the timer is done," which can cause anxiety, you can say, "Let's see if you can work on math for this long" and point to a visual timer. "Come and get me when the timer is done."

Consider Homework Only in Preferred Subjects at First

If your child is struggling with homework, ask their teacher if they can choose homework that incorporates their interests. Even if your child is tired after school, they may be able to practice working later in the day on a preferred task. For younger children, this might look like searching for an item or game to bring to school to talk about. Planning show-and-tell is an example of preacademic homework that combines interests and executive functioning (i.e., planning and organization) without seatwork. For older kids, this might look like making sure homework that is sent home requires a skill they have already mastered, so that you are asking your child only to practice and not to learn something new. For many kids, preferred homework can be reading a book of their choice. Reading with a loved one builds connection, imagination, and social comprehension skills; heightens feelings of security and confidence; and fosters a love of learning.

Consider Creative Ways for Your Child to Show What They Know

Your child might be tapped out on seatwork for the day but still be interested in learning after school. Notice what they gravitate toward. If they are reading independently, building something independently, or creating music or art independently, make sure you tell your child's teacher about this. Send their teacher an email with a story, picture, or video of something your child has learned on their own. Teachers love to hear about all types of learning and may be able to incorporate your child's ideas into classroom learning.

Work on Nonacademic Independence

If your child struggles with academic homework, spend time outside school working on nonacademic tasks, like following a list of household chores, to build their stamina and attention span for nonpreferred tasks. Completing chores helps kids practice sequencing tasks, using fine and gross motor skills, and attending to a task through to completion, which are all executive functioning skills. As we discussed in Chapter 4, emphasize the delayed gratification of how a clean space feels better, how happy we make pets when we feed them, and how rewarding it is to watch plants grow. Share your observations about your child's independence with nonacademic tasks at home with their teacher, and ask what they can do independently at school. The goal is to find a balance between enabling and overwhelming your child so they feel empowered to gain skills.

Strategies for Supporting Executive Functioning Skills

Create Visuals to Support Sequencing Tasks and Make Homework Time Predictable

When we create visual lists, we don't have to rely on our child's ability to remember a plan stated aloud. If you find that you repeat yourself often, write out a homework checklist like this:

1. Take out the materials.
2. Decide which work to do first.
3. Get started.
4. Put the completed homework back in the folder.
5. Put the folder into your backpack.

Designate the same time every day for homework to help your child predict and remember when it's time to get started. Try aligning homework tasks with your child's energy. For instance, if your child runs out of steam as the day goes on, do the hard task before dinner and the easy task after dinner.

Have Your Child Name Their School Supplies

This might sound silly, but when a pencil has a persona and feelings about being left behind, it can help your child remember to "take care" of it. We more easily remember things that have meaning to us. If your child has a certain item that they cannot keep track of, like pencils or a water bottle, it's time to give it a name and a story. Just yesterday I was talking to a sixth grader who loses four pencils a day, one for every class period. This has happened as long as he can remember. He blames it on anxiety about being late to his next class, which makes him leave each class in a rush and forget his pencil in the process. If this sounds familiar, have your child name their pencil and give it a story. Use masking tape for a pencil name tag, and have your child create a dialogue about how Jeffrey the pencil might think "Dude! Don't leave me behind!" or how Tabitha the pencil can't wait to rock those math problems next class period. You might get an eye-roll, but you also might sprinkle in just enough humor to cut through their anxiety.

Create a Folder or Binder Homework System

The first skill to build with homework is remembering to bring it home. At the elementary level, children often have just one homework folder, but by fifth grade they may have a binder of assignments. You have to help your child learn a homework system and practice filing work in their binder. I provide resources, suggestions, and guidance on my website, which you can find at learnwithdremily.com, for how to create a folder or binder system.

Create Shorter Deadlines for Projects

For long-term projects, consider asking the teacher for shorter deadlines, or create your own by portioning out a project to teach time management. Think about projects not just as a way for your child to explain what they understand, but as executive functioning practice. Talk with your child about predicting how long each project task will take, and map out shorter deadlines. Check in at each deadline, and decide if they need to ask the teacher for help. Be cautious about the accommodation of extended time: For some, extra time can encourage procrastination. If your child is susceptible to putting off the work, shorter and more attainable deadlines will likely be better than extended time.

Practice Finding Assignments Online

Parents of neurodivergent middle schoolers are often frustrated that their kids don't know what to do for homework. This is because when the teacher announces an assignment in class, the neurodivergent student may not have the attention, planning, and organization skills needed to write it down. When we were in school, we may have called a friend to find out about an assignment, but now our kids can look at online classroom portals. Sit down with your child after school and come up with a plan. You will need to figure out the classroom portal yourself so you can help your child develop a system for finding what to do and making a checklist to get it done. However, once they begin to show some independence, even inconsistently, step back and become their executive functioning coach. Your goal is to simply remind them to check the classroom portal rather than to walk them through each step every day.

What to Do About Forgotten Homework

Your child will likely forget to bring things home or will leave completed homework on your kitchen table. When we're parenting neurotypical kids, we can often allow them to feel the natural consequence of a forgotten assignment with a poor homework grade, and the sting from this one experience will remind them not to leave their homework behind next time. But for neurodivergent learners, that's not usually how it works. Kids with executive functioning weaknesses are already doing the best they can, and realizing they forgot an assignment, again, usually doesn't make them try harder—it leaves them feeling defeated.

Most elementary teachers don't hold strict homework deadlines, so work with your child's teacher on a system, like a laminated checklist card on their backpack. As your child enters middle school, you will notice teachers holding them accountable with zeros for missing work. Talk with your child about a strategy like a visual checklist before they leave home in the morning. One family I worked with used an acronym to help their child remember: BLAH (Backpack, Lunch, Agenda, Homework). As your child matures, the goal isn't to penalize them, but to prepare them.

Tips for Collaborating with Teachers

Work on Homework for a Certain Time Frame, Not for Completion

The timing and pacing of homework is important. Describe to your child's teacher what their energy is like after school, and let your teacher decide what is important—or not important—for them to try practicing at home. It's often beneficial to wait on requiring homework assignments until a child is successfully completing that task independently during the school day. Another way to adjust pacing is for children to work only for certain amounts of time and not to task completion. It can be hard for teachers to predict what kids can do at home because they don't observe it. If you observe, for instance, that your child's attention span after school is fifteen to twenty minutes, then create a homework routine for that length of time, and turn in what gets done. This plan can help your child build stamina for completing homework, and your child's teacher can see how much they can accomplish in an allotted amount of time.

Collaborate with Teachers About Learning Disabilities

If your child has a learning disability, like dyslexia or dysgraphia, they are likely supported by a special education teacher who knows how to teach them. Since your child's teacher doesn't come home with you, you might research certain methods to use, like Orton-Gillingham for dyslexia; but many parents understandably aren't able to take this extra time or hire a specialized tutor. If this is the case for you, discuss modifying homework assignments for your child, allowing teachers to assign the amount or type of homework they think your child can complete independently.

Be Cautious About the Amount of Homework Assigned to Twice-Exceptional Learners

Children should not be assigned more homework just because they are intelligent. For instance, a neurodivergent learner who is intellectually gifted and has ADHD is likely ready to move their body and play after school, not do more work. Many twice-exceptional learners despise homework because they already understand the material but don't have the executive functioning skills to complete more work. When you collaborate with teachers to accommodate homework assignments, be sure to discuss your child's ability to complete tasks independently late in the day, which should include a discussion of what motivation and effort look like after school hours.

When to Be Concerned: Negative Self-Talk

If your child is resisting homework more days than not, that's a sure sign that something is too hard or too much for them. Sometimes this shows up as a child negatively talking about themself because they assume that not being able to do homework means they are not smart. For instance, they might say, "I can't believe I forgot my folder again. I'm so stupid!" or "I can never remember to turn in my homework. I must be the dumbest kid at school."

Once your child has calmed down, help them understand that intelligence and executive functioning are two separate skills, and that forgetting to turn in homework doesn't mean they didn't *understand* the homework. Remind them of all the ways they are smart, including nonacademic strengths. Validate that remembering their homework is hard for them, and come up with a plan to support them. Talk to your child's teacher about what they are capable of at school and how that differs from what you see at home. Collaborate to find a balance between helping your child make progress with independent work after school and recovering from the stress of school when needed.

Ten years ago I would leave work early to get my son to therapy appointments, and I was stressing about homework. Today I wish I could tell my younger self: *If it's too hard then it's not aligned. Prioritize what is most beneficial to your son's growth, which includes reducing your stress, having time to rest at home, and enjoying each other. One day, your son will be a senior in high school. He will know where to find his assignments, he will email teachers for clarification on his own, and he will learn in so many ways beyond homework.*

Teacher Email Script: Starting the Homework Conversation

Dear Ms. [Teacher],

I wanted to reach out to let you know that we are struggling with homework on a daily basis at home. I'm met with resistance if homework involves writing, and I'm wondering if you are seeing this during the day. I'm not sure if the work is too hard or if [Child] is just out of steam after school. It seems like on some days, she has about ten minutes of stamina for math but none for writing. I'd love to hear more about what you see at school and hopefully come up with a plan to help her practice working independently after school without causing so much conflict between us at home.

Thank you for all your help!
[Your name here]

Kid Chat Script: Helping Your Child Understand the Homework Plan

I talked with your teacher to share the stress you've been feeling after school with homework. She wonders if practicing only math and reading after school would be helpful. What do you think? Would taking writing out of the mix help? Our goal is for you to practice working independently without feeling overwhelmed. What do you think?

Chapter 6

Testing and Memory

"If I fail this test, I can't go to fifth grade!"

The classroom was so quiet, I could hear my own heart beating. As I slowly walked up and down the aisles of desks, I kept thinking about all the student heartbeats to my right and left. Some were surely racing, while others were perhaps comfortably beating with confidence. I had volunteered to proctor the end-of-grade standardized test at my son's elementary school, which meant I was on my feet pacing for three hours, watching fourth graders answer questions about reading passages, making sure no one was cheating, and replacing broken pencils. No one was allowed to talk until every student was finished. Trips to the bathroom were monitored by an adult in the hallway. When students finished, they could read silently or put their head down. This felt like more of a boredom tolerance test than a reading test.

I had plenty of time for my own thoughts. I thought about how often students take standardized tests. I thought about the students with disabilities who were taking their test in different rooms to minimize distractions. I recalled endless bubble sheets from standardized testing in the 1980s, wishing every time was the last time I had to color in those circles so neatly. I smiled thinking about the year my son took a standardized test in a classroom by himself because the only way he could focus was to read the test out loud. I thought about my therapy clients in various schools across the county taking tests that might not measure their skills. I recalled the anxiety that kids have expressed to me over the years in therapy about tests and how I coached them to remember that no standardized test reflects their worth as a person. As time went on, I thought about my training in administering psychoeducational evaluations in a one-to-one setting so different from this group of ten-year-olds. I thought about the test anxiety I experienced as a student and how that shaped my interest in asking the question: How do we accurately measure what kids know?

As the parent of a neurodivergent learner, you can likely conjure up a few memories of times when your child's skills were not measured by a test. You know that your neurodivergent child is full of knowledge, but helping them communicate what they know sometimes requires a different scenario than group testing taps into. Throughout this chapter, I'll explain the science behind memory, explain how your child's anxiety may impact their test performance, and provide strategies to support them not only when taking tests but also in finding other ways to show what they know.

But first I want to share my own experience with pesky test anxiety.

Dr. Emily's Story

The first time I remember feeling panicked about a test was also the first and only time I got caught cheating. As a seven-year-old, I didn't know how to spell a word and was genuinely curious if my neighbor did, so I leaned over to catch a glimpse. My teacher reprimanded me in a quiet whisper that sent an emotional lightning bolt through my gut. I didn't know then that my nervous system had perceived a threat in my teacher's tone, and my body was checking in for safety. All I knew was that I wanted to never feel that way again, so no more cheating for me. I quickly learned how to play the game of school and luckily had the executive functioning skills to do it. Teachers seemed to like students who worked hard, had neat handwriting, and didn't cause them any trouble. I could do that. So I stuffed my emotions down deep into my gut, leaned into my love of organization, and became a perfectionist.

What I couldn't do most of the time was take a quiz or test without an overwhelming amount of anxiety. I combated this test anxiety with overpreparing, which worked until I took honors chemistry in tenth grade. You have to understand what you're studying to be able to recall it, and I did not understand chemistry. I made it through by never missing a homework assignment, which balanced out my low test grades, but I started to notice something: My classmates didn't need to study as long as I did, and they also weren't as wound up as I was on test day. No one ever suggested that I should drop back to a standard level chemistry class—I was "too good of a student" for that.

Where I thrived was English class. I decided in eleventh grade that I wanted to be an English teacher. My mother was an English professor. I loved reading novels and dissecting the stories of the characters. I loved writing. This was it. It wasn't until my senior year in high school that I started to question myself. I don't remember the questions on the Advanced Placement (AP) English exam; I only remember that I got a 2. That's the score that gets you nothing, no college credit and definitely no bragging rights. I remember feeling really embarrassed. How could I love writing so much and be so bad at it? Turns out, it depends on what I'm writing about. But I didn't know that as a seventeen-year-old. I just thought that after two years of AP English, this test score meant my hard work wasn't good enough.

I pushed on and, as a college freshman, declared English as my major—because it certainly wasn't going to be biology or math. But the testing problem found me again when I was studying abroad one summer at Oxford University. I was taking Shakespeare and eighteenth-century poetry in an immersive experience that involved attending plays in London and reading sonnets in the garden while sipping tea with classmates. This experience was every aspiring English teacher's dream; however, I realized that while I could spend days interpreting a Wordsworth poem, I was terrible at recalling quotes from Shakespeare. My test anxiety would wipe my brain in these moments, so I started dreading Shakespeare. I was so caught up in doing well on tests that I was losing my love of learning.

Back on campus that fall, as the leaves changed hues, I took my first psychology class. Something shifted inside me. I loved human stories—the more complicated, the better. I realized that all the literature I loved was about marginalized characters, trauma, and resilience. I wanted to be a psychologist, not an English teacher.

I spent the following summer in the North Carolina mountains as a camp counselor and noticed that the classroom and the outdoors are very different contexts for learning. Campers who were rock climbing had to pass safety standard tests by correctly tying knots and locking carabiners, and those learning to kayak had to complete timed slalom courses to demonstrate that their paddling skills were strong enough to take on a river. Recalling how to tie a knot or turn your paddle to steer yourself down a rapid is a sensory-motor movement coupled with the motivation to stay safe—which is very different from recalling what Hamlet said in Act III.

By the time I returned to campus for my graduate studies in school psychology, I was already thinking beyond what standardized tests could measure. I was fascinated by how we learn, how we show what we know, and how standardized tests can't possibly measure it all. These experiences got me thinking about the limitations of how we measure what kids learn in school. While school districts need test data to track progress across systems, as I tell all kids I work with in therapy, those results are for schools to measure their teaching. There are many other ways to measure what you know.

Understanding One-on-One Evaluations

Often parents assume that group-administered standardized tests provide all the information they need to know about their child's learning. While it's true that for neurotypical children, report cards and standardized test scores adequately track progress, most neurodivergent learners at some point will need an individualized evaluation to more accurately measure their skills. These one-on-one evaluations with a psychologist remove the variables of testing for three hours straight in a group environment. Your child likely had one of these evaluations when diagnosed with autism, ADHD, intellectual giftedness, or a learning disability; I want you to fully understand the purpose of this process.

The evaluation process in public schools has three goals: identify what is interfering with a student's learning, use this data to help the IEP team determine if a student meets eligibility to receive special education services, and provide recommendations for learning and emotional-behavioral support. Evaluations completed by a school psychologist don't result in a clinical or medical diagnosis but rather identify which special education category your child qualifies for to receive services. An evaluation by a psychologist in a hospital clinic or private practice provides a clinical diagnosis and a report you can share with your child's school team.

Psychological evaluations are given by psychologists investigating either a person's intelligence (IQ) or mental health. A psychoeducational evaluation is conducted by a psychologist investigating IQ, emotional/behavior functioning, and academic achievement in order to determine any differences in development or mental health that may be interfering with learning. Neuropsychological evaluations are similar to psychoeducational evaluations, but are conducted by psychologists specially trained in neuropsychology. If your child has a medical condition, like epilepsy, or has had a traumatic brain injury that can impact memory, a neuropsychologist is often the best fit.

Psychoeducational evaluations are designed to figure out *how* students learn, not simply *what* they know. These evaluations are crucial parts of identifying what our children struggle with and determining how we can help them learn. Still, intelligence tests are not blood tests or brain scans, so while psychologists are trained to administer tests in the same way, each child brings their own attention span, effort, and mood to every testing session. Psychologists are also ethically bound to let parents and teachers know if we think any of those variables interfered with the validity of the test results, because sometimes they do.

While it would be fascinating for every child to receive a thorough individualized evaluation to dissect their learning profile, we do not have enough psychologists to do this—and it's not necessary. As I mentioned earlier, most children will not need to be evaluated by a psychologist because they learn well within the general education classroom and their achievement is tracked effectively through report cards and annual group testing. However, we need to dig deeper into student learning when something isn't working, which is often the case with neurodivergent learners. The goal of having your child tested is not to find out what is *wrong* with their learning but rather to discover how the way they engage, think about, and remember information is *not aligned* with the systems around them at school, at home, and in the community.

While the purpose of an individualized evaluation is to determine a diagnosis, in my opinion, the most helpful part of conducting these evaluations is observing a child's attention, effort, stamina, pace, and persistence. For instance, if I'm testing a child who struggles to attend to a timed pencil-and-paper task while sitting in a quiet room, I can only imagine that their attention span will be shorter in a classroom with the buzz of chatter and movement. For some neurodivergent learners, group-administered standardized tests end up measuring a child's attention span rather than their reading comprehension. If you have watched your child become a ball of stress around standardized testing time, or if you feel that the results of your child's standardized testing don't capture your child's skills, it might be because the way they show what they know is out of alignment with how the questions are asked. When bringing your concerns to teachers and school administrators, it's helpful to understand the different ways we learn and retain new information, also known as our memory skills, and how these skills vary across neurodivergent learners.

Lived Experience

"I know [testing] is so that the teachers know how the work is for you. But it's just so many hours of sitting still, wanting to move but having to keep your hand working, moving, writing!" —Alicia, age eleven

"The academically/intellectually gifted teacher at my child's school recognized his need for intellectual rigor despite his test scores not demonstrating his official qualification for the program. As a parent of a 2e kid herself, she saw the spark in him and went out of her way to provide this educational opportunity in a different setting." —Natalie, mom of a ten-year-old

The Science Behind Memory Skills

Parents of autistic learners are frequently perplexed when psychoeducational testing shows a weakness in their child's memory. "But he can remember everything he has ever read at a museum about any type of dinosaur. How is this a memory problem?" I then ask if he can remember multistep directions, and I usually get an agreeable "Ahhh, okay."

We have different types of memory skills that rely first on our attention span, followed by the various ways that we take in, store, and recall or recognize information in order to demonstrate what we understand. Many of the academic difficulties encountered by neurodivergent learners are unrelated to their intelligence and have to do with how their executive functioning, communication, or anxiety interferes with their ability to remember new information. Understanding how our memory works is the first step in understanding how some test formats fail to capture the capabilities of neurodivergent learners.

How Our Memory Works

Memory is the process by which we collect, encode, store, and retrieve information we come across throughout our lives. Information first enters our nervous system through our sensory memory, a process lasting only a second or two, where we involuntarily absorb information through our senses. This new information then enters our working, or short-term, memory, where we hold it while deciding what to do with it. Our working memory is like a cognitive notepad lasting from seconds to minutes, and unless we grab a literal notepad, we lose the information. Just this morning, I was walking my dog and saw a house for rent. It reminded me of a friend moving to town, so I wanted to remember the information on the sign. I was going to take a picture, but my excitable goldendoodle lurched for a squirrel running across the street, forcing me to keep moving. I took note of what street I was on and glanced at the name of the realty company, which was an acronym. For the next few moments, I repeated the name of the realty company in my mind, a strategy called rehearsing, and made an extra effort to remember it so I could later search for a link to send my friend. We are bombarded with similar information all day long, and our attention and working memory help us hold on to the relevant information and release what we perceive to be irrelevant.

Once our brain decides that a piece of information is important enough to hold on to, it makes its way into our long-term memory for safe storage. Our long-term memory is made up of declarative memory (learned information we talk about like facts and events) and nondeclarative memory (learned information we can demonstrate, like rock-climbing or paddling). Many gifted and autistic learners have strong declarative memories, especially for details that are of high interest to them, like the child who can remember all the facts about dinosaurs at the museum. Being interested in a topic strengthens our attention to it, so usually the more focused we are on something, the more we can remember about it. In other words, intelligence is not all that's needed to learn; we must also rely on our memory. One study illustrated this by tracking the literacy and math achievement of seven-to-eleven-year-olds with learning difficulties and found that a child's working memory scores were better predictors of academic achievement than were their IQ scores.[1] Therefore, if we don't accommodate memory weaknesses in neurodivergent learners, we're setting them up for failure.

According to the psychologist Gretchen Schmelzer, information moves from our working memory to our long-term memory in only three ways: through urgency, repetition, or association.[2] Urgency is most often paired with stress hormones and brain chemicals that strengthen the connection between neurons and synapses, leading to memories that can last a lifetime. Repetition, most commonly used in school, occurs when we rehearse facts, like multiplication tables, or actions, like getting dressed, over and over until they're automatic. Repetition strengthens the connection between our neurons, which makes skills easier for us over time.

One of the downsides of repetition and testing is that once the test is over, we are no longer motivated to practice the information, and that synapse (neural connection) begins to weaken. In other words, if we don't use it, we lose it. But when we learn by association, new information connects to already-existing information in our brains. Learning by association is the reason we can recall information we learn through songs rather than text. Music is a multisensory experience that involves multiple parts of our brains, including memories of how the music made us feel. While it can feel annoying to remember that song about U.S. capital cities but not where you put your keys, thinking about different types of memory sheds light on how misalignment between our knowledge and how we are asked to recall it matters. Figuring out how our kids take in information and show what they know can make all the difference in their learning experience.

Recall and Recognition

Once we have encoded information into our long-term memories, learning is complete. Except, in order to measure learning, we have to demonstrate our knowledge. Think about your child and how they express what they know. Are they able to recall information without prompting, or do they need to recognize it? Question-and-answer, essays, and fill-in-the-blank without a word bank are examples of recalling information, while multiple choice and matching formats, as well as fill-in-the-blank with a word bank, are examples of recognition. Once you understand what your child is capable of and what they need support with, you can help plan testing accommodations for them.

Testing accommodations may include testing in a separate setting to improve focus and reduce anxiety, allowing extra time to aid slow processing, or for students with a reading disability, having a math test read aloud to them. Notice when your child does well on quizzes, tests, or assignments, and talk with their teacher about formats of testing that seem to be working. If you have a psychoeducational evaluation report from a psychologist, be sure to share it with your child's teacher. These reports often have recommendations to support your child's attention and memory. (For a "Mapping Out Skills" template based on the results of your child's evaluation, go to learnwithdremily.com/downloads.)

Attention and Memory

When I hear that a child is "not listening" I always want to know if the child is not attending, not understanding, or not remembering the verbal directions. These are all different skills that call for different strategies. The child who struggles to attend may need to move their body or incorporate an interest; the child who doesn't understand may need the information chunked into smaller portions or explained in a different way; and the child not remembering the directions may need a visual list to reference at their own pace. In my experience as a therapist to neurodivergent kids, seeing their face light up with excitement to share their interest is the most authentic form of attention, and it appears effortless. For instance, I can feel the engagement coming from an autistic child talking about their interest versus a topic they find boring. Engaging with interests increases attention, which in turn strengthens a child's memory in the moment. As we discussed in Chapter 3, attending to uninteresting information is effortful and exhausting for most neurodivergent learners, so it's easy to see why our kids find tests stressful. Even when neurodivergent learners arrive to school on testing day rested with a full belly, most will benefit from accommodations to ensure they can show what they know.

Helping Your Child Show What They Know

As the parent of a neurodivergent learner, you will notice that at any given moment, your child's interests, energy, attention, and mood may become barriers to their ability to perform on a test. The best way to help children show what they know is to (1) increase their engagement so more information can get into their memory to begin with, and (2) offer flexible ways to demonstrate knowledge. What follows are strategies for helping your child show what they know and for supporting them in situations where their skills are being measured in ways incongruent with how they learn.

Strategies to Support Your Child's Memory Skills

Make Multistep Directions Visual

As we have previously discussed, visuals can accommodate short attention spans and increase autonomy. There is a common misconception that visual schedules are used only in preschool, but remember, the executive functioning support needed for many neurodivergent learners extends into elementary and middle school. This is because the visual is not only helping them *understand* what to do next; it's helping them *remember* what to do next. Once children can read, visual tools simply become easier to use. Parents and teachers no longer have to draw pictures to communicate the plan; they can simply use lists.

Something as simple as a brightly colored sticky note with three steps on the kitchen counter could be the difference between you repeating yourself until you're overwhelmed and your child feeling capable of checking their list if they forgot what you said. Many families use small whiteboards posted in their kitchen or entryway to catch their child's attention. Your child's teacher could also use this strategy when your child takes a quiz or test with the following steps:

1. Pencil and notebook out.
2. Read directions.
3. Begin.
4. Ask for help if needed.
5. Look over answers when finished.
6. Turn in to the teacher.

Not only do visual lists help kids remember what they are supposed to be doing; they minimize the child's anxiety about forgetting what they are supposed to be doing, freeing up mental energy to show what they know. In other words, it's hard to remember how to do fractions when you are panicking about losing your pencil—again.

Create Routines to Encourage Rehearsal and Automation

Much of the school day is predictable and routine, which is why some neurodivergent learners do well at school but struggle at home. When we can rely on a routine, our brain goes into autopilot, and we don't have to use our working memory as much. So if your child has weak attention or working memory, making the morning, afternoon, and bedtime routine as predictable as possible will likely give them more stamina for the school day. If your child is struggling with transitions or following directions, ask their teacher about the routine at school, and see if you can practice some of these routines at home. For instance, if your child is asked to throw away their own trash in the classroom, have them do it at home. If your child is asked to put their backpack away before sitting down to eat a snack, have them do that at home. Consistency is usually the most effective way to support weak attention and memory skills, so keep routines as predictable as possible across home and school settings.

Consider Medication If Your Child Understands the Content but Needs Help Focusing

Most of my pediatric and psychiatric colleagues recommend medication to support attention if you feel your child's ADHD symptoms are interfering with their ability to learn. In conversation with your child's teacher, try to figure out if their struggle to show what they know largely stems from difficulty focusing. Think about how they focus during academics compared to how they focus in a nonacademic situation like sitting to eat, building with Magna-Tiles, or baking cookies. If your child can sit still or focus only when looking at a screen, this indicates a possible difficulty with sustained attention for you to discuss with your child's provider. When considering medication with your child's pediatrician or a psychiatrist, make sure to discuss your child's movement, sleep, and nutrition quality as well.

Support for Testing

Request Accommodations for Group Standardized Tests

One elementary administrator shared with me that he doesn't find standardized tests very helpful in determining individual student progress, as results rarely show all that kids know. He went on to say that teachers in his school gain more information from classroom assessment, observations, and cooperative learning activities. Still, most schools require at least one group standardized test per school year to track student progress. Talk to your child's teacher about what would help lower their test anxiety and support their attention and memory skills. Commonly requested accommodations include extended time, a separate setting to minimize distractions, or testing with a familiar adult.

Increase Predictability on Testing Days

Many testing situations are routine because they are done the same way every time. However, because testing disrupts the school routine, it's important to prepare routine-driven children for this change in the schedule. Keep life outside school, including the mornings and evenings, as predictable as possible. Ask the teacher or school administrator for the testing day schedule, where your child will be in the building, and which staff members will be there so that you can prepare your child for this "wacky day." The goal is to help your child save all their energy for taking the test.

Thinking Beyond the Test

Redefine Success as Your Child's Happiness and Not as a Test Score

It can be hard *not* to pay attention to test scores. Most parents today were raised in a generation where the higher the grades, the better the opportunity, no matter if our sleep or mental health suffered. However, due to the variable energy of neurodivergent learners on any given day as well as their uneven skills, your child's test scores might be inconsistent. This is when it's helpful to have a psychoeducational evaluation so that your child's skills are assessed in a one-to-one setting to minimize factors like distractions and fatigue. However, if testing situations are challenging for your child, remember that your child is more than a test score. Begin measuring their success by their joy. Notice your child's laughter, satisfaction, and pride because these are the moments they are experiencing success.

When "Good Students" Need Support

Because group standardized tests may not capture the full range of your child's knowledge, it's possible—for twice-exceptional learners especially—to ace standardized tests but struggle to complete daily assignments. This is because some kids have weak attention skills but excellent memory skills. When test scores are the most valued measure of success, struggling neurodivergent learners can slip through the cracks because their grades are "fine." These are the students who never take notes and never turn in homework but make A's on every test, so they look like B students on paper. This is an unsustainable plan for these students when the workload increases in middle and high school because they will likely not have had the executive functioning skill practice to keep up. If this sounds familiar, talk with your child's teacher about what study skills seem lacking and come up with a plan.

Tip: Help Your Child Understand That Intelligence and Attention Are Two Different Abilities

If you hear your child say, "I failed the test because I couldn't remember the answers! I'm so dumb!" it's easy for us as parents to say, "That's not true, you're smart!" but that can feel invalidating to a child, given that they don't feel smart at the moment. Instead, we can say, "I know it feels that way, but understanding the information and being able to focus during the test are two different skills. Let's ask your teacher if you can take the next test in a quiet room so it's less distracting."

Seek Out Learning Opportunities Outside School

Because standardized tests don't allow for the flexibility of using a child's interests to increase engagement, we have to provide opportunities outside testing to increase their confidence with learning. If you find that something outside school brings your child joy, follow their interest. You will never go wrong nurturing your child's confidence, no matter how unrelated it feels to school. Any type of learning is valid, even if it can't be measured by a standardized test. (Read more about nonacademic learning in Chapter 9.)

When to Be Concerned: Relying Too Much on Test Scores

For the most part, educators and parents are in agreement about test accommodations, mainly because parents want to reduce their child's anxiety and school administrators want students to perform as well as they can. As a psychologist, I get concerned when school teams rely solely on test scores to plan support for a child, especially if those scores don't accurately represent the child's skills. This could look like a child with high test scores that mask their need for executive functioning, mental health, or social support. Or this could look like a child with low test scores and strengths in areas not measured by tests. For example, many autistic learners struggle with reading comprehension not because they aren't paying attention when reading, but because they struggle to make social inferences about the character's actions in a story. The weakness isn't about literacy but is rooted in social pragmatic differences associated with autism. A twice-exceptional learner can succeed at making A's on a test but not be ready for the organizational and planning skills needed to handle taking seven classes in middle school. If you think standardized group testing is not capturing your child's strengths or weaknesses, talk to your child's teacher about looking beyond testing to determine strengths and needs for support.

Teacher Email Script 1: Communicating Anxiety About Standardized Tests

Hi, Mr. [Teacher],

Thank you so much for all your help this year supporting [Child]'s high energy and enthusiastic interest in speaking French (even though I'm pretty sure he's the only fourth grader in your class who greets you with "Bonjour!"). Your curiosity in his interest has made him feel happy in your class.

As you know, [Child] is very anxious about the standardized end-of-year English/Language Arts (ELA) test. He gets down on himself about his low test grades in ELA because, as he says, "I know how to speak English really well!" I just wanted to share what [Child] and I have discussed so you can support him with a similar conversation if this comes up.

I've explained that since everyone gets the same test but has different interests, it's impossible for the test to ask him everything he knows. He understands that some parts might feel easy, like finding details in the passage, and some parts will be harder, like predicting what happens next. We've encouraged him to do his best, but he understands that this is just one way to measure his knowledge. He added, "Yeah, because I bet this test doesn't include any French!"

Please let me know if you have any other ideas for supporting his anxiety during this process. I'm so grateful for your partnership.

Thank you!
[Your name here]

Teacher Email Script 2: Communicating New Testing from a Private Psychologist

Dear Ms. [Principal],

I wanted to reach out to share an update on [Child]. Over the summer, we had [Child] evaluated by a private psychologist to take a closer look at his attention and memory skills and investigate a diagnosis of autism. I'm attaching the full report and copying last year's teacher, this year's teacher, and the school psychologist. Based on the evaluation, [Child] was diagnosed with autism and there are recommendations listed in the report to support him during instruction and testing at school. Once you review this information, please let me know when we should meet to discuss adding this new data to [Child]'s IEP. I am available to set up a phone call, or we can go ahead and schedule an IEP meeting to make the appropriate changes.

Thank you for your collaboration!
[Your name here]

Kid Chat Script: Easing Your Child's Test Anxiety

Even though every student in your class has different interests and skills, schools need a way to measure how the class is learning as a group. So every year starting in third grade, students take a test in reading and math. Because every kid gets the same test, it's impossible for the tests to ask about everything you know. Your teachers know that there are many ways to measure what you know, and this is just one way. Because the test is long, you will take it in a room where you will be able to move around for breaks when needed. I've talked to your teacher, and no matter how you do on this test, you will still go to fifth grade.

Chapter 7

Finding Friendship

"They think I'm weird."

"I'm just so sad for him," Kristin said, after reading me an email sent from her son's teacher. Aiden, an autistic second grader, had frightened his classmates at recess when he growled at them while holding a rock in his fist. Even though no one was hurt, Aiden's teacher emailed to let his parents know and to see if they could figure out what was upsetting Aiden so much. Kristin put her phone back in her purse and exhaled. "I have no idea. It's so hard for him to make friends."

While making friends is often the goal, we have to first understand the social milestones that form the foundation of friendship. Developmentally speaking, infants begin socially interacting through eye gaze and facial expressions with caregivers before they can even sit up. Once they gain mobility, children will crawl or walk across the room to grab an item of interest or hand a toy to someone else. These early milestones of noticing, grabbing, and offering lay the groundwork for social connection prior to the development of spoken language. Toddlers then begin to play beside each other, known as parallel play, which is followed by more collaborative play as they learn to use language to request, wait, take turns, and make social predictions about what another child is going to do next. During the preschool years, social interactions become more creative as pretend play skills emerge, and children are not only playing with objects they see but also engaging with ideas in their imagination.

For the neurodivergent child, these early social milestones might be interrupted by differences in communication skills and impulse control, or by interests that misalign with those of their peers. Differing communication skills can make it hard to request a turn or share a play idea. Impulsivity can hinder a child's ability to wait or lead to emotional outbursts when something doesn't go as they expected. Having interests that significantly differ from peers can limit social interactions. Even while learning alongside each other, children can be like ships passing in the night.

So it's not surprising that autistic adolescents report poorer friendship quality and more feelings of loneliness than their typically developing peers.[1] Children with ADHD have similarly been found to have fewer friends, lower-quality friendships, and poorer social interactions.[2] And due to uneven skill sets, twice-exceptional children often struggle to figure out where they fit socially.[3] To help neurodivergent children make friends, we must consider how their early play and communication develops, strengthen any lagging skills, and provide them with social opportunities where they can find others with shared interests. We can explicitly teach children social skills like greetings, asking questions, and taking turns, but forming and maintaining friendships takes experience and practice. It also takes kind, patient, and accepting peers.

Aiden's Story

After talking with Aiden's parents and teacher, I had gathered enough information to determine that he was not trying to hurt anyone at recess but rather had been pushed outside his window of tolerance by classmates interrupting his play. His teacher described how he often wandered around the playground at recess, looking at the ground and talking to himself. Aiden's mom had told me that the idea of him walking around alone made her sad, but his teacher shared that he seemed happy doing this—as if he were using the time and space outdoors to recover and restore a sense of calm.

However, on this particular day, Aiden had paused mid-wander and was digging in the dirt—right in front of the soccer goal. The teacher watched from afar and saw a small stack of rocks beside the hole. She knew Aiden loved rocks and minerals. He was so focused on collecting his rocks that he seemed unaware of the boys shouting at him to move out of the goal box. While Aiden's teacher was walking over to get his attention, one of the boys kicked over the tower of rocks. Aiden stood up, a stick in one hand and a rock in the other, and let out an angry growl at the boys. His teacher arrived just in time.

Because Aiden and his teacher had an established, trusting relationship, she was able to convince him to come with her by saying, "Let's move your rocks to a safer place." Once he was emotionally regulated, Aiden's teacher gathered all the boys together and explained that the rocks were important to Aiden, and they needed to ask for help when Aiden didn't respond to them. After some conversation, Aiden decided that he wanted to keep digging but agreed that the soccer goal wasn't the safest geological site.

Even though Aiden's teacher masterfully supported the boys who didn't understand the importance of Aiden's rocks, this situation could have easily ended with Aiden throwing rocks and hurting someone, or the boys starting to call Aiden names. Aiden wasn't trying to hurt anyone; he was simply reacting to the boy kicking his rocks. It had likely felt abrupt to him, as he was hyper-focused on his rocks and hadn't noticed the soccer game or the boys shouting. Aiden was struggling to make friends, but he was also having a hard time with the foundational skills of noticing his surroundings, predicting social outcomes, and problem-solving. I wanted to get to know Aiden and his play skills better, so I had his parents bring him in for a play therapy session.

On the day Kristin brought Aiden to my office, it was pouring rain outside, so they were both peeling off wet jackets and boots when I greeted them in the waiting room. I mentally noted that the sensory experience of being wet and sticky didn't seem to bother Aiden. This made sense given how much he loved spending time in nature. Aiden was immediately curious about who I was and what we were going to do, so he separated from his mom with little hesitation. Once in the playroom, I told Aiden that he could play with anything he found interesting. I wanted to see what he noticed first. His voice was somewhat monotone, so it was hard to gauge his excitement from his inflection alone.

However, when he opened the bin containing every single character from the movie *Cars,* he jumped up and down and exclaimed, "Ka-chow!" (Lightning McQueen's catchphrase). Aiden quickly pulled out the bin and dumped the cars everywhere in excitement, saying that he had seen all the *Cars* movies *lots* of times. He loved Mater the most, but he also liked Radiator Springs because it was built into the red rocks—and he *loved* rocks. His enthusiasm made me smile, and my play therapist wheels were spinning as I observed him playing with the cars and voicing the characters. Aiden's imaginative play, often a weakness in autistic children, appeared to be well developed within this interest, but over time, I saw that his lagging skill was not in how to play but in expanding the ideas of his play.

Even playing one-on-one in a quiet playroom, Aiden struggled to tolerate my play ideas, speaking sternly in protest when I voiced a character and tried to join in. He seemed to have a play plan in mind, and he was frustrated when I didn't follow it. So we had three goals:

1. Help Aiden expand his awareness of what was going on around him so he could have more social experiences.
2. Build enough trust so that Aiden would let me into his play without becoming overwhelmed.
3. Once Aiden was better able to tolerate me joining his play, find social experiences outside my office to foster friendships.

After playtime, Aiden and I sat on beanbags and completed an activity I call the Friendship Circle, which I learned from a speech/language pathologist colleague. I drew a small circle with several concentric circles on a piece of paper—in pencil so they could be revised later. In the bull's-eye, I wrote Aiden's name and explained that no one knew Aiden as well as he knew himself, which put him at the center of the Friendship Circle. We decided to call the second circle "brothers and cousins," because Aiden said his brothers and cousins were his best playmates. The next circle was "friends," and the outer circle was "classmates and neighbors." I asked Aiden to write in each circle the names of the kids that fit the given category.

After writing his brothers' and cousins' names, he paused. "I don't have any friends," he said with a shrug.

He seemed a little sad, so I said, "Okay, do you want a friend?"

"I guess it would be nice to play with someone at school," he replied.

"So let's think of some potential friends," I said. "Can you think of classmates who you would like to be your friend?"

He looked down and said, "No, they all think I'm weird."

Aiden was more aware of his surroundings than the adults had given him credit for. He explained that he had been called weird for liking rocks more than soccer and for not responding to classmates when they asked him a question. We started by identifying what qualities a potential friend would have, such as kindness and an interest in cars, rocks, or nature.

Lived Experience

"Recess is the best time to try and make friends. Most friends are not my type, and I cannot make many friends." —Sarah, age nine

"The best learning I do is with my friend, Evan. We are really interested in utilities and outdoor warning sirens. We learn all about them by collecting utility flags and then going out to observe how things like gas flows are marked in our neighborhood." —Nolan, age nine

What the Science Says About Friendship

Research has shown time and again that quality social connections lead to longer and healthier lives. The first causal link between social relationships and mortality was documented in 1988,[4] and since then studies have focused on the quantity and quality of social bonds. Quality relationships have been proven to help us manage stress, reduce anxiety and depression, and protect us from heart disease, stroke, and dementia.[5] As social beings, we rely on human connection for support when we are stressed, celebration when we are proud, and shared laughter when we need cheering up. The key to emotional health is not to avoid our emotions but rather to avoid being alone with our emotions.

Our ability to form social connections evolves from infancy

through adulthood. In early childhood, friendships are formed predominantly for companionship and fun, while teen friendships serve additional needs of trust and emotional support.[6] For neurodivergent learners who experience communication differences or social anxiety, these social development timelines are more variable. In order to understand how kids make social connections and why socialization is harder for some, we first have to understand a core concept of social development called theory of mind.

Theory of Mind

Theory of mind was first studied by scientists David Premack and Guy Woodruff in 1978 to investigate whether chimpanzees could understand human intentions.[7] In the context of human development, theory of mind is a social cognition skill that develops during early childhood and allows us to recognize that every person has their own thoughts and interests. This skill helps us see things from another's perspective, make predictions about how someone might react, and feel empathy even when the situation is not happening to us. Children develop theory of mind over time, as they do with other developmental milestones. In neurotypical development, infants and toddlers with caregivers who are attuned to their needs begin building the foundations of theory of mind through everyday interactions. For instance, infants and toddlers begin paying attention to those around them and imitating sounds and facial expressions as a way to play, which leads them to understand how the actions of others are connected with their own experience.[8]

One of the most significant social milestones for toddlers is *joint attention,* in which the child sees something, looks at another person's face to see if they also see it, and then turns back to look at the object *with* that person. Joint attention is often paired with a gesture, like eye contact or pointing. For instance, when a child spots an airplane in the sky and points at the airplane with excitement, joint attention occurs when that child shares their excitement with their dad by looking to see if he also sees the airplane. If the child feels they have their dad's attention, whether by meeting his eyes or by seeing his face turn, they will wait to see their dad's reaction so they can look back at the plane and experience the wonder together. This entire interaction often occurs in seconds, without spoken words, and is a building block for developing theory of mind.

As theory of mind develops into the preschool years, usually around four and five years old, neurotypical children are able to make predictions about others' actions based on guessing what their thoughts might be in a given circumstance. The best-known theory of mind experiment is the false-belief task, where a child is shown a box that is labeled as having candy inside but is then shown that the box is actually full of pencils. The child is then asked what another child, one who has not been in the room, will think is in the box. Most neurotypical four-year-olds will predict that the other child will think it's candy, because that child will not know about the pencils, while most three-year-olds will say pencils, because they are not yet able to predict that the other child's knowledge will vary from their own.[9] What this might look like on a playground is a child watching peers go down a slide, noticing that the child who repeatedly goes down the slide must like it, and predicting that if they jumped in front of that child without waiting for their turn, that child might be upset. So the first child makes a plan to wait for their turn, leading to a playful interaction that builds trust and belonging. Over time these peers are more likely to become friends because they have had fun together on the slide.

Now imagine a child who is very active and impulsive and climbs up the slide so quickly that he misses the frowns on the faces of peers waiting at the top. This child may be overwhelming his playmates and is missing their social cues to adjust his intensity. Or consider a child who has an enthusiastic interest in a topic that is not interesting to his same-age peers, like Aiden and his geological knowledge. This child may struggle to gain play experience in traditional settings because he can't relate to the recess interests of his same-age peers, like soccer.

Establishing social connections requires taking another person's perspective, predicting what they like and don't like, communicating desires, and negotiating compromises—all skills that are challenging for many neurodivergent learners. But what if these challenges are more difficult because we're asking neurodivergent brains to socialize in neurotypical ways? In other words, for years autistic individuals have been assumed to have difficulty with theory of mind and expressing empathy, but many autistic adults assert that this isn't a *deficit* but rather a *difference* when trying to socialize with neurotypical people. This is called the double-empathy problem.

The Double-Empathy Problem

Theory of mind is now understood as a complex construct that goes beyond predicting what a peer will think is in a box. Researchers have noted that theory of mind involves joint attention, play pragmatics, empathy, intentionality, and the ability to distinguish appearance from reality.[10] Multiple studies have documented that autistic children experience differences in their development of theory of mind, which can lead to difficulty attending to social cues and making inferences.[11] While many autistic children do struggle with social skills that are rooted in theory of mind, most research to date has defined social interactions based on the way neurotypical individuals socialize.

This discrepancy led the autistic researcher Damian Milton to introduce the idea that autistic individuals don't have a deficit in communication; rather, they experience a misalignment of communication styles when interacting with neurotypical people.[12] Milton called this the double-empathy problem, meaning that when an autistic person and a nonautistic person have difficulty communicating, the trouble doesn't come from a lack of empathy and social attunement on the part of the autistic person. The difficulty is due to a mismatch of social perspectives and communication styles. Another way to think about this is through the lens of a deaf person using American Sign Language (ASL). We don't require the deaf person to go to speech therapy until they can speak so a hearing person can understand. We simply understand that they will communicate using ASL and that we will need an interpreter. While many autistic children receive social skills therapy to help them interact in the world around them, classmates and neighbors also need to learn more about how their autistic peers socialize.

Making Versus Keeping Friends

While neurotypical children often gravitate toward children who look like them or who are involved in the same activity, neurodivergent children seem to be drawn toward matching energy and sharing interests. For example, autistic children tend to say exactly what they are thinking, which may turn off nonautistic peers, but two autistic kids will likely enjoy the energy of a direct conversation about facts they both find fascinating. Two high-energy kids with ADHD who love riding bikes are a fit for each other compared to a peer who likes to draw quietly. While not all neurodivergent children will be drawn to other neurodivergent children, they will certainly pursue what makes them feel joyful. And while finding our people is incredibly important to making friends, that's only the beginning. Once our child finds a friend, then we have to help them learn how to keep a friend.

Many children with ADHD are impulsive, get into others' space, and interrupt often, all of which can annoy a friend. As a child psychologist, I often help parents differentiate between the social weaknesses of autism and ADHD by explaining that while autistic children may not know how to start a conversation, children with ADHD can easily initiate a social interaction and make friends; it's the keeping of friends that is hard. One study comparing theory of mind skills between autistic and ADHD boys in a "research setting" found that autistic boys showed weaknesses in theory of mind, while boys with ADHD performed well on these tasks. However, these solid theory of mind skills for ADHD boys did not carry over to the "applied setting." In other words, once the ADHD boys were socializing out in the world, their parents rated them lower than the neurotypical control group and closer to the autistic group in theory of mind skills.[13] One possible explanation is that emotional regulation skills, not theory of mind skills, are more socially impactful for kids with ADHD.[14]

I'm familiar with this pattern as I've heard many times from parents and teachers who say things like "If he would just slow down, maybe he wouldn't annoy his friends" or "If she would just stop and think before she speaks, then maybe she would be able to keep a friend." It's in these moments that children with ADHD can feel bad about themselves—when a friend becomes distant or excludes them because of something they feel they can't control. If you feel your child is losing friends or missing out on social opportunities because of hyperactivity, inattention, or impulsivity (which sometimes shows up as big emotions), it's time to talk to your pediatrician or a therapist for help.

Also remember that because neurodivergent children are such a heterogenous group, there is no one way to measure social success. At the end of the day, what matters most is not how we as adults measure social success but how we identify social *satisfaction* in our kids. When a parent is sad about their child being alone at recess or lunch, my next question is always "Is your child sad about it?" I'm only concerned if the child is not socially satisfied, feels lonely, and wants more social interaction. Many times neurodivergent kids do not enjoy socializing in large groups and often use downtime to recharge themselves. Notice how and when your child feels socially satisfied, and provide more of those opportunities.

Classmates Versus Friends

Young children often view peers as "my friend" or "not my friend," depending on who they sat next to at snack time or played with on the playground. Teachers in the preschool and kindergarten years often emphasize the idea of everyone being a potential friend by calling all students "friends." But around second or third grade, children shift from playing with everyone to gravitating toward preferred peers. These connections grow stronger in the middle school years as children creatively play less and more often socialize by talking about interests and participating in organized games, sports, and activities.

Around the time children begin to prefer certain peers, you may notice that your child isn't meshing well with a certain peer and that every time they are together, it turns into a firestorm of emotions. You may have heard your child say, "I don't have to be nice to them. They aren't my friend." In this moment, it's imperative to teach the difference between a friend and a classmate. You could replace *classmate* with *sibling, neighbor,* or *kid in your cabin at camp last summer,* but the sentiment is the same: Even though we might not be friends with someone, we must still be kind and helpful to those sharing space with us. Classmates grow up to be coworkers, neighbors, and the guy in front of us in line at the grocery store, so children need a category in their mind for people who are not friends but are nonetheless worthy of kindness.

Helping Your Child Find Friendships

As I told Aiden's parents in my office that day, children have many layers of social development to nurture before they can make a friend. In response to the predicament of Aiden *almost* throwing rocks on the playground, I helped his parents reframe their friendship goals for him to include peers who share his interests and match his energy. Aiden was likely not going to find friendships with the soccer kids, but he could learn to share space with them as classmates while his parents looked for social circles that shared his enthusiasm for geology. Aiden's mom soon discovered the importance of honoring his desire to seek socialization on his own terms while also finding social opportunities to stretch him.

Over time Aiden was able to realize that there was nothing weird about loving rocks and minerals—it was just that most kids his age were not into it. He used his sessions with me to unmask and completely be himself. He brought me rocks that we named, and we used the rock characters to help expand his ideas in play. I shared his progress with his parents and teacher, who continued to support him in social situations to notice others, to talk through what they were doing, and to decide whether he wanted to join in.

Some children will be socially satisfied by attending school alongside classmates, whereas others will want as many friends as they can get. What's important is for each child to identify the social experience that makes them feel they belong. Ultimately, we want all children to learn that they don't have to be friends with someone to be kind to them, which we will discuss in Chapter 11. Fostering empathy among everyone involved, as Aiden's teacher did, is a crucial part of positive social relationships within our collective neurodiversity. Here are more ideas to support your child in finding friendships:

Embrace Your Child's Uniqueness

Understand the Benefits of Solo Play

There will be times when solo play is socially satisfying and soothing. Many autistic children enjoy solo play because sensory demands are low, and no one interrupts their plan. Some neurodivergent learners experience unnecessary social anxiety from being in group situations before they are ready. For them, learning in a group at school is enough togetherness for the day. As kids' nervous systems mature, however, they are able to handle increasingly complex sensory experiences and social situations. Sometimes we have to convince a child that playing in a group has benefits, which is why it's important to introduce group play intentionally. (More on that follows.)

Let Your Child's Mood Lead the Way

Too often as parents, we let our mood lead the way, but our moods are laced with prior experiences that might have been sad for us but won't necessarily upset our child. You may have felt sad that you were left out of a birthday party, for example, but your kid may not care one bit about not getting an invitation. In order to determine your child's social satisfaction, let your child's mood be your guide. Are they content and calm, and do they seem satisfied with the frequency and type of socialization they are involved in? If so, then keep on keeping on with what you are doing. Do they seem overwhelmed, dread activities you've signed them up for, or flat-out refuse to attend social events? This means that their social environment is not aligned with their skills or interests, and it's time to reevaluate what makes them happy. Or are they lonely, sad, and feeling left out? If they are lonely, you will notice a sadness that can manifest as mild annoyance or boredom, meaning your child wants more connection. If this feeling isn't debilitating, it can serve as motivation to try new things, investigate interests, or find activities to try. If their sadness leads to continued reluctance to socialize, it's time to talk to a mental health professional for support.

Validate That Your Child's Interests May Differ from Those of Same-Age Peers

Neurodivergent learners are often surrounded by peers whose interests and skills differ greatly from their own. This creates an environment where it can be difficult to know how to connect. You can validate this reality for your child by saying something like "I know it feels like no one in your class knows as much about geography as you do," which helps them know that there is nothing wrong with them; there's simply a mismatch of interests. Of course, it's best to follow this up with a plan of action and say something like "Let's look for some online groups of geography enthusiasts." (A great resource for this is outschool.com.)

Tips for Building Social Skills

Teach the Difference Between Friends and Acquaintances

Some autistic children are hesitant to talk to anyone while others, as my grandmother would say, "have never met a stranger." One of the downsides of a weakness in theory of mind is that your child might view everyone as friendly. Many autistic children are also very concrete in their thinking patterns, so you will likely need to teach them rules for interacting with others. Just as I taught Aiden to use the Friendship Circle, you can describe the level of information you would share with each of the groups, but be sure to define the relationships in concrete terms. For instance, acquaintances are people we've met once or twice rather than "people we don't know well." We greet acquaintances, and we save our personal information, like interests, feelings, and plans, for those we have known longer. The closer we get to the center of the Friendship Circle, the more we trust those people—a correlation that helps kids differentiate among social connections.

Teach Perspective-Taking in the Moment

Elementary-age children primarily connect through play and having fun. This feeling of fun keeps them coming back for more time with each other, creating trust and friendship. But spending time with a playmate who is impulsive, rough, or talks constantly may create social tension. Kids with ADHD often have the ability to take another child's perspective, but they may struggle to slow down long enough to recognize it. This is why it's crucial to help them understand the perspective of others and likewise to teach neurotypical children patience and grace for kids who are working hard to control their impulses. Maintaining friendships shouldn't be the responsibility of the neurodivergent child alone. The playmate must also communicate what they do and don't like so the neurodivergent child can practice self-control. As the adult stepping into these conflicts, you can coach both children to stop and listen to each other to support the growth of their perspective-taking.

Help Your Child Understand How Their Energy Matches with Others

Have your child rate their energy on a scale from 1 to 10, and then challenge them to notice and rate the energy level of their sibling or playmate in that same situation. This is a great starting point to help them build insight into the fact that we play best together when we match energy as much as we can. The caveat is that you don't want your child to try to tamp down their energy all the time and in turn become someone they are not—so make sure you also expose them to situations where they can unleash their energy with peers who can match it.

Teach How Positive Actions Build Trust in Friendship

When children are young, maintaining friendships is less of a concern because kids tend to join in with whoever is playing around them. But as kids mature, they begin to make predictions about each other. For instance, if a child is always rough, a peer might avoid playing with them. Or if a child impulsively grabs the ball or quits a game when they're losing, they could gain a reputation as a "quitter." It's hard for many impulsive children to think beyond the present moment, so we have to map it out for them. Draw a flowchart to show them the cause and effect of their actions on others' feelings and how those feelings then spark reactions. Sketch the chain of events on a whiteboard and literally connect the dots for kids. Understanding that controlling their impulses can help others trust them and want to play with them more can motivate kids to work harder in the moment to control their reactions. However, if you don't think your child can control their impulsivity, or if they are mean to others when upset, it's time to consult your pediatrician or a child therapist.

Nurture Group Play Skills

Introduce Group Play Intentionally

As you balance your child's tolerance for crowds and noise with their desire to interact with others who share their interests, helping them practice playing with others is the best way to help them gain group experience. Begin by engaging in preferred play with your child at home, then expand the preferred play to a sibling, cousin, or neighbor who can be a familiar and reliable play partner. Ideally the partner (often an older child) is someone who is patient, flexible, and aware that the play is practice for your child. Once your child can engage in preferred play with familiar people, try changing the location of these play interactions or extending the length of the interaction. For instance, if your child loves to play UNO with you at home, help them learn to play UNO with others, and then learn to play UNO at school, at Grandma's house, or at an after-school program at the YMCA. The familiarity of the card game will keep them comfortable while their nervous system does the work of adapting to new social scenarios.

Understand That Group Play Will Be Simpler Play

One of my most helpful takeaways from my DIR/Floortime play therapy training was understanding that as the complexity of play increases, the social engagement of autistic children decreases. For instance, pretending to be a team of superheroes is more complicated than throwing a ball back and forth. So a child may be able to play a structured game throwing a ball with a group, but they may not yet be able to engage in pretend play with those same peers because there are too many possible social scenarios happening at once. As you expose your child to more opportunities for group play, know that they may revert to simpler or even parallel play when they are with peers. I've seen autistic children create elaborate pretend worlds when they feel safe playing by themselves or with a sibling, and then wander around the school playground, playing alone, often because they spent their energy learning in a group and don't have any gas left in the tank. These are just different kinds of play, and all play is okay.

Know When a Playdate Is Over

Many active and impulsive children, as well as those who run out of steam suddenly, need their playtime to be structured with a time limit. Plan a start and stop time for the play to prevent your child from becoming overwhelmed with fatigue or boredom. Choose activities to match your child's energy and their playmate's energy.

Swimming pools, playgrounds, and trampoline parks are favorites for high-energy children, while museums, libraries, and nature walks are often fun for kids who move at a slower pace. Ending a playdate with ice cream is usually everyone's jam.

When to Be Concerned: Bullying

As a therapist to neurodivergent children, I find that the topic of bullying comes up often. Parents are worried about their child being bullied and unsure how and when to intervene. First, know that not all negative peer interaction is bullying. All kids are learning to get along in a group, and sometimes kids experience emotional overwhelm caused by a classmate who is annoying or rude but not intending to upset them. However, some are truly being bullied, defined as persistent cruel behavior from a peer who knows it's hurtful. It can be hard for children with social pragmatic weaknesses to tell the difference, putting them at risk for overreporting and underreporting bullying. We have to help them discern the difference and learn to speak up.

As the parent of a neurodivergent child, I know we want to immediately jump in and defend our child at all costs, but it's most helpful to try to get the whole story before you decide how to respond. For instance, if your child says, "The boy next to me in class won't stop bothering me!" follow this up with a calm "Tell me what he's doing." Stay curious, listen, and decide if it's a situation where your child needs coping skills for handling an annoying noise the peer is making or if the peer is doing something the teacher needs to know about. If your child describes name-calling, stealing of materials, or physical harm of any kind, reach out to your child's teacher to start a discussion on how to respond. These are sensitive situations, and while we want to give all children the benefit of the doubt because everyone is learning to get along in a group, your interest is in keeping your child physically and emotionally safe so they can learn.

Here's an example of an email you could send the teacher if your child says they are being called names at school but you are unsure of the severity:

I want to let you know that [Child] told me after school today that [Peer] has been calling them names on the playground. I've talked with him about how it is never okay for us to call each other names and that these names are not a reflection of who he is as a person. We also talked about how sometimes kids are mean when they are having a hard time, which is not an excuse but an explanation for their actions. He let me know that sometimes [Peer] breaks [Child's] pencils, too, so please be on the lookout for that as well. Have you seen anything else that you would consider bullying? We reviewed the idea of tattling versus telling, and I hope [Child] speaks up if this happens again so you can support both of them in these moments.

Tip: Tattling Versus Telling

Tattling versus telling is a helpful skill for all children to have. Tattling is when a child tells the teacher about something that is not hurting anyone, like "He's picking his nose again!" Telling needs to happen when someone could get physically or emotionally hurt, like "I saw her trip him and I think he's hurt." In other words, tattling is trying to get someone in trouble, and telling is asking for help. If you are concerned that your child *is* the bully, it's time to talk to a mental health professional. The goal of social experience is to help kids practice problem-solving peer conflict, but more intervention and supervision is required if they are hurting others or becoming feared by their peers.

Teacher Email Script: Checking In on Peer Relationships

Hi, Ms. [Teacher],

[Child] has been coming home recently talking excitedly about [Peer]. I would love your perspective on when and how they are interacting throughout the day so that I can help [Child] grow this possible friendship. I'm not sure if you know, but this is the very first time [Child] has talked about having a friend, so this would be a major social milestone for her! Also, please let me know if you need volunteers to read to the class, host a holiday party, or join you on a field trip, because I would love to help foster this friendship in real time.

Thank you for all you do!
[Your name here]

Kid Chat Script: Encouraging Peer Interactions

I've heard you talking more lately about [Peer]. When do you see them at school? [Child: During recess.] *What do you like to do together?* [Child: Search for insects.] *Cool! Would you like to invite them to go to the Natural Science Museum sometime? It sounds like you are both interested in insects, and you know they have lots of insects to learn about at the museum. I could get in touch with their mom or dad, and we could all go together.*

Chapter 8

Anxiety

"Hold on, the school is calling."

Amanda and Jim were exhausted. No one in their house was sleeping well, and they were at a loss about what to do next. Stella, now eight years old, often had difficulty sleeping, but last night had been particularly rough. She had come into her parents' room so many times that Jim ended up moving into Stella's room, and Stella climbed into bed with her mom. This arrangement wasn't sustainable, so we started brainstorming ideas to help Stella stay in her bed. "Hold on," Amanda said, looking at her smartwatch. "The school is calling."

My parent sessions have been interrupted by calls from school before. I've also been the parent on the receiving end of those calls, and it's a helpless feeling. When teachers call home because a child is having a hard day, it means that something isn't working. Either a child doesn't have the skills to stay emotionally regulated throughout the day or the teacher doesn't have the skills, time, or staff to support them, or all of the above. Sometimes the child and teacher are doing all they can, but something about the environment is eliciting too much anxiety. And as I had just heard from her parents, Stella was tired, which often exacerbates anxiety.

While I waited for Amanda to finish her call, I reflected on my work with Stella.

Stella's Story

I first met Stella when she was four years old. She had just received an ADHD diagnosis, and one of our biggest therapy goals was to build her vocabulary of feeling words so that she could identify and communicate her emotions more easily. At the time, Stella struggled with emotional regulation in social situations; however, the evaluation determined that she did not meet diagnostic criteria for autism. She had some social strengths that did not appear aligned with autism, like strong pretend play skills and initiating conversations with peers. Still, autism can be harder to diagnose in girls because it presents differently than in boys, so I monitored Stella's development just as I do with any young girl who has anxiety and ADHD. As she matured, she might be able to convey her internal experience of social demands and sensory overwhelm more clearly, which many autistic women express as a core feature of their autism.

Autism and Girls

Autistic girls don't always have the same communication and play differences seen in autistic boys, causing early diagnosis to be more difficult to determine. Also, autistic girls tend to mask, or camouflage, their autistic traits more than boys, leading to delays in diagnosis. A 2022 study from Stanford University using artificial intelligence to compare the functional magnetic resonance imaging (fMRI) brain scans of 637 autistic boys and 136 autistic girls found significant differences between the brains of autistic boys and girls. Autistic girls had "different patterns of connectivity than boys did in several brain centers, including motor, language and visuospatial attention systems." Previous research had shown that autistic females tend to be "less severely affected, especially in the restricted and repetitive behaviors (RRB) symptom domain, than males," meaning their patterns of rigidity and repetitive behaviors like stimming, rocking, and flapping were not as severe as those found in boys, but the reasoning behind this is unclear.[1] Research on autism in girls is in the beginning stages, and my hope is that we will eventually have better diagnostic tools to identify the needs of autistic girls earlier in life. Early identification enables earlier intervention and support, and it helps autistic girls understand themselves better.[2]

Stella was a talkative preschooler who made great progress in articulating emotions such as anger, sadness, and fear. We played games at each session to associate situations with feelings and acted out scenarios to practice reading others' nonverbal cues. She also received occupational therapy, which taught her to notice her body in space, as well as the impact her actions had on others. Stella's parents used visuals at home to support her during routines, which reduced her persistent questions about the schedule and maintained their positive relationship. Stella made a smooth transition into kindergarten and benefited from frequent movement and sensory breaks.

Amanda and Jim had requested to meet with me now, in the middle of second grade, to see if I could figure out what was going on with Stella's sleep and school avoidance. Her sleep had worsened at the start of the school year, and she was also arguing about doing things she perceived as boring or difficult. When I asked Amanda what was different this year, she recalled that Stella's kindergarten class had only twelve kids with two teachers, which afforded Stella's teachers the availability to meet her needs quickly. Her first-grade teacher had a firm but encouraging style, communicating expectations to Stella without creating anxiety for her in moments of confusion. But there were a few calls home about pushing classmates who invaded her space during transitions. After Stella worked with the occupational therapist to practice body awareness during classroom transitions, the situation improved. However, Stella and her second-grade teacher were "not meshing." Her teacher was very structured, which usually worked well, but there seemed to be a lack of encouragement, or an impatience, that was making Stella anxious. Now, on top of the sleep disturbances at home and Stella's resistance to tasks, the school was calling to report a problem.

Amanda ended the call and took a deep breath. "She's okay and no one is hurt. But that was the principal," she said, her eyes wide. "He found Stella crying in the hallway, and when he couldn't get her to return to class, he brought her down to his office. Every time he suggests going back to class, Stella shuts down and becomes upset again. He said he could keep her in his office this afternoon or we could pick her up. I told him I'd call him back after talking it over with you both."

We had two decisions to make: (1) what to do right now to support Stella and (2) how to better support Stella moving forward. Amanda and Jim agreed that pushing Stella to return to class that day was too much because she was tired from not sleeping well. Sending her back into a stressful environment with low energy was only going to cause more distress. After further discussion, I learned that Stella and the principal had previously bonded over their shared interest in cats. I also learned that Stella had recently developed a maladaptive coping strategy of avoiding discomfort. She would refuse, argue, or ignore anytime her parents tried to help her problem-solve. It was possible that picking Stella up early from school would reinforce her avoidance, triggering a cycle of struggle whenever she encountered difficulty. Amanda and Jim decided to have Stella remain until the school day was over and complete her work in the principal's office, since she felt safe there. Amanda called the principal to relay this plan and request a meeting to determine why Stella was avoiding the classroom.

Identifying the Problem

Through the lens of neurodiversity, the child is not the problem. The problem stems from the misalignment of the child's skills with the demands of the environment around them. Recall the window of tolerance from Chapter 1 and how we cannot learn unless we feel emotionally regulated and safely connected to those around us. New circumstances and challenges push us to the edges of our window and lead to new learning, but when we are forced outside that window, our nervous system is overcome with stress, and our brain and body go into survival mode. Many times I have seen children struggle in learning environments to the point of not learning at all. When we lower sensory demands, slow the pace, or move them to a classroom with fewer students, their anxiety lessens and problematic behavior improves.

Unfortunately, we are inclined to see the child as the problem because special education is rooted in the medical model. This model defines a problem, assigns a treatment, and tracks progress. As a psychologist, I was trained on the medical model to evaluate a child to determine what was "wrong" with their learning or behavior and give them access to support. But the medical model is geared toward physical problems, not neurodevelopmental ones. For instance, if my child has a broken arm, they need to have it fixed so they can use it again. Neurodevelopment is more complex. If my child is anxious, I need to know more about the triggers, their previous experiences, the sensitivity of their nervous system, and their ability to emotionally regulate—or their access to coregulation from attuned caregivers. The neurodiversity movement demands that we look beyond the medical, or deficit, model and embrace kids who play in different ways, learn in different ways, and communicate in different ways.

As long as a child is not hurting themself or others, their behavior needs to be viewed as different rather than dangerous. As the autistic scientist and author Temple Grandin says, autistic individuals are "different, not less." There are times when a child's anxiety does pose a danger, such as physical aggression or running from a building, and these children need more support or a different learning environment. However, most neurodivergent learners, like Stella, are capable of learning in the general education classroom—even though they will go through tough seasons where accommodations are needed. It's in the tough seasons that parent-teacher collaboration is paramount in order to make decisions in the child's best interest. We must answer tricky questions like the following: Can they tolerate us setting a boundary, or will they become so anxious that they will shut down or become aggressive? Is their anxiety causing them to avoid something, in which case rescuing them from this situation will reinforce the avoidance? Collaboration allows us to make informed decisions as we balance providing support with fostering autonomy.

This is what I call the art of setting limits. Begin by assessing your child's skills across various areas, and compare those skills with expectations from the people, environment, or demands they face. The size of the discrepancy between the child's skills and the expectations is often the size of the child's anxiety. Every child's anxiety manifests differently. Their behavioral response to experiencing anxiety can look like frustration, avoidance, anger, aggression, or running from the classroom. When a child is pushed outside their window of tolerance, we have to pinpoint what type of problem is happening and the strategies that regulate their nervous systems back to homeostasis.

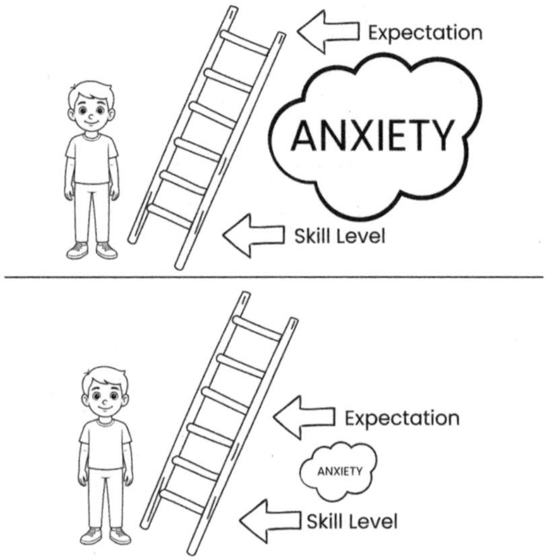

Emily W. King, PhD | Learn with Dr. Emily® | www.learnwithdremily.com

Types of Problems That Can Lead to Anxiety

In order to get to the bottom of what might be causing your child's anxiety, think about these dynamics your child experiences every day.

Student-Environment Fit

If a child is overwhelmed by sensory demands like crowds, noise, or smells, this may show up as avoidant behavior, like not wanting to get out of the car, transition into the hallway, or join the group at the lunch table. If school is calling home about your child's avoidance, something is causing anxiety or overwhelm at school.

Student-Curriculum Fit

If your child is struggling due to the pace of the curriculum, or if the topic isn't engaging enough, sharing how your child engages in non-academics like art and music, follows a recipe, or completes multi-step directions can help compare skills across settings.

Student-Teacher Fit

If your child struggles to process information from a teacher with a stern voice because they think that they are in trouble even when they are not, or your child would benefit from a structured teacher to help keep them organized, share this with a school administrator to brainstorm solutions.

Student-Student Fit

If your child is frustrated by turn-taking or loathes group work because they worry about being picked as the "reporter," look for a pattern of avoidance that occurs when your child is asked to work with peers, because the student-student fit might be the problem.

None of these situations is a significant concern if they happen only once or twice. In fact, you likely won't hear from the school if one of them happens occasionally, and that's a good thing. We want our kids and their teachers to solve problems together to gain frustration tolerance and confidence to regulate without you. But if your child's teacher is repeatedly reaching out to you or your child continues complaining about the same situation, it's time to investigate.

Lived Experience

"I think that one of the biggest sources of anxiety is the fear of being rejected by peers or teachers. He is very worried about getting in trouble and as a result follows the rules very closely." —Amy, mom of an eleven-year-old

"He just wants to get everything right. He strives for perfection and is really hard on himself when he doesn't achieve it." —Carly, mom of a twelve-year-old

What the Science Says About Anxiety and Learning

Anxious feelings are hard to ignore. Our anxiety is an evolutionary strength that keeps us alive in the face of danger. As we learned in Chapter 1, when we are met with danger, our nervous system launches into a response to power up our energy reserves and either fight or flee from danger. If that doesn't work, we slip into a freeze response, essentially "playing dead" until the threat is over. When we are in a survival state, our executive functioning is impaired, because we don't have the bandwidth to learn or create. Once our anxiety level is back within our window of tolerance—with the help of soothing sensory activities and safe relationships—our executive functioning comes back online, and we feel open to learn and create again.

When a child is emotionally dysregulated or shut down, they do not process verbal information in the same way they do when they are regulated. As the neuropsychologist Lisa Jacobson puts it, "An anxious child without a calm and safe learning environment who is unsure of what is expected of him or her will feel threatened, and the child's brain will have a difficult time learning new things."[3] Remember: "They are not giving me a hard time; they are having a hard time." If you've tried to talk to your child when they are upset and received a "Don't tell me to calm down!" or a physical recoil upon touching their shoulder, they are outside their window of tolerance, still in a sympathetic state, and not ready for talking, problem-solving, or learning. So, it's incredibly important to determine *what* triggers your child's anxiety, *how* they use coping strategies during emotional dysregulation, and *when* to step in and assist.

Let's explore how anxiety impacts different types of neurodivergent learners.

Anxiety and Autism

Autistic children are twice as likely to be diagnosed with an anxiety disorder as their nonautistic peers.[4] For preschool and school-age autistic children, anxiety is likely related to sensory sensitivities, sleep disruptions, and behavior problems.[5] However, the specifics vary from child to child. Some will exhibit separation anxiety, avoidance, somatic complaints, or selective mutism, while others engage in obsessive-compulsive behavior, aggression, or perfectionism. In my work with parents raising autistic children, anxiety often causes more disruption to daily life and learning outcomes than autism itself. This makes sense given what we know about the effects of anxiety on the brain and nervous system. In order for an autistic child to achieve more optimal outcomes, we need to reduce their anxiety across settings.

For many children, reducing anxiety does include medication, but with caution: Since we need anxiety to sense danger, we don't want medication to turn off anxiety completely. I think of anxiety medication like a dimmer switch rather than a light switch. Talk with your child's pediatrician or a child psychiatrist about the potential benefits of turning down your child's anxiety so they can access more of their skills throughout the day. The goal is not to change their autism but to ensure that they feel safe to communicate, engage, and learn.

Anxiety and ADHD

According to the Centers for Disease Control and Prevention, 35 percent of six-to-eleven-year-olds with ADHD are diagnosed with an anxiety disorder.[6] For parents and educators, it can be challenging to distinguish which behaviors are associated with which diagnosis. Imagine a child who is so nervous that they fidget in their seat to settle their emotions. Or a child who is consumed by worries and stares out the window, appearing inattentive. It's important to accurately diagnose these symptoms, because the medications used to treat ADHD can increase anxiety, and the medications used to treat anxiety can lower a child's inhibitions. If you're contemplating medication as part of your child's support plan, work with a pediatrician or child psychiatrist who can help you differentiate between anxiety and ADHD.

Anxiety and Learning Disabilities

Learning disabilities hinder a child's ability to read (dyslexia), write (dysgraphia), and understand math (dyscalculia). As you can imagine, sitting in a classroom where the curriculum is moving forward without you might cause anxiety. In fact, a meta-analysis from 2011 reported that 70 percent of children with a specific learning disability (SLD) experienced significantly more anxiety than their peers without a learning disability.[7] But what comes first, the learning difficulty or the anxiety? If your child displays anxiety only in academic settings, or if they progress in sports or the arts but not in academic classes, they might have a learning weakness to investigate. However, if your child is anxious in the classroom, during extra-curriculars, and at home, this would indicate anxiety across settings.

Anxiety and Twice-Exceptionality

Let's consider what we know about anxiety paired with autism, ADHD, and learning disabilities thus far and add in intellectual giftedness. In her book, *The Gifted Parenting Journey,* the clinical psychologist Gail Post explained that gifted children are prone to overthinking, perfectionism, and social isolation, especially when they realize that others don't think as quickly or deeply as they do.[8]

Twice-exceptional learners can be more easily annoyed, feeling capable but failing to grasp why they can't achieve it. Because of this, twice-exceptional learners can be mistaken for being "lazy" if adults notice they are smart but not putting forth effort.[9] Their gifts often mask their disabilities, and their weaknesses mask their strengths, putting them at risk for inadequate support because they are "doing okay." Of all the neurodivergent learners, twice-exceptional children are most likely to fly under the radar, with your first clue of distress often being anxiety or self-defeat. As we identify neurodivergent learners' neurobiological and environmental triggers, we must also consider the role that our own anxiety plays in our efforts to support them.

The Impact of Parental Anxiety on Children

Admitting that we could be part of the problem is tough. But children of anxious parents are five times more likely to have an anxiety disorder than children without anxious parents.[10] While anxiety is proven to run in families, researchers haven't been able to pin it all on genetics. Research has also connected anxiety in children with parent behaviors, including high levels of criticism and control, low levels of warmth, and restrictions on a child's autonomy.[11] One study following parents diagnosed with social anxiety disorder found them to show less positive affect and more criticism and doubt of their child's competency compared to parents without social anxiety disorder.[12] This all makes sense if we think back to our first trip to the playground as new parents. We worried that our child would get hurt, so we hovered closely, even if they didn't need help. We may have gasped in fear when they stood at the edge of the ladder, and even though they actually weren't feeling scared themself, they heard our gasp and felt our anxiety. Consistently over time, this type of anxious behavior from a parent can send the message to a child that they should be worried for their safety despite not feeling they were in danger prior to noticing their parent's reaction.

That said, when raising a neurodivergent child, there are instances that spark parental anxiety and rightfully so. Physical aggression, impulsivity, and social aloofness are all behaviors that can put children in unsafe situations. Parents of neurodivergent kids must spend more time thinking about, planning, and advocating for their children within systems that often misunderstand their child. Multiple studies have documented that "behavior problems" in autistic children correlate with stress in mothers, which then culminates in anxiety and depression for the mother.[13] While fathers of autistic children are less stressed than mothers, they have been found to be more stressed than fathers raising neurotypical children.[14] Parental stress is similarly high for parents raising children with ADHD due to their emotionally dysregulated behavior and their need for support.[15] Parents raising twice-exceptional children report high levels of stress as well.[16] These findings corroborate what many of us already know: When our child is upset, we are more stressed. And when we are unsure of how to help them, or don't have the resources to help them, our stress levels drastically increase.

So if the emotional dysregulation of our kids leads to parental stress and anxiety, and our anxiety potentially makes our child more anxious, we have a cyclical problem. By the time families reach my therapy couch, everyone is anxious. We start by sorting through areas of biological anxiety based on family history. Next, we think about the child's neurodevelopmental wiring related to sensory integration, which is associated with a higher likelihood of developing anxiety later in life.[17] This anxiety, as we've learned, is more common for neurodivergent children and is closely related to the problematic behavior we see when they are overwhelmed.

The best way to break a cycle of relational anxiety—cyclical anxiety between the parent and child—is to help the person with the most emotional regulation skills first, which is usually the parent. Most of the parents I've worked with over the years have benefited from therapy themselves. I know from personal experience that having my own therapist has allowed me to sort through my triggers, recognize when I experience them, and slow down to support myself along this journey. While you continue supporting your child through accommodations and interventions, know that they will also benefit if you reduce your own anxiety. Seeking out therapy for yourself, finding activities you love that are restorative, and joining communities that make you feel seen and welcomed are all ways to take care of your own mental wellness. Parenting neurodivergent kids is hard work, and you deserve support, too.

How to Reduce Your Neurodivergent Child's Anxiety

When Stella's parents met with the principal and her teacher, they figured out that Stella had difficulty resuming work after recess. Because Stella started her work independently every morning, her teacher didn't realize she needed to support her in the afternoon. Amanda and Jim shared the sleep difficulties that Stella had been having—even on the weekends she seemed to need rest in the early afternoon. The day the principal found Stella in the hallway, he didn't know what had happened, only that Stella was unwilling to go back into the classroom. Once she was feeling calm and safe in the principal's office, she was able to express that she couldn't pay attention in the afternoon and that it was "so embarrassing!"

The team collaborated to assemble a plan for the added accommodation of a visual checklist in the afternoons. Stella felt less embarrassed because if she lost focus, she could independently reference her list. Her teacher and parents maintained communication about her sleep so that the following day her teacher would know how much to push her or support her. In sessions with me, Stella's parents and I came up with a plan to improve her sleeping environment with a sound machine and a weighted blanket. Amanda and Jim also started walking Stella back to her bed every night she came into their room, so that she got used to staying in her bed when she woke up. They consulted with her pediatrician about supplements that could help calm her body at night. Over time Stella's sleep improved, which helped her have more energy to manage her anxiety and learn in the afternoons at school.

Anxiety shows up in different ways for every child. Some kids quietly avoid work by putting their head down, while others flip desks and create an unsafe environment for those around them. Because neurodivergent kids are more easily pushed outside their window of tolerance, parents and school staff have to collaborate to support children in distress and protect the learning environment for others. Here are some of those patterns and ways to address them.

The Autistic Learner

Rigidity and Transitions

Autistic children often think concretely about the world, perceiving things as all or nothing and struggling to interpret nuance. These gray areas must be filled in by making inferences, which can be difficult for them. Interestingly, most of us become rigid when we are anxious, making all-or-nothing thinking errors in times of overwhelm. When we are outside our emotional window of tolerance, we think the problem must go away for us to be okay; however, once we emotionally regulate, we realize we will survive the situation. Most of us fear the unknown, but we can predict that even if we're uncomfortable, we will be safe. Because the gray areas are hard to predict, autistic children often feel anxious when the next move is unclear or unpreferred. Autistic learners may feel "stuck" and struggle to transition or think about something in a new way because it's scary when the next step is unfamiliar. Coaching an autistic child to "see" what comes next through pictures, schedules, and demonstrations can ease their anxiety and, by extension, their transitions. Adding familiar people or activities when going to a new place helps the anxious autistic child feel safer. You can also support transitions by making them routine so they are not a surprise.

Changes in Routine

Autistic children often like routines because they are predictable and safe. As parents, we can use our children's love of routines to get them through self-care tasks, teach them to follow a bedtime or screentime schedule, and help them feel a sense of security in their daily life. However, life doesn't always go as planned. We have to strike a balance between preparing our child for change and not telling them so much that they will be upset. You know your child best, but there is usually a window of time between a child knowing about a change too far in advance, which can interfere with sleep, and not knowing about it soon enough, which leaves insufficient time to process the change. Communicate anxiety-inducing changes when your child is rested and fed. Introduce the new plan in the way they learn best, whether in talking, writing, or pictures, and support them while they process their emotions about the change.

Somatic Complaints

Since our emotions are felt in our nervous system as well as in our brain, we all have the capacity to feel aches and pains when we are anxious. Stomachaches are probably the most common complaint of anxious children due to the neurotransmitters in our gut. It's also not uncommon for a child to complain of a stomachache, leave school, and have their stomachache magically disappear once they are home. In these instances, it's likely connected to somatic symptoms of stress. When talking to kids about stomachaches, it's helpful to distinguish between what I call a "virus stomachache" and a "nervous stomachache." Both are valid complaints but with difficult solutions.

Some clinicians recommend using exposure, or continued school attendance if that's the stressor, for somatic complaints to help children process that they are safe over time. This approach often works for a neurotypical child who relies on experience to evaluate safety, but if the child has unmet sensory needs, relational conflict, or misaligned academic demands, repeatedly sending them into an overwhelming environment without accommodations will likely intensify their anxiety and possibly give rise to school trauma and persistent school avoidance. When you are troubleshooting avoidance for a neurodivergent learner due to anxiety, start by supporting their sensory and energy needs; then as the child continues to go to school, make academic interventions in parallel with establishing safe relationships. Because somatic complaints are a symptom of anxiety, when they fade, you'll know you're on the right track.

The ADHD Learner

Inattention and Worries

Inattention and anxiety represent the classic chicken-or-egg situation. Sometimes a child is overwhelmed by worries running through their mind, which makes them lose focus. Other times a child is biologically wired to be less attentive and becomes anxious about missing something because they have lost focus. Look for the patterns in your child's attention span. If they are inattentive only when overwhelmed, the source might be anxiety. If they are inattentive even when their anxiety is low and they are having fun, they might have a biological difference in attention regardless of anxiety level. If you are stumped, have your pediatrician or a psychologist collect data to compare symptoms of anxiety and inattention across home and school settings. If a child is biologically inattentive, visual supports like lists, schedules, and digital calendars are helpful so your child can check back when they realize they've lost focus. If a child's mind is filled with worries, then they need to talk with a trusted adult about their anxiety or engage in other strategies to process their thoughts, such as journaling, drawing, or music. If anxiety is interfering with eating, sleeping, learning, or socializing, it's time to talk to a mental health professional.

Lying

On average, children with ADHD lie more than their neurotypical peers due to a combination of impulsivity, shame, and difficulty predicting the consequences of their actions. For example, if a child sneaks a cookie and is caught in the act, their anxiety immediately spikes into fight-or-flight. Without the self-awareness and insight granted by maturity, they impulsively "flee" by saying, "I didn't eat a cookie," even when you can see the chocolate in the corners of their mouth. Because they often act without thinking, children with ADHD are reprimanded more regularly, which leaves them feeling like they are "always in trouble." This combination of impulsivity and shame may cause a child to lie more often, breaking down relationships over time. It's important for parents and caregivers of children with ADHD to separate a child's intent from their impulsivity when sorting out an instance of dishonesty. Help your ADHD child practice the skills of asking permission and of accepting a *no* if what they want is not allowed. If they have already lied, remind them that you can help them solve the problem faster if you know the truth. The focus is then on building trust rather than feeling defeated for not telling the truth. Help them understand that the more they tell the truth, the more you will trust them, which will lead to you being able to give them more autonomy.

Emotional Explosiveness

The intensity of an ADHD child's emotions can catch us off guard. Many parents assume that ADHD is just inattention, hyperactivity, and impulsivity, but some children experience impulsive spikes in emotional dysregulation. When this happens, a child's words and actions appear to come out of nowhere and can look like an emotional explosion. They might lose a game and storm off the basketball court. They might throw something across the room if they can't get it to work. Or they might insult someone who makes them angry without thinking about the social consequences. I describe this symptom of ADHD as emotional impulsivity. Kids with ADHD know that they sometimes act without thinking, and sometimes their emotions "explode" without thinking, too. Your instinct may be to provide immediate consequences, but these are the parenting moments when it is important to help your child emotionally regulate first. Then at a later time, when everyone has calmed down, you can decide whether or not a consequence will help them learn to respond differently next time. The goal is to help your child learn that it's okay to be upset, but not to hurt others.

You can work on tolerating explosive emotions by practicing losing board games and card games, but start slowly. For instance, take the wild cards out of a game like Candyland so your child can experience it without the anxiety of getting sent back to the gumdrop. Take the "draw four" wild cards out of UNO to practice the unexpected feeling of their opponent changing the color on them without having to draw extra cards. Other strategies include teaching them to walk away at the first sign of upset, before they say something hurtful. While cognitive behavioral therapy and medication can aid emotional regulation, sometimes time and maturity are the answers.

The Twice-Exceptional Learner

Perfectionism

Perfectionism is actually a maladaptive coping strategy for anxiety, allowing us to avoid anxiety by sidestepping negative feedback. If we are "perfect," we can avoid the anxiety that comes with failing, making mistakes, and being judged. Perfectionism is commonly mistaken for achievement and is rewarded by others; it's therefore common among gifted learners. As a result, we must pay close attention to how much effort gifted children are putting into their work. Are they spending excess amounts of time to unnecessarily overachieve? Are they getting stuck on a project and missing out on time for play? Twice-exceptional kids can become perfectionists as they try to control their achievement in one area because they struggle in another. We can help perfectionists learn that "less is enough" by having them adopt these categories for their work:

1. My best work
2. Good enough
3. Messy is okay

To use handwriting as an example, if a child is writing a note to remember something, messy is okay, writing their name on their paper is good enough, and writing a paragraph that will be graded is their best work. Helping perfectionist kids outline categories of effort allows them to learn where to put their energy, because pouring all their energy into absolutely everything will lead to burnout.

Overthinking

Like perfectionism, overthinking is also a maladaptive coping strategy. Many gifted individuals overthink, sometimes to the point of having existential questions spinning in their brain on a daily basis.

Imagine being a child and wondering about big problems like climate change, global hunger, and gun violence but not having the power to vote or speak out. These ideas may be swirling inside a child's mind in the middle of third-grade math class. Such overthinking, of course, leads to anxiety. If you are raising an overthinker, pay attention to the big questions they have, and research the people and organizations who are doing something about it, together. Your child can contribute by raising money or volunteering. If they are overthinking on a smaller scale, like worrying what others think about them or if they will make a mistake, normalize that no two people think alike and that mistakes are exactly what they should be doing because they lead to new learning. Rather than overthinking and overpreparing to handle everything, we need to help overthinkers and perfectionists put energy into what they are capable of and trust others to do the rest.

Masking Abilities/Disabilities

Twice-exceptional learners who are also diagnosed with autism, ADHD, and/or a learning disability are at risk of slipping through the cracks. They work hard to camouflage struggles in one area as the standardized curriculum minimizes opportunities for them to show what they know in other areas. Being misunderstood as a twice-exceptional learner is anxiety-provoking because these kids often do not feel seen. They question their skills and wonder if anyone will ever "get" them, which in turn undermines their confidence. If you are parenting a child who doesn't believe in themself due to uneven abilities, fill them in on how their brain works. Collaborate with teachers and therapists to determine which parts of your child's learning need support and which just need the right opportunity to flourish. When children feel seen and understood by others, they will come to understand themselves, leading to more independence and autonomy.

When to Be Concerned: Aggression

The most common reason a school administrator calls a parent is physical aggression. Similar to a child whose anxiety turns into a stomachache, a child who reacts with physical aggression, or with a "fight" response, has an overwhelmed nervous system. The difference, however, is that a stomachache doesn't put others in danger, whereas aggression clearly can. Furthermore, a stomachache disrupts the learning of only one child, while aggression has the potential to disrupt the learning of an entire classroom or family. Because aggression impacts those around the child, the first priority is safety, which is accomplished by either removing the child from the environment or removing everyone else from the environment. Once everyone is safe, the focus turns to the child's emotional regulation. Coregulating with a physically aggressive child is challenging and requires an adult who has a well-established and authentic connection with a child.

There are no magical solutions for aggression, because every child's nervous system responds differently. Thus it's an all-hands-on-deck situation where parents, educators, and professionals must collaborate to figure out the best combination of treatment and support at home and at school to prevent the aggression from happening. Many times children who are aggressive at school are not in the best learning environment for them. To prevent a recurrence of aggression, notice the patterns of sensory, social, and academic demands that may have led to the emotional dysregulation, and consider if something about the school environment can be changed.

Communicating with teachers and administrators in these situations can be emotionally draining. Here is an example of what you might say to your child's teacher after your child is physically aggressive at school:

Thank you for keeping everyone safe at school today. We are heartbroken that [Child] became so upset that he caused an unsafe situation for his classmates and teachers. [Child] was exhausted when we brought him home, and he slept most of the afternoon. After talking with him, he was able to explain that the other students got in his space, which felt threatening, and he pushed them into the bookshelves. He feels terrible now that he realizes that a few of the boys were hurt. We are in agreement that it's time to discuss moving [Child] to a smaller classroom so that he has more adult support to help him in moments like this.

Teacher Email Script: Explaining How Anxiety Relates to Transitions

Ms. [Teacher],

Thank you for letting me know that [Child] is having a hard time cleaning up and transitioning to lunch. He used to have difficulty transitioning when he was younger, but he doesn't struggle with this at home anymore. After talking with him about it, he was able to explain that your voice feels loud and startling to him when you ask the whole class to clean up and transition. When he is startled, he tends to freeze and is not able to move until his anxiety passes. I think this might be the problem. He doesn't feel your voice is startling when you're talking to just him, so I'm wondering if you could instruct him a few minutes before everyone else to begin cleaning up or even have him help announce that it's time for lunch? I just wanted to share this idea because whenever I involved him in the transition when he was younger, it helped so much!

Thank you for all you do for him,
[Your name here]

Kid Chat Script: When a Child Comes Home with a Stomachache

It sounds like your stomach was hurting at school today. Did it feel better when you came home? [Child: Yes.] *Did you know there are two different types of stomachaches? One type of stomachache happens when you have the flu or you ate something that made you feel sick. When those types of stomachaches happen, we need rest, sometimes medicine, and time to feel better. The other kind of stomachache happens when you have worries or are nervous about something going on around you or something that might happen later, and your stomach might feel tight and rumbly, or you might even feel like you want to throw up. This is because when we feel anxious, our brain sends our body a signal that we don't feel safe. Once you got home, you felt safer so your stomach felt better. What type of stomachache do you think you had today? If you think it was a nervous stomachache, let's figure out what was making you feel that way so we can try to fix it.*

Part III

Empowering Your Learner

Chapter 9

Interests and Extracurriculars

"This is my thing!"

"What are your child's interests?" This is the first question on my psychology practice intake form. It doesn't matter if your kid is into superheroes, cats, or ceiling fans; I want to know what catches their attention because that spark is our entry point into connection. Next, I want to know "Where is your child successful?" because something about that setting or activity helps them feel safe, connected, engaged, and capable. This search for success is the opposite of the medical or deficit model, which dictates that we look for problems and design solutions. While there is a time for solving problems, in my experience, nurturing a child's development involves focusing on areas of success. Rooted in positive psychology, the success mindset allows us to find what's working and expand from there.

When we allow interests to take center stage, anxiety decreases, engagement increases, and neurodivergent children thrive. This is true for all children, of course, but interests are necessary for neurodivergent learners. Interests help kids find joy, connection, and eventually a blooming part of their identity. We tend to think that we discover interests during adolescence, but many neurodivergent kids know what they like at a younger age, often going deep into their interest to learn vast amounts of information.

Even if your child's interest is academic, the structure and pace of the standardized curriculum can restrict the time they spend with their interests as well as the depth of their exploration. For instance, an autistic child may want to dive deep into George Washington for hours rather than hit the highlights of the American Revolution. An active child with ADHD may struggle to remain seated in class but captivate a crowd when given a stage and a microphone. An intellectually gifted child may find little in common with classmates but cultivate connections with docents at the science museum. Ultimately, engaging with interests is fundamental to the joy of learning, which protects the mental wellness of neurodivergent learners. I hope this chapter will widen your view of how your child learns beyond the classroom and of the power you have to nurture that gleam in their eyes.

We know that interests work. Let's see how they worked for Isaac.

Isaac's Story

I don't usually sit in front of the door to my therapy playroom, but at our last session, Isaac had run from my office. Elopement for autistic individuals occurs when they run from a setting due to a burst of emotional dysregulation, disregarding potential dangers. I have worked with kids who run from classrooms and school buildings because they have been pushed beyond their window of tolerance by the demands around them, but I had never had a child run from my office. Even though Isaac seemed to feel safe and connected in our therapy sessions, he experienced intense internal emotional dysregulation that was hard for others to recognize and impossible for him to control.

Many autistic individuals have difficulty expressing their emotions both verbally and nonverbally. For instance, adults will notice that a neurotypical child is in a bad mood by a change in their usual posture or facial expression. But some autistic children don't show their emotions in their body or face, which means that the adults around them might miss brewing emotional dysregulation. For Isaac, not only did his body language and facial expression conceal the internal intensity of his emotions, but due to weaknesses in interoception, he struggled to recognize his feelings until they were too big to communicate. When parents and teachers tell me that a child's behavior "came out of nowhere," it's often because it was hard for the adult to predict the surge of emotions. But Isaac was running from school, home, and now my office, so it was too dangerous for us to continue missing his emotional cues. We had to figure out how to support him sooner by noticing subtle changes and helping him identify and communicate his feelings.

I scheduled a session with Isaac's parents, Lisa and Jason, to learn how they notice his dysregulation so we could brainstorm a safe and effective plan. Lisa shared that Isaac is safely within his window of tolerance when engaged with his interests: math and climate change. But because Isaac was able to complete math well above his grade level and his peers did not share his passion for renewable resources, the school day was very lonely for him. Jason also shared that Isaac's triggers at school seemed to be writing tasks and smells in the cafeteria.

There was no writing in my quiet playroom. However, during the session when Isaac ran, we were talking about his problems at school. His parents and I realized that simply talking about the issues in an attempt to process his emotions was sending his nervous system into a sympathetic survival state. I imagined that if I inadvertently pushed him outside his window of tolerance simply by talking about school, then experiencing it on a daily basis was not sustainable.

We made a plan for one of Isaac's parents to join us in future sessions as his emotional coregulator and translator. They were both able to recognize when his emotions were rising, usually by a slight shift in his posture. We also flipped the script and started talking through what *was* working. Sometimes Isaac would bring up school problems, and when he did, we used math equations to represent the size of his emotions, often using exponents. He would create formulas to explain how variables in each situation led to certain outcomes. Using math to communicate allowed Isaac to stay emotionally regulated while talking about overwhelming topics. Over time I began to notice Isaac's subtle patterns of dysregulation, and he developed the skill of dropping to the floor rather than running when overwhelmed. When he slumped to the floor and rolled under the table, this was my cue to stop talking and give him time and space to self-regulate and reenter our conversation when he was ready.

Isaac's parents also provided him with interest-based opportunities outside school. Two of his biggest milestones were attending a city council meeting focused on sustainability and confidently teaching a group of peers and staff at summer camp how to compost. We started to notice that when we followed Isaac's interests, we found his joy. This joy led to emotional regulation, stamina to tolerate challenging environments, and a newfound confidence.

Lived Experience

"When I'm not in school, I learn by going outside and reading in nature." —Grayson, age nine

"I do one-on-one singing lessons. I read a *huge* amount of books with my mum and dad. I love to watch birds and collect plants and leaves." —Alicia, age eleven

"I use Duolingo for Japanese, Korean, Spanish, French, German, and the thing that they recently added that is not in the slightest a language, chess." —Ben, age twelve

What the Science Says About Interest-Based Learning

As the parent of a neurodivergent learner, you likely already know that pairing your child's interest with a nonpreferred activity increases their engagement in the task. You also know that you'll get more resistance from your child if something bores them. Interests matter.

Interest Development

Based on the works of researchers Judith Harackiewicz, Jessi Smith, and Stacy Priniski, there are two types of interest: *situational interest* and *individual interest*. Situational interest is the momentary capture of our attention by something that is enjoyable. Individual interest emerges after we put forth effort over time to reengage with an interest across settings.[1] In other words, a situational interest refers to something that catches a child's attention, while an individual interest develops as a child repeatedly engages with that interest because they find it intrinsically rewarding.

These ideas are based on the work of researchers Suzanne Hidi and Ann Renninger, who developed the Four-Phase Model of Interest Development.[2] According to Hidi and Renninger, we journey through four phases to deepen our interest as learners.

1. *Environment*: We are triggered by an interest, often based on novelty or wonder (emerging situational interest)
2. *Meaning*: We maintain our interest because we find it enjoyable or valuable (developed situation interest)
3. *Reengage*: We continue seeking opportunities to develop our interest (emerging individual interest)
4. *Self-sustaining*: We make plans to engage with our interest across settings (developed individual interest)

When I think about neurodivergent learners within the context of these stages of interest development, I wonder about the child with a short attention span who struggles to move beyond the *environment* of novelty in the moment. I wonder about the child who finds *meaning* in an interest but is too anxious to share that interest with others. I wonder about the child whose weak planning skills inhibit their ability to *reengage* in opportunities to develop their interest without a parent planning for them. And I wonder about the child who is hyperfocused on a special interest, which fast-tracks them to a *self-sustaining* interest but may cause them to miss out on other opportunities. Supporting the interests of neurodivergent learners involves keeping these roadblocks in mind while finding interest-based learning opportunities that align with a child's skills. This formula of interests plus skills minus roadblocks will lead to positive outcomes.

The Benefits of Interests

The research is clear that interest-based learning is better for neurodivergent learners. A meta-analysis of twenty-four studies on incorporating interests into early intervention for autistic preschoolers found that interest-based interventions significantly increased prosocial behaviors and decreased negative behaviors.[3] Another study comparing the sustained attention of gifted children receiving the standard curriculum versus an "enriched education" (defined as schools providing various curricula for the children rather than simply accelerating the curriculum) found that gifted learners receiving the "enriched education" performed better on sustained attention tasks.[4] The path to positive outcomes will differ based on the child's interests and skill sets, but it's evident that interest captures attention.

When thinking about how to nurture your child's interests, figure out where their interest and attention span intersect. If you're not sure what your child is interested in, start by following their joy. This joy may show up in a smile, a squeal, or the pull of your hand toward an activity over and over again. Or joy might be an internal experience that shows up as improved emotional regulation, better sleep, and reduced irritability, so notice those patterns, too. Seek out opportunities for them to engage with interests to promote new and deeper learning on their own terms.

Interests That Regulate

So much of the world pushes our kids outside their window of tolerance, but interests bring them back to emotional homeostasis. While regulating experiences vary from person to person, here are some common interests that neurodivergent learners find regulating, as well as the science behind them.

Animals

You may have noticed that your neurodivergent child connects more easily with animals than with humans. Often this is due to the predictable patterns of animal behavior, the unconditional love they offer, and the fact that they don't talk. Imagine being an autistic eight-year-old and not understanding why your classmates act the way they do, fearing rejection if you say the "wrong" thing, and feeling lonely as a result. These worries don't exist when you are spending time with animals. Multiple research studies have documented the benefits of service dogs for autistic children, including socialization, safety, independence, and language development.[5] While service animals are costly and training is time-consuming, pets are valuable companions when they form a compassionate connection with your child. One study of "companion animals," not only dogs, found similar results for autistic children, adding that the fit of the animal with the family was necessary for beneficial outcomes.[6] The same benefits have been linked to horseback riding. At the end of a ten-week study, autistic children who rode horses had significant improvements in irritability, hyperactivity, and social communication compared to autistic children in the control group who completed barn activities.[7]

Another fascinating study compared the social stress and anxiety of autistic children with their neurotypical peers across four situations: (1) reading silently, (2) a scripted classroom activity involving reading aloud, (3) free play with peers and toys, and (4) free play with peers and guinea pigs. Results showed significantly more stress among autistic children than among their neurotypical peers in all situations—except when the guinea pigs were present. Specifically, the autistic students' stress decreased 43 percent during free play with peers and guinea pigs compared to playing with peers and toys.[8] My theory is that animals help us emotionally regulate, and we are better able to play and learn when we are inside our window of tolerance.

Research on animals and neurodivergence isn't limited to autism; children with ADHD have also been proven to benefit from time with animals. One study followed children with ADHD who received group social skills training either with or without a therapy dog present. While both groups showed a reduction in ADHD symptoms over the twelve-week treatment plan, the group with a therapy dog showed a greater reduction in severity of symptoms.[9] Another study looked at 571 children ages eleven to fourteen with diagnoses of either ADHD, anxiety, or depression and found that exposure over time to a "highly attached" dog or cat reduced the risk of adolescent mental health disorders.[10]

Not all children connect with animals, especially if they have had a traumatic experience with an aggressive animal. But for the ones who do, there is no denying the soothing benefits of time spent with a furry friend. The same is true for getting outside in nature.

Nature

Something magical happens when we take neurodivergent learners outdoors. For children who struggle with mood regulation, hyperactivity, and distractibility, being in nature, moving their body, and experiencing the awe of Mother Earth has a calming effect that is backed by science. When researchers analyzed twenty-four studies on the impact of nature-based interventions for autistic children, they observed significant reductions in irritability, hyperactivity, and distractibility.[11] Similar results were seen in a review of seven studies tracking the effects of nature on children with ADHD, which indicated a consistent reduction in ADHD diagnoses and symptom severity regardless of age, gender, and household income.[12]

The benefits for gifted children being in nature extend beyond emotional regulation into limitless options for exploration.[13] If you are raising a gifted child whom you feel might just be smarter than you are, the best thing you can do is expose them to the world and notice what catches their eye. While some neurodivergent learners will gravitate toward nature because they love rocks, trees, or bugs, many keep coming back because the rhythms of nature are emotionally regulating to their nervous system and the wonders of the earth are awe-inspiring.

Movement

Spending time with animals and being in nature reminds us that we are among the rhythms of all living things. Moving with, and not against, the current of our nervous system benefits emotional regulation. As children develop and feel more autonomy in their bodies, they begin to find their own unique rhythm. Long before we used the word *neurodivergent,* parents and teachers often described quirky kids as "marching to the beat of their own drum," which feels accurate.

Moving to the beat of someone else's drum, like staying seated longer than we want to or controlling our impulses to wait, takes effort. We have to learn how to wait so we can play, learn, and work effectively in groups, but there is a limit to conformity. Helping a child understand how their body likes to move is one of the healthiest lessons we can teach them.

Some neurodivergent children will have barriers to movement, such as a weakness in gross motor skills, coordination, or sensory overwhelm. Others will be met by social overwhelm when movement involves sports teams or dance ensembles. But the research overwhelmingly shows that physical movement helps children diagnosed with autism or ADHD emotionally regulate, so we must help our kids find ways to move. In a review of sixteen studies analyzing the impact of movement on autistic children ages three to six years old, physical movement was found to significantly reduce social difficulties and repetitive behaviors.[14] Meanwhile children with ADHD often love physical play because their body feels better in motion. A review of fifteen studies on movement and ADHD in children found that physical exercise improved attention, executive functioning, and motor skills; however, exercise did not significantly impact hyperactivity, depression, social problems, or aggressive behaviors.[15] So while movement doesn't solve all concerns for children with ADHD, it's still an effective part of their support plan.

Movement on land can have sensory challenges, such as heat intolerance, so movement in water is preferred for many neurodivergent kids. Parents of autistic children often prioritize swim lessons as soon as their child is able to learn because approximately 80 percent of autistic children have some form of motor weakness that puts them at a higher risk of drowning.[16] But beyond safety, learning to swim has other benefits as well. Multiple studies have shown that swimming improves gross motor and social skills as well as reduces repetitive behaviors for autistic children.[17] Swimming is also beneficial for children with ADHD. One randomized trial of a twelve-week swimming intervention for kids with ADHD found significant improvements in behavior, impulse control, and academic performance.[18] When a child's energetic nervous system is given the opportunity to channel that energy, benefits abound.

Music

Music has a similar effect on emotional regulation, which is why so many neurodivergent learners gravitate toward listening to music, dancing to music, singing, or learning to play a musical instrument. It feels good! The benefits of music interventions for autistic children are well established, with one study indicating significant improvements in social communication and functional brain connectivity.[19] Furthermore, some neurodivergent learners have exceptional musical gifts, such as perfect pitch,[20] that positively reinforce musical engagement by building confidence. Music has also been proven to enhance learning. For instance, in a study on teaching autistic children about emotions, listening to background music that represented each emotion significantly improved the child's understanding of that emotion compared to learning only through verbal instructions.[21] Sung directions, compared to spoken directions, were also found to significantly improve autistic children's engagement, language learning, and socio-communicative responsiveness.[22]

Music helps children with ADHD, too. Music therapy for children and adolescents with ADHD increases serotonin and decreases cortisol, blood pressure, and heart rate.[23] In a study of sixth and seventh graders, listening to music while reading increased comprehension for children with ADHD, whereas children without ADHD showed worse comprehension when listening to music.[24] The benefits of music are similar for gifted learners. Among intellectually gifted children, music has been found to support emotional expression, motivation, self-regulation, and awareness.[25] Plus, music can expand into interests like dancing, musical theater, or just singing in the car with family, which all foster more social connections. The joy in these moments might lead them to find their "thing"!

Art

While music regulates us through hearing, visual arts and crafting can be soothing and satisfying through vision and touch. Many neurodivergent kids find happiness in jewelry making, crocheting, or painting. Autistic children who engage in creative arts have shown improvements in processing skills and social interaction.[26] Art therapy has proven beneficial for autistic children because it provides a safe place for self-expression and cooperation with others in a natural setting. Being creative also cultivates a sense of autonomy for autistic learners, which is often in contrast to the structure of their school day.

If you are parenting a child with ADHD who is interested in drawing, they have likely been called out for doodling in class. Doodling is a form of fidgeting that helps us improve focus and relieves stress. Many times kids with ADHD doodle to seek novelty in a situation they find boring and cannot escape. You might even be parenting a child with an undeniable artistic gift. Continue creating opportunities for them to hone their craft, because it might be the only time they feel confident and in control during their day. All types of creative art activate the reward centers in our brain, increasing dopamine and reducing cortisol. When a neurodivergent learner uses art to regulate emotions or to simply take a break from life and experience joy, we need to encourage and celebrate it.

None of these interests is superior to the others; however, every single one involves rhythm. This makes sense because our nervous systems have their own rhythm. Our interests sort themselves out as our brains and bodies take stock of the skills we have to access the nervous system regulation we need. If a child has weak fine motor abilities, they may avoid drawing. If a child struggles with gross motor skills, then mountain biking may not be their thing. But if they have an ear for music and enjoy learning to sing or play an instrument, their interests may quickly move from a situational interest to an individual interest, because they will keep coming back for more. It's crucial for neurodivergent kids to find their thing, because this alignment of interests and skills will bring them joy.

Special Interests

Neurodivergent children engage in special interests for different reasons. Autistic children may latch on to an interest and go deep with facts and knowledge, becoming irritable when parents transition them away from the topic. Children with ADHD tend to get lost in activities like building in Minecraft, reading a novel, or playing a musical instrument—so much so that they don't hear you calling their name. The specific interests of gifted children seem to align with their academic strengths. Unfortunately, special interests among neurodivergent learners have historically been redirected by well-meaning adults who deem them off topic or a distraction from the task at hand. However, in the last decade, research is proving what many autistic, ADHD, and gifted learners have known all along: Engaging in interests increases attention, mood, and socialization.

Around 75 percent of autistic children and teens have special interests, and 50 percent have more than one. The most common interests are sensory based, followed by interests in transportation, fictional characters, television and movies, computers and video games, mechanical objects, animals and plants, and attachment to specific objects, with females having more creative special interests than males.[27] Specific interests in autism are typically attributed to detail-oriented processing combined with executive dysfunction, which makes change difficult, creating a brain that thrives on repetition and sameness. More recently, research has shifted to view interests as a positive way to improve social skills and learning.[28] I sensed this shift in my psychology practice about ten years ago when I used cognitive behavioral talk therapy less and allowed neurodivergent kids to just talk about their interests. I've had kids tell me about their cats, analyze Taylor Swift songs, and bring me their collection of clocks, which let their joy blossom and helped restore their overwhelmed nervous system in our time together. Once they could identify that feeling of joy, I could help them recognize how different it felt to be involved in a task that was empty of joy, and we were able to work on identifying and expressing those emotions.

When children with ADHD engage deeply in an interest, it's called hyperfocus and presents as complete absorption in a task, to the point where they appear to tune out everything else.[29] In hyperfocus, children with ADHD lose awareness of time and their surroundings. This is why parents will report that their child seems to not hear them until they have repeated their name multiple times or raised their voice. Hyperfocus is even more prevalent when a child is focused on a screen. The best way to transition a child away from technology is to join them in the moment and ask about the game or video they are watching, and then once you have their attention communicate your message. When we work *with* a child's pattern of hyperfocus rather than *against* it, we can help them plan their time to go deep into an interest rather than always feeling in trouble for tuning us out.

The interests of gifted learners usually align with their strengths, and they often want to connect with others who share them. However, their interests are commonly referred to as divergent interests because of how drastically they differ from those of same-age peers. According to the Davidson Institute, a nonprofit providing programming for profoundly gifted youth, interests of the gifted learner often align with a niche topic or vivid imagination that causes them to seek out older children or adults, or they may connect with younger children who match their imagination.[30] When a child realizes that another person, regardless of age, understands the same complicated thing they do, they feel validated and seen.

Enjoying learning with another person enhances meaning, helps kids reengage, and leads them through the final phase of interest development—self-sustaining—where they maintain their own interests by seeking out additional learning opportunities. Our biggest hurdle as adults is to stop assuming that children should be interested in something based on their age or grade level and instead encourage them to follow their interests into moments of deep engagement, connection, and meaningful learning.

Success Stories

Think of how engaging with interests has led to positive outcomes for the neurodivergent learner in your life. Consider these success stories:

- The child who was miserable in school until she started taking a drama class where she found her people and her confidence.
- The child who was anxious to talk to his classmates but had an interest in dates and could remember everyone's birthday, so he wished everyone a happy birthday, which led to more peer interaction.
- The child who struggled to stay seated throughout elementary school but won medals for running track as a teenager.
- The child who struggles to read in front of the class but shines on stage when singing.

Neurodivergent learners find success in many ways beyond the classroom. We just have to pay attention to their interests and keep an eye out for the barriers holding them back.

Helping Your Child Learn Through Interests

Isaac never ran from my office again, but school continued to be overwhelming. Knowing his sensory, academic, and social triggers for emotional dysregulation, along with his strategy of regulating and engaging through his interests, his school team and parents decided to move him to a smaller special education class. There he had fewer sensory triggers and the opportunity to learn at his own pace, sometimes faster and sometimes slower than his peers. His school team also recognized his profound gifts in math, and when he was allowed to attend math class two grade levels ahead, he had no problematic behavior. Once Isaac felt successful, his math skills soared, and his ability to communicate his emotions improved because he was no longer overwhelmed by them. The principal also allowed him to design a recycling program for the school so he could use his interests in nature and climate change to feel a sense of belonging. The joy he felt while sharing his interest with others was palpable.

When we expose neurotypical children to a variety of experiences, activities, and opportunities, they usually find their thing without much coaxing. But if you are parenting a child with a limited scope of interests, or a child who struggles to maintain attention long enough to persist beyond their initial excitement, you'll likely need strategies to help them find what they enjoy. When we use an interest to capture a child's attention, whether for a moment or for several months, aligning their goals with the natural rhythm of their nervous system, developing their skills, and embracing their interests will help them thrive. Here are more ideas to capture your child's interests.

Nurture Your Child's Interest

Follow Their Joy

A common concern I hear from parents in my practice is that their child doesn't have any interests. When we dig further, we see that they do have interests, but perhaps they are outside cultural expectations or are unusual given the child's chronological age. Go ahead and throw all your age-based expectations out the window, and follow your child's joy. Whatever brings a smile to their face or ignites the light behind their eyes is a budding interest. Instead of trying to shift an autistic child toward something they don't find interesting, which is futile, use your energy to create opportunities for your child to explore their joy.

I have worked with children in elementary school who are gifted in engineering, music, and math, and they come alive when we incorporate these ideas into our conversations. For instance, one child absolutely loved fans. He had a collection of fans that he would show me from time to time, and he built a battery-operated fan to keep the toy characters "cool" in my playroom.

One day he asked if he could bring a fan to our session, and I replied, "Sure!" His mom looked uncertain and explained that the fan was in a box in the back of the car. Turns out, my client and his mom had been thrifting for fans. He strode in holding a giant box of ceiling fan parts and grinning from ear to ear. We sat on the floor of the therapy playroom and talked about all kinds of things while he assembled, then disassembled, the 1980s brass and ivory ceiling fan. We marveled at the fan's condition and decided that someone must have taken good care of it. This was the bridge I needed to talk with him about taking care of things, as he was working on being responsible for his space and belongings at home.

You might feel silly at first, Googling where to find opportunities for your child's offbeat interest, but the moment you feel their authentic excitement, you'll be hooked.

Schedule Their Joy

In contrast to autistic children, ADHD learners tend to have lots of interests. In fact, some have so many interests that their parents need to limit their extracurriculars due to family time or budgets. Because their attention spans are short and emotions can be big, it's also common for kids with ADHD to struggle settling into activities. They often like lots of things for a short amount of time. I've seen this in preschool classrooms, where children flit from center to center, unable to settle into play. And I've seen older kids unable to decide what to do first because they are so excited about everything they see. Once kids find their thing, or things, we have to help them make a plan to stick with it, sometimes for a certain amount of time. If your child tends to quit easily, but you know they may learn to love it if they just stick with it, you might have a family rule to try something three times (more on this follows), or for a season (depending on the best time frame for your child), before deciding if they enjoy it.

Expand Their Joy

There is no denying a neurodivergent child's interest when you see it. They simply must dive deeper and explore further. The difficulty arises when their interests are not found in their school day. When neurodivergent learners have access to gifted programs or elective options for expanded learning that align with their strengths, their mood will improve. You can also find opportunities beyond the classroom through movement, nature, engineering, or the arts. Again, disregard their chronological age and look for opportunities that light up their eyes with excitement.

Make It Routine

Interest-Based Opportunities Are Not Contingent on Success

Once you discover your child's thing, make it a routine opportunity that they can look forward to. If they love math calculations, give them a whiteboard of equations to complete while eating breakfast. If they love the dollar store, go together every Saturday morning. If they love history, incorporate museums into family travel. (Our family has visited six presidential libraries—so far.) The joy is not only in experiencing the interest but also in trusting the consistency of that experience no matter how tough their day, week, or school year has been. Interest-based opportunities should not be contingent on completing chores, earning grades, or controlling impulses. These are joy-filled moments where your child, who may not find their joy at school, can feel happy and connected to the thing they love. In other words, if your child marches to the beat of their own drum, help them find their own rhythm section.

Get into the Groove

In my experience, children with ADHD become very excited about a new activity, only to resist it at the first sign of a learning curve. Many parents ask me if they should let their child quit an activity or push them to stick with it, especially if the child has a pattern of wanting to quit the moment it gets tough. First, make sure activities are routine, or at least have a predictable schedule, to help your child get into the groove of going. When your child gets into the routine of an activity, they will be able to focus on their lesson, their art project, the game, their teammates, and their dance moves, rather than thinking about when it will happen. Committing to a routine sets the precedent that they are going to stick with something for a certain amount of time and then decide if they are enjoying it enough to keep going.

Use the Try-It-Three-Times Rule

The try-it-three-times rule asks kids to commit to a trial period that doesn't overwhelm them and makes a new experience feel more doable. The first time, a child is usually so excited or anxious that emotions get in the way of figuring out if they even like the activity. The second time, they settle a bit and start forming relationships with others. By the third time, things are either clicking or they aren't. You will know by observing your child's mood before and after. If they continue to be uncomfortable after the third try, that experience might not be the best fit. Checking in after the third time to see if they want to continue gives you more confidence that your child isn't simply avoiding due to anxiety about trying something new and gives them autonomy in the decision-making process.

Interests and Skills

Pair Interests with New Skills

Many neurodivergent learners struggle with transitions because trying new things causes anxiety. When there is no prior experience with a situation, it's hard to trust that it will be safe. Familiarity adds trust, and interests add distraction. If you're taking your child to a new place, think about what might catch their eye. If your child loves music, have them listen to music on the way. If they are meeting a new person, help that person understand your child's interests so they can engage them from the start. You can also use interests as rewards for hard work. For instance, after trying something new that you know is effortful for your child, reward them with additional time spent doing their favorite thing. Think of your child's interests as a regulation tool they can use when faced with new or challenging situations.

Pair Interests with Weak Skills

Because it can be hard for neurodivergent children to stick with things that require effort, it's almost always necessary to incorporate their interests when working on a challenging skill. Interests act as a balm for their frustration in these moments, creating motivation where there was previously none. Similar to routine-building, motivating through interests keeps kids coming back for more, or at least tolerating practice when they are having an off day. If trying to stick with something is overridden by emotions, loving the activity is extremely helpful. As with new skills, you can also use interests as a motivator: When your child has to do something they don't like, following it with an enjoyable activity helps teach them how to recover by having fun. And yes, it's okay if it's their favorite video game.

Technology Interests Can Be Motivation

Screen time is a hot topic for parents. As you know, not all screens are created equal. Aside from using them as assistive devices to aid communication, I think of screen use in three categories: educational (computers, learning apps, quality children's programs), social (video calls, texting, social media), and entertainment (video games, movies and TV, funny videos). While I do not recommend social media for children until age sixteen or access to a smartphone for children under thirteen, if your child has an interest in technology, you can nurture it while still keeping them safe. Use parental control to set boundaries on times of day and days of the week that your child uses screens for entertainment. In our house, the wi-fi is turned off between nine p.m. and six a.m.—for all of us. Another great rule is no screens in bedrooms and a public charging station, like a hallway or the kitchen, for all devices. Some families have one phone or tablet to share and use in a communal space, both to promote enjoying it together and for supervision. You get to make the rules, so with your child and family in mind, find a balance between nurturing interests, teaching how to use technology, and setting boundaries to promote the mental wellness of everyone in your family.

When to Be Concerned: Depression

You may be familiar with one of the *DSM-5*'s diagnostic criteria for depression that reads, "Markedly diminished interest or pleasure in activities previously enjoyed." This is not the same thing as when a neurodivergent child is interested in only one thing. It's also not the same as a teenager's change of interest from spending time with the family to hanging out alone in their room. But if a child once deeply cared about something and no longer does, especially if the change is accompanied by a negative mood and irritability, that is a cause for concern. Depression in neurotypical children under age twelve is uncommon, with only 0.08 to 1.7 percent of kids diagnosed.[31] However, depression is more common (8 percent)[32] among autistic children and even more prevalent for autistic children who have anxiety (35 percent).[33] According to the Centers for Disease Control, 10.8 percent of children ages six to eleven with ADHD also have depression.[34] If your child displays a significant loss in interests along with an irritable mood, negative self-talk, sleep disturbance, changes in eating, or thoughts of self-harm, it's time to talk to a mental health professional. In the meantime, check in with your child's teacher to see if there are any differences in interest or mood at school.

Teacher Email Script: Helping Connect Interests with Engagement

Hi, Ms. [Teacher],

I want to thank you so much for noticing [Child]'s interests and incorporating them into the daily routine! As you know, [Child] loves calendars, holidays, and dates, so letting him lead Calendar Time is his favorite thing about school! I have an idea I'd like to share with you. [Child] is anxious to talk to his peers, but he loves learning everyone's birthday and being involved in the planning of anything special those days. Do you think he could help you with a birthday bulletin board or planning something on the day of classmates' birthdays this school year? I think it could really help him connect with his peers.

Thank you for all you do!
[Your name here]

Kid Chat Script: When Your Child Wants to Quit

Can we chat? I've noticed that when it's time to go to dance, you seem to be in a grumpy mood about it, but when I pick you up, you seem happy. [Child: I never know when it's dance day and can't find my stuff.] *Oh, okay, we can solve that problem. I'll make sure all the dance classes are on the family calendar where you can see it, and we will make sure your dance bag is ready to go the night before. Let's make a checklist of things that go in the bag, and we will keep it in the same spot so you can find it. Let's give this plan a try, okay?* [Child: Okay (and a hug).]

Chapter 10

Supporting Self-Care

"I don't care if my hair is clean!"

We all begin the parenting journey as caretakers of helpless infants. We feed them, wipe them, and dress them, assuming that we won't be caregivers forever. However, once our kids feed themselves, use the toilet independently, and have opinions of their own, caregiving becomes less frequent. We care for our children when they are sick or hurt, but generally speaking, as our children gain skills to take care of their bodies, belongings, and bedroom, we take care of them less often. Our goal is to put ourselves out of a job, but this process happens much more gradually when raising a neurodivergent child.

This is because many neurodivergent kids experience memory, motor, and sensory integration differences that impact self-care milestones. Self-care skills, which clinicians refer to as *activities of daily living,* include toileting, grooming, and dressing. However, your child may be able to read anatomy books beyond their grade level but not yet take care of their body. Or they might be able to build a robot but unable to find both of their shoes. Many neurodivergent learners also struggle to find the motivation for self-care tasks. We assume that kids will begin to care about how they look and smell when they hit puberty, but some autistic children are not socially motivated to please others. We predict that kids will be able to pack their belongings for team practice, but many children with ADHD don't have the executive functioning to do this no matter how much they love baseball. In other words, our kids' neurodivergence may cause them to be great at one skill and, at the same time, struggle with another skill.

Let's look at how Annie's uneven skills baffled her parents and led to many arguments at bedtime, leaving everyone feeling defeated.

Annie's Story

I first met Annie when she was ten years old. She had just been diagnosed with ADHD in addition to her already-identified sensory processing disorder. Annie experienced sensory sensitivities that made washing and brushing her hair extremely difficult. She was making progress in occupational therapy, and medication helped her focus at school, but her parents struggled to help her get through her bedtime routine because by then her medication had worn off. Annie's parents would find her sitting on the floor reading a book in her underwear, having become distracted on her way to take a shower. She seemed to hear her parents when they gave verbal reminders, but as soon as she was in her room, she forgot what she was supposed to be doing and noticed only what was right in front of her. Due to her weakness in following verbal directions paired with sensory sensitivities, washing and brushing her thick hair at a time of day when she was already tired felt like a monumental task.

One day Annie's mom, Caroline, caught my eye in the waiting area at the end of the session and asked for five minutes of my time. Caroline shared that she had recently received a diagnosis of ADHD herself after years of feeling she just couldn't keep up with life. This newfound understanding of her past had opened up room for more compassion with Annie. Caroline realized that when Annie said, "I don't care if my hair is clean!" she likely did care, but saying she didn't care was easier than admitting that she struggled to wash and brush her hair as an almost middle schooler. Caroline wanted to support her daughter, but Annie resisted her help.

I was so grateful that Caroline shared her ADHD diagnosis with me because I could now check in each time I recommended strategies to see if they were doable for her to remain consistent or if we needed to come up with a more actionable plan. When the apple doesn't fall far from the tree, strategies have to support both the apple and the tree.

I also recommended that Caroline share her diagnosis with Annie. When our kids know they are not alone in their neurodivergence, they feel seen and connected. Joining each other as teammates for self-care tasks or chores is often better than constantly arguing and kids feeling they are falling short. As a parent, it's also helpful for you to understand what the science says about memory, motor skills, and sensory sensitivities when you're planning self-care goals for your neurodivergent learner.

Lived Experience

"Make time to listen to your child. They are the only ones who know exactly what's happening in their brains and bodies, and with time, they'll be able to communicate their desires and needs." —Andrea, age forty-one

"A few strategies that work for our family have been (1) never fighting a battle to wear 'fancy shoes,' (2) making my son's bed as comfortable as possible, and (3) packing food for him when we go out or travel." —Allison, mom of a nine-year-old

What the Science Says About Neurodivergence and Self-Care

In order to understand how a child's neurodivergence impacts their ability to take care of themself and the space around them, we first have to look at the science behind memory, motor skills, and sensory sensitivities, all of which are used when completing multistep self-care tasks.

Memory for Verbal Instructions

As you may recall from Chapter 6, we use our working memory to take in new information, hold on to it, and then take action before it's gone. Weaknesses in working memory are most obvious when we ask a child to follow verbal directions. Following verbal directions requires a child to pay attention, understand what is being said, hold the information in their mind, initiate the task, hold the next step in their mind, control their impulses to skip ahead, and continue paying attention while also recalling the verbal instructions previously given. Most neurotypical children gain the ability to follow multistep verbal directions by the time they reach elementary school; however, delays in attention, language, and cognitive flexibility greatly influence a child's ability to remember verbal instructions and therefore affect their ability to follow them.

As you can imagine, relying only on verbal directions is often unsuccessful when supporting neurodivergent learners. One study comparing the ability of children with and without ADHD to follow instructions found that children with ADHD struggled significantly more than their non-ADHD peers to complete multistep directions, especially when the instructions were only spoken. Interestingly, both ADHD and non-ADHD children benefited from instructions being demonstrated.[1] Another study found that children with ADHD struggle to complete activities of daily living due to inattention and memory weaknesses more often than to hyperactivity or impulsivity, indicating that supporting attention and memory is necessary when completing self-care tasks.[2] Based on these results, kids need us to show them what to do rather than simply tell them, especially if they are inattentive.

Demonstration helps kids visualize how to do self-care tasks, but many still need visual support to remember the steps. We often assume visual schedules are used only for young children, but we all use a planner or digital calendar to support our working memory. Further, numerous studies support the effective use of visual schedules for children diagnosed with autism and ADHD.[3] We just have to figure out which system works best for our kids and then teach them to use it. For children who are not yet reading, we use pictures to convey the plan. When we provide visual structure in the form of pictures or lists, the neurodivergent learner can see the steps and reference them if they lose focus or need to know what's coming next.

Motor Skills

You may feel confused that your bright child struggles with self-care tasks. One study among autistic children found that motor skills, not intelligence, were the primary predictors of self-care skills.[4] Motor skill weaknesses are common in autism, with prevalence rates ranging from 50 to 95 percent.[5] Many autistic children have an additional diagnosis of dyspraxia, or developmental coordination disorder, which can present as clumsiness, poor coordination, and trouble sequencing tasks, and they can benefit from working with an occupational or physical therapist.

Motor weaknesses to look out for include those involving fine motor skills (using hands and fingers), such as writing, zipping, and buttoning, and gross motor skills (using arms, legs, and whole-body movements), such as running, climbing, and cycling. Some children also struggle with tasks involving two arms—like washing hair, tying shoes, or holding a cup while pouring—or two legs, like riding a bike or swimming. Weak fine motor skills commonly lead to messes at home, causing a stressful interaction between parent and child. If your neurodivergent learner has weak fine motor skills and you tend to do things for them to avoid a mess, try to reframe your goal from clean to safe. As long as they are safe, being messy is part of the learning process.

Research on the prevalence of motor weaknesses and ADHD is mixed, with most studies finding that about 50 percent of children with ADHD also have a motor coordination disorder.[6] The most common fine motor weakness among children with ADHD is handwriting, but these skills also impact tying shoes, brushing teeth, and eating with utensils, which require hand strength and dexterity. One study looking at fine motor skills among children with and without ADHD found that those diagnosed with ADHD (combined type) and ADHD (inattentive type) performed significantly lower than non-ADHD peers on the Grooved Pegboard Task, which measures manual dexterity.[7] Interestingly, ADHD (hyperactive/impulsive type) did not differ in fine motor skills from the non-ADHD group, indicating that fine motor skill weaknesses correlated with being inattentive.

Given how common motor skill weaknesses are for neurodivergent learners, it's important to seek an evaluation with an occupational therapist if your child has any weaknesses or avoidance of daily self-care tasks involving hand strength, dexterity, or motor coordination. That said, even when a child understands what they are supposed to be doing and has the motor skills to complete a task, some will avoid self-care tasks because of the sensory experience.

Sensory Sensitivities

Sensory processing differences are more common among children diagnosed with autism, ADHD, and anxiety.[8] If you have ever watched your child lie on the floor crying about their socks "not feeling right," you are well aware of sensory sensitivities. Children with sensitive sensory systems can often feel the difference between clean clothes and dirty clothes, smell an onion being cooked from the other side of the house, and gag on food because of its texture. If you think about your child's sensory experience when getting dressed, brushing teeth, washing hair, using the toilet, cleaning dirty dishes, or taking out the trash, you may start to see a pattern of avoidance related to sensory sensitivities.

In Chapter 1, we discussed the sensory overwhelm that can happen in a classroom, often due to the sights and sounds in a group learning environment. But the sensory overwhelm that most commonly interferes with self-care skills relates to touch, smell, and taste. You may have heard the term *tactile defensiveness,* which describes kids who avoid getting dirty, recoil when touching sand, or complain that their clothes are itchy because the feeling of touching a certain texture is overwhelming. Teachers and parents may see these behaviors as problematic, but as a therapist who listens to neurodivergent kids describe their sensory experiences, it's clear to me that their brains are *defending* them from an overwhelming sensation that they perceive as uncomfortable or even painful.

Pioneering occupational therapist Jean Ayres first identified children with sensory processing differences in 1972, when she documented children who struggled to integrate multiple sensory stimuli at once. More recent research has identified three patterns of sensory differences: (1) hyper-responsiveness, (2) hypo-responsiveness, and (3) sensory-seeking behavior. Hyper-responsiveness is related to certain sensations feeling more overwhelming than others. Hypo-responsiveness occurs when the brain doesn't register pain, temperature, or touch as readily, so hypo-responsive children often enjoy rough-and-tumble play and may not notice when they get hurt. Sensory-seeking behavior is seen in children who repetitively rub textures as a way to soothe themselves, and they often enjoy deep pressure like squeezes, hugs, and weighted blankets.[9] While we can make accommodations for our children's sensory differences so they can become comfortable interacting with the world at their own pace, we also have to find a way to help them tolerate tasks that keep them healthy. In order to stay healthy, children need to eat, bathe, brush their teeth, and play outside. We'd also prefer they wear clothes while doing it.

As my son says, "Food really isn't my thing." However, our kids have to eat. When considering breast or bottle feeding, we are told that "fed is best," and any parent of a child with food sensitivities will tell you that fed truly is best, but we have to pick our battles. "Fed is best" for a school-age child might mean that they eat the same five foods every day, or they eat only at certain restaurants, or you have to pack their food when you travel.

Autistic children experience significantly more feeding problems and take in significantly less calcium and protein than do their non-autistic peers.[10] Because a child with food sensitivities may eat the same foods in fourth grade as they did when they were four years old, you might fall into a habit of continuing to prepare food for them after they are physically capable of helping you, especially if they never show an interest in preparing food. This makes sense because when food "really isn't your thing," you don't want to be around it longer than you have to.

Food preparation, as well as chores like washing dirty dishes and taking out smelly trash, can be hard for kids with a sensitive sense of smell or a sensitive gag reflex. If your child is struggling to tolerate the sensory experience of being around certain smells or textures, start by teaching them how to help you make their favorite things and complete chores without smells. For sensory-sensitive children, we can often help them gain independence by teaching them to prepare their limited menu or doing certain chores they can tolerate before they will be successful completing tasks that trigger their over-responsive sensory system.

These oral and olfactory sensitivities, and the anxiety that comes with it, are most severe for kids who have avoidant restrictive food intake disorder (ARFID). ARFID (previously called selective eating disorder) occurs when an individual restricts their food variety or intake, frequently based on the sensory experience of eating, to the extent that it disrupts their health. While those with ARFID are not attempting to lose weight, their restrictive eating impacts their nutrition and energy and can affect growth and development.[11] Not every child with sensory sensitivities will be diagnosed with ARFID, but if your child's eating is so restrictive that they are not growing, it's time to talk to the pediatrician and an occupational therapist who specializes in ARFID.

When it comes to difficulty with self-care tasks and chores, try to resist the urge to assume that your child is "lazy." They might appear "lazy" when they are unmotivated to complete tasks, but stay curious to figure out the reason behind their avoidance. Try to determine if it's a *can't* or a *won't*. A *can't* means that there are skills involved that your child has not yet developed, so you might be asking too much. A *won't* indicates that they are capable but struggling with motivation, which means that something about the task is hard and they need support. Think about the structure your child needs so they can do the task. Do they need a visual list to support their memory of the steps to put away their belongings after school, or extra time and demonstrations to practice eating with a fork, or different clothing or bathroom products to reduce sensory overwhelm?

Next, I will share strategies to help your child feel supported enough to complete self-care tasks, but without heaping on so much support that you inadvertently enable them and impede their budding autonomy. This is the dance.

Applied Behavior Analysis

If your child has been diagnosed with autism, you may have been recommended applied behavior analysis (ABA). While there are proven benefits to ABA, I recommend proceeding with caution. ABA is an intervention rooted in behaviorism first identified by clinical psychologist Ivar Lovaas in the 1960s at the University of California at Los Angeles. During ABA therapy, an autistic child is given an instruction and rewarded for a certain response in an attempt to increase positive and reduce negative behaviors over time. While Lovaas mostly used positive reinforcement, he also used punishment in the form of electric shock to stop children from engaging in self-injurious behaviors.[12] By the 1970s, electric shock was replaced with spanking during the Young Autism Project at UCLA. Spanking was phased out by the end of the decade.[13]

In 1987 and 1993, Lovaas and colleagues published results discussing the "recovery" of nearly 50 percent of autistic children who received "intensive" ABA treatment, defined as an average of forty hours per week for several years.[14] This research had a significant impact on the autism community at the time, giving hope to parents who yearned for their children to make developmental progress. In response, ABA became the standard of care for autistic children in the 1990s, and a board-certified behavior analyst certification program was created in 1998. In 2007, the American Academy of Pediatrics (AAP) included ABA among its recommended interventions along with structured teaching, developmental models

(Denver, DIR/Floortime, relationship-development intervention), social skills instruction, speech/language therapy, occupational therapy, and sensory integration therapy. However, at the same time, the AAP cited three studies[15] finding that intensive ABA was significantly more effective than equally intensive "eclectic" programs using combined models of intervention.[16] By 2019, all fifty states in the United States had passed mandates for insurance companies to cover ABA sessions, making it one of the most accessible interventions for families.

The Lovaas Institute website currently defines the Lovaas approach as "a highly individualized teaching strategy with an emphasis on the utilization and development of positive reinforcement strategies."[17] However, many are critical that the model still recommends that young children engage in an average of forty hours per week of discrete-trial training to cue a behavior, elicit a response, and receive reinforcement. While forty hours is similar to how many hours children spend in school each week, as parents, we have to take into account our children's need for other interventions, socialization, and the time and cost demands placed on families for such an intensive approach. Some parents also argue that ABA is too rigid and becomes stressful, especially for anxious children, while many ABA professionals say that their approaches are individualized and flexible. Additionally, some autistic adults report traumatic memories from their own ABA therapy sessions where they felt trapped until they performed a certain "neurotypical" behavior. At the end of the day, our goal for any therapy should not be to make a child more neurotypical but to help a child feel safe, more capable, and gain autonomy.

While we can all agree that we want our children to gain more skills, there is no singular therapy that suits all autistic children. The most recent recommendation from the AAP in 2020 noted that "treatments should be individualized, developmentally appropriate, and intensive, with performance data relevant to treatment goals to evaluate and adjust intervention," indicating that no one therapy is the best fit for every autistic child.[18] As the parent of a unique child developing on their own path, you will have to make the best decision for your child at each step in their development. Many families turn to ABA to help teach children how to complete daily living skills; however, occupational therapists specialize in treating the sensory integration or motor weaknesses your child may experience while learning. Always look for providers who practice assent-based care, which prioritizes the child's voluntary willingness to participate. Consult with providers who know your child well, and understand different types of interventions, to help you make the next best decision for your child.

How to Promote Self-Care Skills for Your Neurodivergent Learner

Annie's parents decided that hair brushing was necessary because her very thick hair would become matted and even more painful for her if tangled. Caroline decided that while brushing Annie's hair was a must-do, Annie did not yet need to do it independently. Annie and her mom worked out a plan to research detangling products and to brush and braid her hair when it was wet, which helped her tolerate the sensation of hair-pulling. Annie was motivated for hair brushing to be less painful, so Caroline eventually taught her how to brush and braid her own hair. Watching her mom brush and braid her hair in the mirror helped Annie learn that while it was uncomfortable, she could handle it. Annie picked the music they listened to while brushing and braiding her hair, which helped her not dread it so much. Balancing the uncomfortable task with the pleasurable experience of music helped Annie and her mom stay consistent with this routine, which led to more autonomy with this task over time.

We often try to assign tasks based on our child's chronological age when we instead need to scaffold daily living skills based on their developmental ability. If you feel your child has the capacity to take on more independence, start by adjusting your expectations to include only must-do activities. While every family is different, initial must-do's for a child might include taking care of their body by eating, sleeping, wearing clothes, playing, bathing, and brushing teeth. As your child gains skills, expand your must-do's to include caring for their space, such as taking their plate to the counter, putting shoes in their spot, and cleaning up toys. When they are ready for more, add taking care of others, such as feeding a pet, reloading the toilet paper in a shared bathroom, and emptying small trash cans. Read on for more ideas to promote your neurodivergent child's independence with self-care tasks.

Attention and Memory Skills

Everything Has a Home

Keeping track of belongings is a common struggle for kids with weak attention skills. In order to support this weakness, create a home for each thing. Your child's backpack, shoes, toothbrush, hairbrush, water bottle, and other belongings are all assigned spots called home.

The backpack's home is on the bench, and your shoes' home is in the basket. This way items have a final destination and an expected place to find them. You can make it visual by taping placemats to surfaces and outlining the object to be placed there. The more routine this becomes, the more empowered your child will feel, always knowing where their things can be found. You will likely need to add "put your school stuff in their home" on their after-school list to help them practice, which brings me to my next point.

Calendars, Lists, and Reminders

Once a task becomes rote for us, we go on autopilot to free up space in our brain to actively think about something else. This happens when we drive places while talking to a friend or when we fold laundry while listening to an audiobook. The motor tasks of driving and folding laundry are automated, so we can focus on our friend's latest or anticipate the fate of our favorite character. Children with attention or working memory weaknesses need help outsourcing rote tasks by putting in the reps of routine. Calendars help kids know what to expect, lists help them know what to do, and reminders help them not become overwhelmed by another verbal reminder from us; in conjunction, these three increase their autonomy for completing tasks. Many kids benefit from a four-to-five-step list in the morning, after school, and at bedtime to help them gain more independence with routines. However, parents with ADHD may struggle to create and implement these systems consistently due to their own executive functioning weaknesses. Digital lists, family calendars, and automated reminders are often most helpful for parents with ADHD.

Help Your Kid Visualize What Done *Looks Like*

Children with executive functioning weaknesses struggle to translate our verbal language into the visual picture of what it looks like to be finished with that task. Examples of showing your child what *done* looks like could include taking a picture of them fully dressed, their clean bathroom, or an organized binder. Whatever you are working on with them, show them what *done* looks like and reverse-engineer the steps from there. Some children benefit from a picture of every step, and once they see all the steps, they will understand what to do. Art and science teachers show students what *done* looks like when presenting an example of a final project. You can do the same with a morning routine or by showing your child what a play area looks like when it's cleaned up. Some children respond well to watching a video of themselves getting dressed or cleaning up, and watching again and again to add repetition to their learning.

Add Music to Associate with the Task

Years ago, when my son struggled with bathtime transitions, we added a music playlist to his bathtime routine. He chose the playlist (interest-based), with only a few songs (time-limited), and it was the same every time (predictable). Adding music or movement to routine tasks can help cut through the fatigue, boredom, or sensory demands of the moment. Try music when brushing teeth, bathing, or getting dressed and see what happens!

Tip: The Sticky-Note Strategy

My favorite strategy for supporting kids who forget what they are doing halfway through an activity is to make their plan visual and portable. This plan can be as simple as writing down three words on a sticky note for them. If a child is completing multistep directions in one location, like (1) find a pencil, (2) sit down, and (3) get out your homework, then place a sticky note with these short phrases on the table next to them. However, many times following multiple steps involves leaving the first location, doing a task in another location, and then returning to the first location. A sticky note works well in this scenario because your child can take it with them. Handing your child a sticky note that says (1) take dirty socks upstairs, (2) put them in the hamper, and (3) bring down a clean pair of socks provides more support than verbally saying "go get some clean socks." At first, kids will get distracted and lose the sticky note, and you will have to coach them, but over time, they will learn to look at the note in their hand when they forget why they are standing next to the hamper.

Motor Skills

Fine Motor Play

One of the most important things I've learned from my occupational therapist colleagues over the years is that fine motor skills are not just about being able to hold a pencil. Handwriting involves core strength, postural support, shoulder and arm positioning, and hand strength and dexterity. Young children develop most of these skills through play when they are climbing, running, digging, building, and creating. When I speak to elementary educators, many report that kids have poor core strength, posture, and handwriting. While some blame time spent indoors during the pandemic and some blame screen use in the preschool years, the solution is the same: Children under five years old need to play outside as much as possible. For neurodivergent learners who might have motor weaknesses, encourage fine motor play throughout the elementary school years, too. Activities like building with magnet tiles, opening Play-Doh containers, and squeezing Silly Putty to fidget are all ways to increase hand strength. Climbing on playground equipment, falling down and getting up on their own, and swinging all strengthen a child's core muscles and postural control. Time spent playing eventually helps children feel more capable in their body when unloading the dishwasher, unscrewing the toothpaste tube, and getting dressed.

Demonstrate Motor Tasks

For children who have dyspraxia, motor skills involving two hands can be tricky. If your child has struggled to learn how to ride a bicycle or swim, it could mean that they struggle to cross midline, which is what happens when our right hand reaches over to do something on the left side of our body and vice versa. Bilateral hand movements impact tasks like putting on socks, tying shoes, putting away dishes, and folding laundry. If your child has motor weaknesses, they will likely need to see repeated demonstrations of these tasks. You can join your child to demonstrate these tasks or make a video of the task for them to watch more than once. The repeated information will help support your child's practice of skills that they may find easy to give up on. It's also okay for your kid to wear slip-on shoes as long as necessary. We pick our battles.

Give Extra Time for Practice on the Weekends

I commonly hear from parents that they do things for their child in the morning because their child doesn't move fast enough. I have experienced this with my own kids, but I also know that when we always do something for our kids, we interfere with their opportunity to practice the skills themselves. Think of all the times in the week when you do have time to wait for your child to take ten minutes to pack their bag and get their shoes on. Weekend mornings are a great time to help your child practice getting dressed, making breakfast, and brushing teeth. You can still give more support on school days to hurry the process along without taking away all their learning opportunities. Or you can move back the start time on school mornings so you have time for extra practice. Remember to base your expectations on your child's skill development and not on their chronological age.

Occupational Therapy

Parents sometimes question the recommendation for occupational therapy because it can seem like a big investment for what appears to be just "play." But for a neurodivergent child, that play is actually hard work, and important. Occupational therapy helps your child develop strength and control over the muscles and movements that will lead to more autonomy with daily living skills. If your child has motor weaknesses or sensory differences, or both, they will likely benefit from occupational therapy and the exercises that an occupational therapist recommends for you to do with your child at home.

Sensory Differences

Why Won't My Kid Wear a Coat?

Not needing a coat may indicate that your child is underresponsive to cold temperatures. Some kids are also underresponsive to heat, pain, and hunger, which is related to interoception (discussed in Chapter 3). Talk to your child's teacher about the necessity of a coat and if, at the moment, it is even a must-do. If your child does need a coat due to the climate you live in and they are not motivated by the warning "But you'll be cold later!" then create a coat-wearing routine. Many kids are not motivated to please us or to agree to a coat if they don't feel cold at that moment, but kids can learn to follow a routine. If your kid loves to check the weather, give them a number to focus on, and if the temperature falls below a certain degree, then it's time for a coat. I also use this strategy when teaching kids to decide if it's a day for pants or shorts. I have worked with many kids who struggle in the first cold week of the fall when they have to adjust to the feeling of pants again. Practice jackets and pants on the weekend, and let their teacher know this is a work in progress, so you might be late some mornings.

Make Bathtime Preferred

Often children will struggle to transition into a bath or shower and then get so comfortable in the water that they resist getting out. This has more to do with their senses processing the change in temperature than it has to do with giving you a hard time. So don't take it personally, and instead brainstorm strategies for support. Experiment with bubble bath, bath bombs, shower gel, and anything else that makes your child excited about being in the bath or shower. Incorporate soft lighting, toys, and music. My son, who is hyperlexic and taught himself to read at age three years old, was motivated to get in the bath to play with foam letters that stuck to the tiles. Kids who struggle to manage time will need help knowing when to get out of the bath or shower. You can tell them that it's time to get out when the song or playlist is over. This way you are in control of the time frame, but they are cued by their favorite music. You may also have to add a favorite story they are moving toward next to help them leave the music behind.

Turn Toothbrushing into an Experiment

Many different textures, tastes, and temperatures impact sensitivity to toothbrushing. Toothbrush bristles, toothpaste flavors, and water temperatures can all affect a child's experience. However, if you take into account your child's opinions of these products, you will lower their anxiety by giving them a sense of control. You will also likely increase their willingness to try new things once they know that they can say it doesn't work for them. The experimentation strategy also works for trying out clothes and bedding for the best feel. Involve your child in decisions about how their body feels so you can be sure they are comfortable and rested.

Food Prep Independence Before Variety

You might feel worried that your child eats only five things, but as long as your pediatrician is not concerned about their lack of nutrition, put your energy into helping them gain independence with preparing their favorite snack rather than by trying to get them to eat a variety of snacks. Your child will feel empowered to pour their own drink, put grapes into a snack bag, or open their own bag of crackers. Variety will come with time and exposure, so don't let a limited food list stop you from helping your child gain autonomy in the kitchen.

My teenage son has eaten eggs, yogurt, and applesauce for breakfast since preschool. When he was in middle school, we taught him how to scramble eggs. He has made himself breakfast every weekend since, but we still scramble eggs on school mornings to give him an extra ten minutes of sleep. When he went through a growth spurt, we added another egg rather than trying to introduce meat. This plan worked for us, and you will find a plan that works for you, too.

Enuresis and Neurodivergence

Enuresis, or involuntary urination, is common for children diagnosed with autism or ADHD and is more prevalent in boys than in girls.[19] In autistic children, both daytime and nighttime enuresis occur more frequently than in nonautistic children of the same age,[20] often due to issues with sleep, sensory integration, constipation, and bladder control development. For children with

ADHD, enuresis occurs more frequently than for children not diagnosed with ADHD, likely due to differences in sleep, impulsivity, and attention. I talk with so many parents in my psychology practice who don't realize their child isn't the only one struggling with this developmental milestone. Unfortunately, many preschools require a child to be toilet trained to join the classroom of three-year-olds. Some children experience anxiety around toilets, which also needs to be taken into account. If your child is still working on toilet training past age three, that is okay! Talk with your pediatrician, an occupational therapist, and your child's preschool teacher to come up with a consistent plan to work on this skill.

For neurotypical children, bedwetting usually stops sometime between ages five and seven, so most medical professionals don't consider bedwetting before age seven to be a concern. However, nighttime dryness can take a few more years for neurodivergent kids, even if they are successfully toilet trained during the day. Try stopping liquid intake before seven p.m. and emphasize independence with disposable underwear. For instance, instead of calling disposable underwear diapers, call them "nighttime undies" and let your child know that when they start waking up dry for a few weeks, they should let you know so they can change to sleeping in cotton undies. A child should never be shamed for enuresis as it's completely out of their control. The goal is to create a plan with them to gain independence to change clothes if they wake up wet and to let you know if they wake up dry.

When to Be Concerned: Cavities, Skin Infections, and Encopresis

There are some limits to choosing your battles with self-care tasks. If your child begins to have medical issues involving their dental, skin, or gut health, it's time to talk to your dentist or pediatrician. Pediatric dentists are well aware that children with sensory sensitivities struggle to maintain dental hygiene, but you may want to look for a "sensory-friendly" dentist. Talk with your child's dentist about options for sealants to prevent cavities while you work with your child on increasing toothbrushing frequency. There are options of fruity or unflavored toothpaste (mint seems to be too harsh for many), fine bristle brushes (nano-bristle brushes designed for babies), and adaptive flossing (long-handled flossers).

Similarly, if a child doesn't bathe enough, they can develop skin infections. But give yourself some grace. According to the American Academy of Dermatology, children between the ages of six and eleven need to bathe only once or twice a week, when they get dirty or sweaty, and after swimming or sunscreen application. It's more important to pick your battle with handwashing to prevent sickness. That said, some children benefit from the calming routine of a nightly bath, so make the decision that is best for your child. Unscented soaps or soaps of a certain scent might be helpful for your child during bathtime as well.

Encopresis is when a child who is already toilet trained passes stool into their underwear or places other than the toilet. Often caused by chronic constipation and anxiety about the pain of having a bowel movement, encopresis is more common among autistic children, who are more likely to experience constipation, interoceptive differences, and anxiety. Encopresis is often out of a child's control, and some children are not aware when it has happened. Talk to your child's pediatrician about their diet and gut health but also consult with an occupational therapist or mental health provider to discuss the intersection of food sensitivities that can cause constipation and anxiety that can lead to holding bowel movements, which worsens encopresis.

Empowering your child to continue gaining independence with self-care tasks over time means that you will have to step back. As you do, expect to feel annoyed, frustrated, and anxious. If you were a punctual person before becoming a parent, you will likely feel annoyed that you will be late more often. Take a deep breath and repeat to yourself, "My kid is gaining skills, and gaining skills takes time." If you are an organized person who feels uncomfortable with messiness, be prepared to be frustrated more often. Take a deep breath and repeat to yourself, "My kid is gaining skills, and gaining skills is messy." If you are a cautious person who worries your child will get hurt, expect to feel anxious more often. Take a deep breath and repeat to yourself, "My kid is gaining skills, and gaining skills takes mistakes." Parenting is a time-consuming, messy, and risky endeavor even when raising neurotypical kids. When nurturing neurodivergent learners developing on their own path, you will sometimes have to guess about what they are ready for next. That's why you have to lean on a village of family, friends, educators, and providers who will help you know what your child is capable of when you are not around. And finding out your kid is capable without you is a celebration.

Teacher Email Script: Checking in on Independence Across Settings

Dear [Teacher],

I hope you are doing well! I'm writing because we are having trouble getting out the door in the morning, and I'm trying to figure out what is a skill weakness for [Child] and what is due to the dynamic between us. For instance, he rolls around on the floor, not wanting to put on his shoes or a jacket. Even though I think he can physically do these tasks, he becomes irritable and resists every morning. Have you ever seen him take his shoes on and off or put on his jacket independently at school? If so, can we partner to work on these skills together? I think it will be helpful for him to receive coaching on this at home and school. Thank you for any ideas you have to share!

In gratitude,
[Your name here]

Kid Chat Script: Making a Plan for Practice

I know you have felt rushed and upset in the morning when I have wanted you to get your shoes on to get in the car. I talked with your teacher, and she said that you also have a hard time with shoes at school. Let's make a plan that I will help you with shoes on school mornings, and you can have as much time as you need to practice putting on shoes on the weekend. How does that sound?

Chapter 11

Finding Allies

"They were so nice to me!"

We send our children to school for academics, but we also want them to learn how to socialize and cooperate with others. However, many neurodivergent learners don't learn social skills through exposure alone, so we have to explicitly coach them along the way. I believe the responsibility of social learning doesn't fall solely on the neurodivergent child and their family but also on the community of peers and adults around them. When neurotypical allies realize the positive emotional impact they can make by better understanding neurological differences, we all win. In order to help neurodivergent learners find their allies, we must support their social development *and* teach neurotypical peers to notice—and not feel threatened by—differences.

When our neurodivergent children are young, we surround them with a carefully cultivated village that has earned our trust—educators, providers, family members, and other parents who "get" our kid. Some people won't make the cut. They may have little patience for our child, they may judge our parenting, or they may want our child to act more neurotypical. It's okay to set boundaries with people who make life harder for you or your child. In fact, it's necessary to teach your child that part of feeling safe in relationships is for them to be able to share their unique needs, strengths, and interests with others without being dismissed or excluded. Over time our goal is to surround our children with people who nurture their individuality and are willing to stay curious about how they can be supportive. This is how neurodivergent kids expand their experiences beyond school and learn in community with others. Sometimes this looks like helping a neurotypical sibling understand certain behaviors, and other times it can be partnering with educators to teach neurotypical peers how to engage your child. In this chapter, we will discuss how to help your child find their people while also helping others understand them so they feel welcome.

Malcolm's Story

As I sat at my desk, finishing up therapy notes from the morning, an email popped up from Malcolm's dad. The subject line read: "GOOD NEWS!" My heart skipped a beat in anticipation. My client families know that I'm always looking for the wins so we can make more success happen. I was scheduled to see Malcolm later that day, but clearly something couldn't wait.

Dr. Emily, we have figured it out! I can't believe it. I have never seen Malcolm so relaxed and happy. We signed him up for an improv camp, and even though he was reluctant at first, after the first day, he was all in! We've unlocked something, and he can't wait to tell you about it!

I knew immediately what a big deal this was, not only for Malcolm but also for his parents. I recalled one of our first parent sessions, when Malcolm's dad had been hesitant to move forward with my recommendation for an evaluation because he worried a diagnosis would label his son as "less than." I explained that leaving differences undiscovered won't make them go away but will result in a child being misunderstood. While the evaluation process can be overwhelming, more information is always better. Malcolm's parents were ultimately grateful to receive the recommendations that accompanied his ADHD and learning disability diagnoses, which helped them make sense of the strengths and needs of their complex kid. In my experience, once people understand a child's strengths and needs, they are grateful to know how to connect and include them. Over time these connections cultivate compassionate relationships and create inclusive communities where our kids thrive.

Recently, Malcolm had not been thriving at school. He was having trouble controlling his impulses, staying engaged when bored, and refraining from interrupting others. School felt incredibly boring for him as he struggled to tolerate the monotony of the school day. While he was included in the general education classroom, he struggled to make friends because he tended to overwhelm peers by getting in their space or interrupting their conversations. He was feeling socially rejected despite his best efforts. Malcolm's parents and I had been talking about where he could find joy outside school, but so far everything had been a bust. He had struggled to participate in sports, attend day camps, and learn musical instruments due to his weaknesses in motor skills and impulsivity. Because Malcolm interrupted others and peers didn't know how to handle his energy, he was often left out of things. In our therapy sessions, we worked to find a balance between building his skills and validating his effervescent authentic self.

Malcolm burst into my office that afternoon with the joy of a thousand sunshines. His mom gestured to him and said with a laugh, "He can't wait to talk to you." Before I had even heard the details, I knew we needed more of this emotion in Malcolm's life.

"Dr. Emily, do you know what improv is?" he said.

"Yes, I do!" I replied. "Your dad told me that you had a great time at improv camp. Tell me all about it!"

Malcolm's words came tumbling out as he described how it was "totally normal" at improv to not have a plan, so if you forget the plan, you just make one up. He asked if I knew about the concept of "yes, and," which I did because another client had taught it to me years ago. "Yes, and" is a foundational concept in improv comedy where you accept your partner's idea, no matter how wild it is, and add to it. Your ideas build on each other to create a shared story. Because no one tells you your idea won't work, creativity has room to bloom.

In addition to the rules of improv aligning with Malcolm's talkativeness and creativity, he shared in utter disbelief, "Everyone was so nice to me!" This was both wonderful and heartbreaking. Wonderful that Malcolm had experienced such acceptance, and heartbreaking that it hadn't happened until he was ten years old. As he went on, I realized that improv had unlocked his sense of belonging. He had found a place where his endless well of ideas was not only welcome but also accepted and encouraged. He also wasn't met with resistance from others reminding him to sit down, stop talking, or move out of the way. He still had to take turns, of course, but he was able to practice impulse control in the context of improv because the reward of being in the flow of creativity was so high for him.

Lived Experience

"The kindest students have been in theater and chorus classes. The leaders in those areas make it a point to create a family within their circles." —April, mom of a seventeen-year-old

"We are immensely grateful for the various sports coaches who have 'gotten' our son. Along the way there have been a cadre of men who have dared to love him and supported him absolutely." —Amy, mom of a seventeen-year-old

What the Science Says About Belonging

What was happening in real time for Malcolm was a budding sense of belonging through the power of inclusion. His parents had helped him find an environment that aligned with his strengths and allowed for his differences. Belonging develops when a child feels emotionally connected to a community.[1] In order to belong, kids need to first feel safe with the people around them, which requires understanding and acceptance. While others' kindness and compassion are essential, they are not enough. As my colleague and inclusion expert Tim Villegas says, "We belong when we have something to contribute." Many neurodivergent learners feel they don't have much to contribute to a group of peers who are more socially at ease. But everyone has something to contribute. We must look to the adults in the room to notice what is needed in a group, classroom, or team, and offer a neurodivergent learner an opportunity to belong.

The Impact of Adult Attitudes

When your child is diagnosed with a neurodevelopmental difference, you quickly become aware of reactions from others, wanting to shield your child from a hurtful gaze or comment. You may feel judgment from people who make assumptions and do not try to understand your child. You will come across others who already "get it" due to their prior lived experience. And you will have to help others understand your child in order to widen their circle of allies. Teachers, extended family members, coaches, clergy, and neighbors will all take their cues from you.

Trusting Others

Being the only adult in your child's life will limit their opportunities for socialization and independence while leaving you burned out.

For neurotypical children, widening the circle to include teachers, coaches, and clergy feels easier because we don't anticipate the children will be misunderstood, and we trust they have the skills to communicate if something is bothering them. In order to widen the circle of allies surrounding your child as they grow, you have to find a balance between sheltering them and trusting others. When it comes to trusting other parents, look for those who make you and your child feel welcome and are willing to learn how to interact with your child. Parents who stay curious about getting to know your child are more likely to talk to their neurotypical child about including yours. In fact, research has found a positive relationship between parent attitudes toward including neurodivergent children in preschool classrooms and their child's social acceptance of peers with disabilities.[2] So increasing your child's social support starts with you finding allies for yourself as a parent on this journey. One of those allies could be your child's teacher.

Teacher Attitudes

From a parent's perspective, the common denominator that determines a "good school year" is often the teacher. A good teacher fit might be due to a teacher's personality, use of humor, or tone of voice. What is also crucial is a teacher's ability to make a child feel understood and included. Much of the research surrounding teacher attitudes toward children with disabilities is within the context of attitudes toward inclusion.

A meta-analysis across fifty-five countries from 2000 to 2020 showed that teacher attitudes toward inclusion were generally positive and progressed over time; however, special education teachers had more favorable attitudes toward inclusion than general education teachers.[3] Even though children with disabilities have been included to the greatest extent possible in general education classrooms for the last fifty years, some general education teachers still assume that they shouldn't have to support students with disabilities. Younger teachers tend to have more positive attitudes toward inclusion, and not surprisingly, lower levels of teacher stress are often paired with more favorable attitudes toward inclusion.[4] The attitudes of the adults in the room do not go unnoticed. Students receiving special education services report feeling less socially integrated in general education classrooms, and the more positive a teacher's perception of inclusion, the more socially integrated the child feels.[5]

We also know that lived experience influences our attitudes toward diversity and accepting others' differences. A study looking at teacher attitudes specifically toward inclusion of ADHD students found that a teacher's professional training was only a secondary factor in influencing their attitude; the most important factor was determined to be the teacher's own diagnosis of ADHD or prior experience with children or relatives with ADHD.[6] As a parent, you have likely felt relieved to find out that your child's teacher "gets it" because they have lived it. This lived experience is reassuring as we trust teachers to accept our child for who they are and help them find their peer allies along their learning journey.

Peer Acceptance

I don't think we talk to kids enough about disability. Because disability has historically carried stigma, it can feel taboo to discuss, especially with children. But if we don't explain why a child needs an accommodation, their peers will make assumptions that often boil down to "That's not fair!" We have an opportunity, especially among school-age children, to explain differences earlier so that neurotypical children can develop compassion for differences and become allies to their neurodivergent peers.

Classmates and Playmates

Neurodivergent learners are surrounded by potential allies in the classroom, on the playground, and in the community. However, as parents, we often focus on protecting our child from bullies rather than looking for allies. This makes sense when considering that autistic children are at more risk for victimization than their nonautistic peers.[7] But in addition to looking for safe and nurturing adults to add to our child's circle, we also need to talk with allied adults to help us identify helpful peers. The first thing to know is that allies may not be the same as friends, and that is okay. As we discussed in Chapter 7, many parents feel sad that their neurodivergent child struggles to find friends, but don't let this stop you from seeing the benefit of an allied peer who helps your child feel included and gives them the opportunity to practice socializing.

Some peers have exceptional social skills and compassionate hearts that make them trustworthy allies. Social maturity is also a factor when thinking about who might be a helpful peer for our kids. One study investigating attitudes about accommodations for five-to-eleven-year-olds found that the older children were more accepting of disability-related accommodations and had a better understanding of how accommodations related to a specific need.[8] As kids mature, they can learn to be allies, but we have to show them how.

Finding Allies

Public schools in the United States use the Multi-tiered System of Supports (MTSS), where teachers think about the information in three levels:

1. Tier 1—Universal support (whole class)
2. Tier 2—Targeted interventions (small group)
3. Tier 3—Intensive support (individual student)

I'd like to propose teaching peers about neurodiversity and identifying peer allies through this framework as well. Think of Tier 1 as your child's classroom, religious community, or neighborhood. This is a random sample of children, and you don't know yet who might become a trusted ally for your child. During interactions at this level, you might share information about your child on a need-to-know basis by responding to peer questions like "Why can't he ride a bike?" or "Why doesn't he talk?" You might overhear a peer ask their own parent a question, and you can jump in and help that parent explain your child's skills rather than leave them to make assumptions or dismiss the opportunity to learn. Over time you will become more confident helping others understand your child, and you will begin to notice your circle grow.

Think of Tier 2 as your extended family, an interest-based activity, or a regular playgroup. These parents and children need to understand your child so that you and your child can anticipate feeling included when you spend time together. Tier 2 allies are the ones you can relax around because you know your child is welcome. Help these Tier 2 allies understand your child's communication style, interests, and energy level. There may be questions about motor skills, sensory sensitivities, or communication that they are willing to accommodate to help you and your child feel comfortable. In some instances, you may feel you're in the wrong playgroup or need to set boundaries with someone. If the situation is causing you or your child added stress, then it may not be worth engaging in that social interaction. I call these moments "not our scene," which is a great way to explain to others why you won't be joining in. When someone asks you, "Why aren't you coming to the school picnic?" but you already know that crowded, loud, and hot settings aren't worth it for you and your child, you can simply say, "That's not our scene. We'll see how it feels next year."

Tier 3 allies are the unicorns. I call these the VIPs (very important people) in your child's life: the teacher, classmate, or camp counselor who takes a special interest in looking out for your child, including them, and truly caring about them as they grow. They think of your child when you're not together. They reach out when they have an idea of something your child can contribute to the community. They ask what they can do to help your child feel comfortable at an event. Hang on to these relationships even if your child outgrows the activities that brought you together in the first place. These are the people you will share milestones with years later when your child finds their own version of success. I can't wait to invite my son's VIPs to his high school graduation!

Siblings

In my clinical work with families, I have seen siblings serve as allies for each other, and I have seen siblings struggle in conflict. These dynamics have a lot to do with the alignment or dissonance in the siblings' personalities and interests, but they can also have to do with birth order, the push and pull of parental attention, and overall emotional (dys)regulation in the household. Even more than classmates, siblings know how to push each other's buttons and often use the phrase "That's not fair!" In order to support your kids in these moments, try to think of them as unique collections of skills and needs. As Rick Riordan, author of the Percy Jackson series, has said, "Fairness does not mean everyone gets the same. Fairness means everyone gets what they need." If we gave everyone prescription glasses, the child with 20/20 vision wouldn't be able to see. If we gave everyone a cast when someone broke their arm, we would reduce the uninjured child's mobility. Everyone might not get the same thing, but everyone gets what they need to succeed.

> You will have to come back to this sentiment again and again when raising more than one child, especially when neurodivergence and uneven skills are in the mix.

How to Help Your Child Find Allies

Malcolm was in an excellent position to identify some allies. Perhaps some peers from his new improv group would become his friends, but even if they didn't, he was experiencing a safe, social, and accepting place where he felt like he contributed to the fun. For my son, this first happened when he joined the youth group at our church. Everyone was welcoming, and youth leaders went out of their way to learn about his interests, to include him, and to accommodate verbal directions into written ones so he could better understand games and activities. The neurotypical kids around him followed the adults' lead, were encouraged to never let anyone sit alone, and asked for help if they needed guidance on understanding a peer. A few years later we have widened our circle of allies that supports my son's social and emotional learning. Start thinking about where your child feels included. Think about whether they participate in that setting. Ask yourself if they are understood and accepted when they participate. What do they have to contribute, and are they aware of their contribution? These are the ingredients of belonging. I've included more ideas in the following pages for helping your child find their allies so they can continue learning beyond the classroom.

Family

Cousins Are Friends

When my son was first diagnosed, I didn't know how to share the news with my brother and cousins, who would need to help their own children understand my son at family gatherings and vacations as they grew up together. This was before the days of group text threads, so I decided to send an email to everyone. I remember feeling so worried, but I was met with compassion and an alliance I didn't expect. Over the years, my brother and cousins have taught their children, and their aging parents, about the behavior, sensory, and attention differences they may notice, which has helped me relax more during family gatherings. When it's hard for a child to establish friendships, there is so much great social learning that can happen with cousins, whether you live in the same town or are on vacation together.

Grandparent Support

Raising neurodivergent children is not a one-person job. You will need parenting partners. One of my favorite requests as a therapist is to have a parent ask if I'm willing to talk to a child's grandparent. Absolutely! We have so much more research to understand neurodevelopmental differences than we did fifty years ago. Grandparents who are eager to relearn how to support a child are some of my favorite people because they are curious. Some provide childcare or transportation or cover the financial costs of treatment, all of which are incredibly helpful. Not everyone has the support of a grandparent, but you can find similar support in other adult allies in your life.

Sleepovers with Extended Family

Neurodivergent children sometimes miss the opportunity to spend the night away from parents, which helps children experience autonomy. Sometimes this is due to the parent not trusting another adult to meet their child's needs, and sometimes this is due to a child not having a peer they would want to spend the night away with. Grandparents, aunts, uncles, and cousins are often great options for sleepovers. You might need to host sleepovers first in order to make them routine for your child before sending them off to another household. But consider if sleeping away from home would help your neurodivergent learner gain new skills, and ask your extended circle for help.

Friends

Don't Get So Focused on Friendship That You Miss Out on Belonging

As we discussed in Chapter 7, social success is often measured by having friends. But social satisfaction is what we should really be tracking for our kids. Some are satisfied with one friend, some with loads of friends, and some are satisfied simply to be included. Don't stay so focused on helping your child make a friend that you miss potential opportunities for them to belong. Look for neurodiverse playgroups and preschool classrooms where you can find parents and peers who support the benefits of inclusion, even if they are raising a neurotypical child. The year before kindergarten, my son attended a preschool where half of the four-year-olds had a developmental delay and the other half didn't. While he benefited from this classroom model, I gained invaluable relationships with an inclusive group of parents who shaped how I view helping my son expand his social learning experiences, even years later. Often it's the moments that start with acceptance, like my son's youth group or Malcolm's improv class, that lead to belonging. However, we can't teach our kids to belong; we have to clear the path ahead by helping others understand and shepherd them toward it.

Help the Adults Understand

It's important for the parents of potential allies and friends to understand your child's personality, strengths, and needs for support because children model their interactions after us. You can start by saying, "Let me know if you're curious about anything [my child] does or the best way to communicate with her." Some parents send an email to all the parents in their child's class to share information that will help them talk to their child about being a helpful classmate. As we spend more time with other families, allied adults will get to know the strengths in our kids' skills or knowledge that will help them connect, and they will be more likely to include our kids in conversations or activities. If something is happening, like an outing or a trip, that your child would love to do but needs you to support them, join in when you can. Chaperoning field trips is an excellent way to be present to support your child and be available if needed. But also keep your distance, and allow them to build autonomy. I will never forget when my son asked me not to ride the bus as the chaperone. I was thrilled he didn't want me there because this meant he saw himself as belonging among peers without my support.

When Peers or Siblings Grow Apart

As children mature into the tween years, their interests begin to shift, from playing with everyone to playing with those who share their interests. Your child may still be in a developmental phase of wanting to play with everyone, or with younger toys, while more social peers are moving on to friendships based on sports, the arts, or a shared love of Pokémon. Sometimes this feels sad because our child might miss a friend who has matured out of the play they shared. You can validate your child's feelings while helping them understand that classmates and siblings sometimes move on to other activities, but they can, too. For instance, when children are young, it's common to invite the entire class to your child's birthday party, but eventually kids invite just their close friends. As my son got older, we realized that he didn't have anyone he wanted to invite to a birthday party. Instead of emphasizing this, each year we asked him if he wanted a birthday party or wanted to go on a weekend family trip. He chose the trip every time and loved visiting cousins or exploring a new city. Plus, travel is one of the best ways to expand your child's learning beyond the classroom.

Community

Learning How to Trust Others

Some parents feel paralyzed by anxiety when thinking about trusting other adults to care for their children. But in order to widen your circle of allies, you have to take a leap of faith. When you feel your child is physically and emotionally safe with another adult, or has the skills to communicate when something bothers them, it's time to widen your circle. Trusting others is healthy for you and for your child. You will need respite along this journey, and your child will benefit from seeing adults and other children do things in a different, but still safe, way. Once my son came home talking about the screen limits at his friend's house. I could see him putting it together that we weren't actually the only parents on the planet that had family rules for technology. When your child is ready, exposing them to new opportunities, challenges, and routines will expand their window of tolerance. Trust your gut and take baby steps to expand your child's experience. If not, you may be limiting opportunities to expand their learning.

Seek Interest-Based Opportunities

Your child will most likely feel confident to seek out new social connections first among those who share their interests. If you ask your child to meet new people while doing something they don't like or don't feel good at, this could overwhelm them, which shuts down new learning. But when surrounded by their passion, they will more easily trust others, engage in new routines, and grow in confidence. Think through the settings where your child seems most confident. If you're not sure, ask their teacher for moments when they appear confident or need less support. These are the first situations to begin looking for allies, and in many cases, peers who share interests will become more than allies—they often become friends.

Find a Compassionate Community

I know it feels overwhelming to talk about your child's differences, perhaps before you have even processed them yourself (more on that in Chapter 12), but you will need allies for yourself. You will need friends who can listen without judging or making suggestions. This might mean you take a step back from some people because your current season-of-life experiences don't align. Help your friends understand your child, but also let your friends know what you need. If you need to not talk about your child while socializing, or if you need to talk about your child without feedback, let them know. Seek out connection online through community groups where you can relate based on your child's developmental stage, interest, or diagnosis. Raising a neurodivergent child is a complex experience, so you will need people to talk to and to connect with when you need a break. Above all, surround yourself with compassion.

When to Be Concerned: Loneliness

While it's okay for children to feel lonely for a few hours, when children feel lonely for days or even when they are with other people, that can lead to sadness. Sometimes we need to help our children feel included by working behind the scenes with the allied relationships we have made with other adults. Teachers, coaches, neighbors, and other mentors in youth activities can be excellent allies for quietly pairing kids or offering a child an option to connect with a peer outside an activity so they feel they belong.

Teacher Email Script: Asking for Social Support at School

Dear Ms. [Teacher],

As you know, [Child] is struggling to make friends as she is hesitant to join conversations at lunch or games at recess. From what she tells me, those situations seem overwhelming to her, and when it's unstructured, I'm not sure she knows what to do. I'm wondering if you could help her identify a peer for her to connect with at lunch? Or an adult she could eat with to talk about her interests? Even better if a teacher hosts a small group of peers at lunch. At recess, is there a game happening that I could help her practice playing so she knows what to do? I think she needs more structure and familiarity around these social times so she can predict what is happening for a better chance to connect with her peers.

Thank you for all you do,
[Your name here]

Kid Chat Script: Offering Your Child a Better Social Option

You know how you told me that your classmates at lunch are talking about all the things they did this weekend, and you'd rather talk about the books you are reading? Well, I talked with the librarian, and she meets with a group of students during lunch, and they talk about books while they eat their lunch. Would you like to join them?

Chapter 12

Embracing Neurodivergence

"I'm neurodivergent and this is how I learn best."

As parents, we often align success with academic achievement and independence, but I want you to start thinking about success for your neurodivergent child as autonomy. While independence often means completing a task without help, autonomy requires knowing your authentic self, and is associated with our psychological well-being.[1] In other words, while independence is the *ability* to do something on your own, autonomy is the *feeling* of deciding to do something on your own because you know you are capable. Autonomy for a neurodivergent learner might look like confidently walking to class without getting lost but also trusting that if you do you'll be able to ask someone for help. A sense of accomplishment and pride accompanies autonomy that we want to nurture in our neurodivergent learners so they embrace their neurodivergence as a part of their identity.

Before a child can embrace their neurodivergence, they have to understand how their unique set of strengths and needs shows up when learning both inside and outside the classroom. But your child can't understand or embrace their neurodivergence until you do. Many parents worry about when and how to tell their child about their diagnosis. This conversation can feel like both a burden and a privilege. We need to explain to our kids why learning is hard for them, but we also get to highlight their strengths that will help them thrive. Remember, this is not just one conversation. Similar to how we explain reproductive health to our kids, we roll out information in developmentally appropriate ways when they are ready to learn more.

I want you to be ready for these conversations, because your child might get in the car after school one day and say, "I have a classmate who said they are autistic, and it sounds a lot like me. Am I autistic?" Instead of feeling overwhelmed and sidestepping their question, you can fill them in on what you understand about their brain and ask if they want to know more.

For instance, you might say, "Actually, yes, you are autistic. You might not remember, but when you were three years old, we met with a doctor who helped us figure out how to help you sleep better and a therapist who helped you learn to talk. They helped us learn about your autism. Autism is different for every person. Would you like to know more about yours?"

"Sure. But can we get a snack first?"

It's possible that your neurodivergent child already notices their differences, but putting a name to it helps them have an explanation rather than assuming something is wrong. For instance, if you are noticing that your child is feeling down about how big their emotions get when they lose, or about how no one else has trouble staying in their spot at circle time, you could say, "You know how your feelings happen big and fast when you lose a game and it's hard to keep your body still when you're on the carpet at school? Well, that's because of ADHD. Many people with ADHD feel their emotions quickly and their bodies need more movement than those without ADHD. Most of your classmates don't have ADHD, but there are lots of people in the world with ADHD. You actually know some!" Then you can read books and share stories of family members or famous people with ADHD. These conversations are necessary to empower neurodivergent learners to understand their brains so they can figure out what they need to be successful and advocate for it in school and in life.

Parents often fear they will "mess up" talking about disability and inadvertently make their child feel "less than." This worry tends to be rooted in the emotional baggage we carry about the stigma of disability and special education from generations past, but we have the power to create a different narrative. I work with many neurodivergent kids who are unencumbered by the stigmas adults experience. I have known autistic kids who feel empowered when I explain that my nonautistic brain cannot remember dates, U.S. presidents, or facts about the solar eclipse—they can't believe I have to Google it!

Thanks to a shifting paradigm that sees neurodivergence not as a medical disorder but as a neurobiological difference, parents are beginning to push back on the stigma by sharing their experiences and listening to neurodivergent voices. Yet we still worry that our child will be judged or shamed for being who they are. This fear was paralyzing Trevor's parents as they struggled to decide when to talk to him about his diagnosis.

Trevor's Story

"He's just like me," Trevor's dad, Matt, said as he looked down, fidgeting with the magnetic rocks I keep on the table next to my therapy couch. "I didn't like school, but I was able to pass all my classes without studying. A friend in college asked me if I had ever considered that I might have autism, because she thought I did. A twenty-year-old figured me out before any doctor could. I remember being offended at the time because all I knew about autism was from the movie *Rain Man,* and I didn't see how I was like that character. But my friend told me that I reminded her of her brother. When she told me more about him, I thought, 'If that's autism, then I have it.' "

"I'm so sorry no one helped you understand yourself sooner," I replied. "We know much more about identifying and explaining all types of neurodivergence than we did in the 1990s. I'm confident that you will be able to help Trevor have a more positive experience understanding his diagnosis."

When Trevor's parents first sought out my help, he was a high-energy third grader who wasn't able to control his impulses, stay seated to complete his work, or keep a friend. An evaluation during preschool had identified Trevor with ADHD, but by second grade, his social difficulties and enthusiasm for specific interests were indicating that autism was also part of the explanation for his developmental differences. After another evaluation, Trevor was diagnosed with intellectual giftedness, autism, and a writing disability, also known as dysgraphia. His parents were overwhelmed by what to explain to him first, not wanting to give him a laundry list of all the ways he was different. They were unsure he was ready to know more, and they wanted to protect him from the stigma of autism as long as possible. However, the way we protect our kids from stigma is by normalizing neurodiversity, not by hiding it. We must talk about neurodivergence not as "less than" but as a difference. As the autistic author Sarah Hendrickx says, "Autism is not a processing error. It's a different operating system." I believe that the beauty of our collective neurodiversity is that we all have a different operating system requiring us to better understand ourselves so we can embrace our identity and know what we have to offer the world.

Lived Experience

"You will absolutely have to parent your child differently than you imagined, but that's okay. I have learned more about my child in parenting him than I ever thought I would. He's taught me patience and understanding and a whole different way of looking at the world. These kids are *amazing*. When times are hard and you are in tears because you don't know what to do just remember, 'This, too, shall pass.' Take a deep breath and know you are doing the best you can. Listen to your child and what they are telling you through both words and emotions. Don't try to change them. Meet them where they are and learn right along with them." —Anne, mom of a nine-year-old

"Be kind to yourself. Give yourself grace; this is hard. No one knows how to do this perfectly, sometimes you are going to get it wrong, but mostly you are going to get it right because ultimately you know your child best. You are their safety net and their best advocate. You will learn when to push them to the next goal and when to hold steady. There will always be another therapy or intervention you can add, but sometimes your kid just needs an afternoon to relax and be at home with the people who love them just the way they are." —April, mother of a seventeen-year-old

What the Science Says About Neurodivergent Identity

Neurodivergent children need to understand how they learn and socialize best so they can understand themselves, find their people, and ultimately feel they belong. If they grow up constantly feeling like an outsider, this can lead to loneliness, isolation, and poor mental health outcomes.[2] We can empower our kids by explaining their differences and encouraging them to embrace their neurodivergence as a part of their identity. Knowing who you are can be challenging when the systems around you, like school, don't always teach in a way that neurodivergent kids learn. So it's important for parents to be aware of resilience factors for neurodivergent teens, which include strong support systems of family and friends, community participation, and acceptance.[3] To best support your neurodivergent child as they grow into the person they are meant to become, it's helpful to first understand how identity forms across human development.

Understanding Identity Formation

The most commonly accepted theory of identity formation comes from psychologist Erik Erikson's stages of psychosocial development, first introduced in the 1950s.[4] Even though some of these terms feel outdated today, it's helpful to understand these stages as a framework:

1. Infancy (birth to eighteen months)—"Trust vs. Mistrust." The infant develops a secure attachment to a caregiver through predictable access to affection and food.
2. Early Childhood (eighteen months to three years)—"Autonomy vs. Shame/Doubt." The caregiver encourages autonomy while providing a safe environment without boundaries.
3. Play Age (three to five years)—"Initiative vs. Guilt." The caregiver encourages and guides the child's own ideas and interests so the child can feel a sense of purpose.
4. School Age (six to eleven years)—"Industry vs. Inferiority." The child develops skills through practice and striving toward expectations at school and in the home.

5. Adolescence (twelve to eighteen years)—"Identity vs. Identity Confusion." Teens compare their lived experience to what they notice is expected of others around them, which leads to figuring out who they are in the context of the world.[5]

Now, imagine how your own child's differences might impact each stage. Perhaps your child was very hard to soothe, so developing a secure attachment was a challenge. Or if they were highly active, setting boundaries with them as they explored the world may have been a struggle. When I look at Erikson's stages and think of neurodivergent learners, I imagine those who are autistic, ADHD, or twice-exceptional dynamically flowing between stages or possibly experiencing more than one stage at a time. For instance, I can imagine a bright, highly active child striving toward expectations in stage four while still learning how their autonomy fits within the safety boundaries set by caregivers in stage two. Or an autistic child whose interest in play extends well beyond stage three and becomes a part of their identity formation in stage five.

Similar to how we have talked about academic curricula being linear but neurodivergent brains being dynamic, these stages are general guidelines based on neurotypical brains that can serve as a framework. Beyond that, think about how your child feels about themself within the social context around them. How we, as parents, anticipate how our children will be treated in the social context of our extended family, neighborhood, religious communities, and school influences how our children feel about themselves. We have the power to model positive resilience for our child that will lead to healthy identity formation, but first we have to check our own fears.

Parent Reluctance to Disclose

As parents, we carry stigmas from our own childhood about disability, but our kids may not have had the same experience. Your child may already have the mindset of "difference is not a deficit" if they have had a teacher speak openly about their own ADHD or seen an autistic character on television. Or they may feel confused when you explain their autism diagnosis, knowing they have an autistic classmate whose skills vary greatly from their own. You may also think that if you don't tell anyone about your child's diagnosis, then they won't be targeted as different. However, it's human nature to notice differences in one another, and unless we provide an explanation, we leave our child open to the uninformed assumptions of others. So why do we as parents fear talking about neurodivergence? Here are a few reasons.

Fear of Social Stigma

Because neurodivergence is a difference not always immediately noticed, meaning you can't look at someone and know they are autistic, ADHD, or twice-exceptional, parents are tempted to conceal their child's diagnosis to prevent bullying. However, when we don't disclose our child's disability to others, we also block peers from the opportunity to become our kid's ally. One study following an autistic child in two summer camp experiences—one where his autism diagnosis was disclosed and another where it was hidden—found that his peer engagement and reciprocal interactions improved at the first camp after he shared his autism diagnosis with his peers. Gains were not observed at the second camp where his autism diagnosis was withheld.[6] Many times a delay in normalizing neurodivergence allows the stigma to persist, which inadvertently harms our kids.

Parents also fear that teachers will make assumptions about their child based on a diagnostic label. Some worry that teachers will lower expectations or treat their child differently. However, in my experience, because teachers are professionals specializing in working with kids, they almost always notice that something is different about a child's development. When teachers understand these differences, they will understand your child better. Otherwise we run the risk of our child being labeled as "weird," "odd," or "difficult." These are not words we want them to internalize as part of their identity. We also don't want our children to assume that something is so "wrong" with them that it is never talked about.[7] Once a child's neurodivergence is identified and communicated to others, we can do the important work of helping others understand, accept, and help our child feel they belong.

Fear of Using Neurodivergence as an Excuse

Some parents worry that their children will begin to use their diagnosis as a crutch, for instance by opting out of things or blaming negative behavior on their ADHD. The truth is, they might. In fact, when interviewing 150 school-age children in the United Kingdom, most children used ADHD as an excuse to attempt to get out of punishment or to explain their emotionally explosive behavior.[8] As a child psychologist, I can assure you that children will attempt to use any excuse to avoid consequences, whether it's a fabricated story about how the dog ate the cookies from the cookie jar or about how their ADHD made them do it. It's in these moments that we teach our kids about honesty and trust, followed up with a conversation about their skills. For instance, there may be a situation where you think your ADHD child has the impulse control to stop themself from touching something, in which case you wouldn't let them use ADHD as an excuse. Withholding the explanation of a diagnosis will not stop our kids from using excuses to circumvent uncomfortable moments, but it *will* rob us of moments where we can help them differentiate between what they are and are not yet capable of.

The How and Why of Disclosure

Our child's awareness of their skills is an important factor in deciding when and how to talk to them about their neurodivergence. The older the child, the greater the chances that they already have an awareness of what it means to be autistic, gifted, or have ADHD or a learning disability.

If your child is diagnosed before kindergarten, you likely have more time to think through how you want to talk to them. For children who are aware of their differences, help them understand their brains as soon as possible, so they don't assume that something is "wrong" with them. Again, shielding a child from their neurodivergence won't protect them from noticing differences between their skills and the expectations around them.

Multiple studies indicate that failure to disclose neurodivergence, especially autism, to your child prevents them from learning to cope with social judgments and learn self-advocacy skills.[9] And not knowing how to explain their differences can make them feel more negatively about themselves, interfering with their journey to embrace their true identity and develop autonomy. In contrast, autistic teens whose mothers had told them about their diagnosis had more positive perceptions of autism than the teens whose mothers had not disclosed their diagnosis.[10] As a child psychologist, I have witnessed how openly talking about neurodivergence within a family normalizes it as a natural part of neurodiversity, reducing stigma and encouraging conversations for finding the best fit in school, activities, and social circles that lead to healthy identity formation. While talking about a diagnosis can be a hard conversation, it is a necessary and nurturing part of the neurodivergent journey.

Difference Versus Disability

Sometimes the word *difference* is used to soften the stigma of talking about a diagnosis, which runs the risk of invalidating the needs of a child with a neurodevelopmental disability. For this reason, it's important to distinguish between these two words. Within the framework of the medical model, being diagnosed with autism, ADHD, or dyslexia, for instance, is considered a disability. However, many neurodivergent adults say that not all aspects of their diagnosis are disabling, just different, but accommodations are needed. Here are some examples:

- Stimming, such as hand-flapping and rocking. Accommodation: Make space around them; teach others that their body likes to move that way.
- Standing/moving while listening and learning. Accommodation: Create space for their body to move safely.
- Concrete thinking. Accommodation: Translate abstract language into concrete terms; allow nonfiction text.
- Understanding instructions better when reading them than when hearing them. Accommodation: Provide written instructions.
- Comprehending stories better when hearing them than when reading them. Accommodation: Provide audiobooks.

Neurodevelopmental disabilities can cause hardship and need to be supported through environmental changes, therapeutic intervention, or medical treatment. Here are some examples:

- Attention or learning weaknesses that interfere with developmental progress
- Stimming that causes self-harm
- Elopement (quickly running away in unsafe areas)
- Impulsivity that disrupts learning or risks harm to self or others
- Emotional dysregulation leading to name-calling, threats, or physical aggression

As a culture, we can do more to become aware of and accept the differences among neurodivergent individuals. At the same time, we need to recognize when differences become unsafe for the child or those around the child, and when more support is needed in the form of a different environment or a therapeutic or medical intervention.

Helping our kids understand their brains is only the beginning of their journey toward autonomy as they move into adolescence. Think of their knowledge of their diagnosis as the foundation that will allow them to ask for what they need, seek out opportunities of interest, and notice social situations where they feel included. As kids mature, they will talk about their neurodivergence in different ways. They may go through phases of being angry about a weakness or feeling proud of their differences. Both are valid ways to feel. Ultimately, we want our kids to understand themselves so they can embrace their neurodivergence, become their authentic selves, and develop a sense of autonomy that fosters their mental wellness.

> "Figure out who you are so your people can find you."
> —Arlan Hamilton[11]

Helping Your Child Embrace Their Neurodivergence

Once I shared the metaphor of autism being a different operating system to Trevor's parents, they realized they were doing him a disservice by withholding information about how he learns. Trevor's dad was especially motivated to create a resilient narrative around autism and ADHD, something that no one had done for him. The following spring I received a voicemail from Trevor's dad—he sounded emotional yet full of pride. Trevor had come home from school saying that a substitute teacher had given all the directions verbally, and he had felt lost. So he walked up to her desk and said, "I'm autistic and have ADHD. I learn best when I can read the directions. Can you write them down for me?" This statement felt scary to Trevor's parents months ago, but he had learned to say it on his own. This sense of autonomy had led to successful self-advocacy and was possible only because Trevor's parents had normalized this language for him and worked with him to understand himself, embrace his neurodivergence, and practice speaking up for what he needed.

When we advocate for our children and nurture their sense of autonomy to self-advocate, we indirectly help every other neurodivergent learner that a teacher, community member, or peer comes into contact with in the future. Here are tips for helping your child understand their brain, embrace their neurodivergence, and nurture their autonomy.

Teach Them About Their Brain

Arm Yourself with Knowledge and Radical Acceptance

Before you talk to your child about their differences, it's important to check in about how *you* feel about their diagnosis. If you feel sad or scared, it's crucial to process these feelings by talking to a trusted friend, clergy, or therapist. You may also find support in online communities of parents raising neurodivergent children. Sharing our stories helps normalize differences and minimize stigmas. Processing your feelings before talking to your child will allow you to sift through any lingering negativity so that you don't pass it on to your child.

It's also important to fully understand your child's diagnosis so you can think through how you want to talk to them about their skills. Your child's evaluation report serves as a road map, and you can always contact the person who tested your child to ask more questions, even after your final appointment. Once you understand your child's skills, interests, and needs, you can more easily make the shift to parenting the child you have, which is an act of radical acceptance.

Redefine Success as Autonomy

A child's mental health is the foundation upon which relationships, learning, and achievement are built. As previously mentioned, autonomy leads to psychological wellness. While focusing on mental wellness is important for all children, it's mandatory for neurodivergent learners who are growing up in a world that was not built for them. Because neurodivergent teens are at a higher risk for depression and anxiety,[12] we have to balance out the challenging moments with helping our kids understand themselves, feel capable, and enjoy their lives.

When to Talk to Your Child About Their Brain

There is no magical age to talk to a child about their abilities. However, we need to talk to kids about their learning style when they begin to question themselves. We don't want our kids believing they are less worthy than their peers who can keep up in class or easily make a friend. Many kids wrongly assume that because they struggle with *one* thing, they must not be good at *anything*.

Begin by thinking about what your child already knows about their skills, and expand the conversation from there. For young children, you can help them understand their abilities and needs even if they are not yet developmentally ready to understand a diagnostic term that explains their constellation of skills. For instance, you can acknowledge that it's harder for them to learn how to ride a bike, tie their shoes, and brush their teeth due to everyone being different, without telling them they have sensory processing disorder and dyspraxia. You can share those terms later when you feel your child will benefit from defining their differences. When you feel your child is ready to understand their diagnosis, you can explain that some combinations of strengths and needs have a name, then help them feel connected to others who also have a brain like theirs.

As children become more aware of their differences, it's important to share what they need support with, as well as point out how their brains can do things that neurotypical brains cannot. Many autistic kids have incredible memories, specific areas of knowledge, or pattern recognition that is an asset. ADHD brains can often hyperfocus and are fueled by creativity. Twice-exceptional children often don't realize how intelligent they are because their executive functioning weaknesses or learning disability is masking their strengths. Pointing out their variety of skills and needs will help them start thinking about how to ask for help.

Help Them Embrace Their Neurodivergence

Focus on Abilities First

We all have abilities, and we all have needs. If you focus only on what your child *can't* do, you will notice more barriers, more challenges, and more frustration. If you focus on what they *can* do, your child will more readily notice their abilities. Borrowing from the framework we discussed in Chapter 3 regarding differentiating between emerging and mastered skills, think through which skills your child can do independently. Mastered skills are those things your child can complete even if they are hungry, tired, or not feeling well—skills you can expect your kid to do without help. When a child knows they are expected to do things they are capable of, they are better able to develop a sense of autonomy that helps them discern what they can do independently and when they need support.

Normalize Variability of Skills

Explaining differences that your child can see, such as a friend who wears glasses or a classmate with diabetes who wears an insulin pump, is a great place to start. Once they have a solid understanding of varying needs, you can then explain that there are some differences we cannot see because they are inside our brains. Many children assume that academic skills are the only way to be smart, but you can help them understand that we have math smarts, reading smarts, music smarts, sports smarts, computer smarts, social smarts, emotional smarts, and the list goes on. Once children are clear on their variety of smarts, we can explain to them that some smarts are weaker than others, and they need a strategy or more practice in those areas.

"It's Not an Excuse. It's an Explanation."

As Oprah Winfrey wrote in her book *What Happened to You,* "Your past is not an excuse. But it is an explanation." While Winfrey was talking about adults living with trauma, her advice has a parallel that parents can use when encouraging their neurodivergent children to embrace their differences. For instance, if you are confident your child is capable of learning to load the dishwasher, but they push back and say, "I can't remember where everything goes because I have ADHD!" you can validate that yes, ADHD does make it harder for them to remember verbal directions, but that doesn't mean they can't learn with an accommodation. Then show them visually, like with a picture of the loaded dishwasher, to help them practice this skill over time. Their struggle is an explanation for why they need a strategy, not an excuse to avoid learning something new. Oftentimes saying this phrase can be an effective way to model this mindset when a task is taking more effort than expected, but you're not going to let it discourage you from trying.

Nurture Their Autonomy

Talk About How It Feels When Something Is Too Much

In order to nurture autonomy, we have to help kids tolerate the feeling of needing help. Once they realize everyone has a variety of skills, it's easier to talk to them about supporting their differences. Disabilities are just a variety of abilities, and some need accommodation. However, realizing you need help is a vulnerable feeling that can overwhelm some children. Kids will first notice differences when an adult, be it a parent or a teacher, corrects them, and this redirection gives them guidance to try again or change course. However, some neurodivergent learners are emotionally overwhelmed by correction (sometimes called rejection sensitive dysphoria)[13] and experience anxiety that pushes them outside their window of tolerance and farther away from their ability to learn.

If a child is overwhelmed by being helped or corrected by others, teach them to speak up when they recognize their own feelings of overwhelm. For some children, the overwhelm will manifest as a somatic symptom, like a stomachache, headache, or fatigue. For others, it will show up as an overwhelming feeling of avoidance or irritability about school. When we see these emotional signals in our children, we can respond by saying, "This seems overwhelming. Let's figure out how to make this feel more doable." Over time your goal is to help your child develop an inner compass to recognize when they are at the edge of their window of tolerance and in need of a strategy that will lead to more autonomy when asking for help.

Teach Them How to Problem-Solve

Neurodivergent learners, like all children, want to feel confident and independent, but many don't know how to get there. We have to help them with strategies to access learning by providing options, experimenting with what works, and persisting to find solutions. Practice identifying strategies like reducing demands, chunking tasks, mapping out a visual homework plan, getting more movement before staying seated, or any other idea that supports their sensory system, emotional regulation, and executive functioning. All help neurodivergent learners gain a sense of autonomy when solving their own problems.

Practice Asking for Help

Even children who can identify when they are overwhelmed sometimes will struggle to ask for help. Difficulty communicating a need can be related to a speech/language difference, social anxiety, or a lack of the executive functioning needed to initiate a plan. Using visual tools to ask for help is often most effective in these situations. For instance, an understood hand gesture between the student and teacher can help them more readily seek help without having to speak up in front of peers. Knowing your child's cues is also very helpful. For instance, when a child comes to snuggle with a parent without saying anything, they could be using physical proximity to ask for help. If your child doesn't know how to get started or problem-solve due to executive functioning weakness, teach them to use a visual checklist and help them become independent with that plan. The consistent use of a successful strategy is just another way the neurodivergent learner gains a stronger sense of autonomy. (For more on this topic, I recommend reading *Autonomy-Supportive Parenting* by psychologist Emily Edlynn.)

Your child is a complex and beautiful personality with a collection of skills and interests that are uniquely needed in this world. As their guide on their path, you have the privilege of walking one step ahead of them, clearing the way to help them feel safe but also stepping aside when they are ready to emerge into their autonomy. It's within this balance of supporting their challenges while celebrating their strengths that you will find a new version of success that is rooted in joy.

When to Be Concerned: Ableism

Ableism is defined as discrimination against individuals with disabilities, as well as the mindset that able individuals are "better than" those with disabilities. While as a culture we have made progress in supporting the civil rights of disabled children and adults, you may come across someone who doesn't believe your child is disabled. Because neurological differences are not as readily visible or understood, we parents often have to explain our children's abilities and disabilities to others. If you feel your child is being treated as "less than" due to their neurodivergence, it's time to speak up. When we educate others about what our child is capable of and what they need support with, we prevent repeated experiences that could lead to our child feeling invalidated or unsupported and instead model for them how to advocate for the life they deserve.

Teacher Email Script: Open Communication About Your Child's Understanding of Their Brain

Dear Ms. [Teacher],

As you know, [Child] receives accommodations and special education support for her dyslexia, dysgraphia, and executive functioning weaknesses related to ADHD. She has made a lot of progress but lately has been talking about how "dumb" she is in comparison to her classmates. This is the first school year that she has noticed these differences, so we have started talking to her about her neurodivergence, and we wanted you to know. We don't think she would fully understand the terms dyslexia *and* dysgraphia *yet, but we have talked to her about having a disability in reading and math, as well as difficulty paying attention, especially when her schoolwork is hard. She knows she has ADHD, and we are working on her not using this as an excuse to avoid work, but rather an explanation to understand why she needs practice using a strategy to stay focused. Please let me know if you feel she is capable of something she is blaming on her learning disability or ADHD so we can help her recognize when she needs help or a break rather than avoiding things that feel challenging.*

Thank you for all you do,
[Your name here]

Kid Chat Script: Telling Your Child About Their Neurodivergence

If your child is diagnosed when they are young, they may have a therapist in their life before you talk to them about their neurodivergence. Often children have positive associations with therapists who incorporate play, so using those memories can be a helpful jumping-off point when talking to your child about their neurodivergence. For instance, you could say:

"Remember Ms. Liz, who you used to play with at OT? She was helping your brain handle the sensations you felt in your body."

"Ms. Robin, who used to play word games with you, was helping you grow the part of your brain in charge of talking so you can have conversations with classmates."

"You saw Dr. Emily to talk about big feelings and practice what to do when something didn't go the way you wanted it to."

Once your child realizes that these experiences were connected with helping them gain skills and you feel they are ready to understand the name of their diagnosis, you can teach them that their unique set of skills and needs has a name. For instance, you could say, *"When people have a hard time feeling the sensations in their body, have differences in their language, and feel stressed when there is change they didn't expect, it's called autism. Everyone's autism is different. Your autism also makes you really good at remembering dates and facts about Super Mario Bros. Do you want to read a book about some other autistic people throughout history?*

Conclusion

Your Child's Path Is the Right Path

As I parked outside the photographer's studio, I could tell my son was nervous. I knew he wasn't nervous to get his picture taken; he had mastered that skill a long time ago with the practice of routine holiday family photo sessions. He wasn't nervous about what he was wearing; his clothes were comfortable, and that's all that mattered. He wasn't even nervous about the fake tuxedo he was going to put on over his shirt; he knew about those from years of looking through yearbooks to familiarize himself with classmates, teachers, and school activities. No, he was nervous because getting his senior picture taken represented that K–12 school was coming to an end.

Some children can't wait to be finished with school, but my son grew to enjoy being with peers and talking with teachers every day. One of his favorite things about high school was pep rallies. (I did *not* see that coming!) Over the years he learned what he needed when he got frustrated, what he needed to help him remember new information, and how to self-advocate. While we all want our kids to go as far as they can in their education, our neurodivergent learners teach us that school is not the only place to learn. Helping my son remember that school was only one part of his life helped him feel less anxious about leaving it behind.

Meanwhile I was bursting with pride that he was getting his senior picture taken! As I watched him follow the photographer's directions to get the best angle for his yearbook photo, it reminded me of how hard yet joyful parenting neurodivergent kids can be. Every single pivot we make as parents, every single teacher who saw my kid for his strengths and supported his weaknesses, and every single moment my son decided to keep going even when it was hard, culminated in this moment.

There is no one thing that will help your child succeed, but many things will add up over time. There will be a teacher who says, "I've got this," and then you will truly believe you can walk away at drop-off. There will be a tutor who helps your child develop an organization system that they actually use. A therapist will say, "You're doing it!" to your child enough times that they begin believing it themself. A doctor will ask the right questions to get to the bottom of a medication side effect. There will be a friend who convinces you to take a nap because you can't pour from an empty cup. A neighbor will coach their kids about your child's interests so they can start a conversation in the backyard. And an aunt will ask about your child's food preferences so they can eat at the holiday gathering. If you're struggling to find these people, keep asking for what your child needs, so others can learn.

Through the lens of neurodiversity, your child is not the problem. The work you are putting in now—whether that entails advocating for your child or stepping back to allow them to figure things out on their own—is not only worth it but exactly what they need to become the best version of themself. Every time you make a decision that follows your child's joy, you are helping them learn to emotionally regulate through their interests. Every time you collaborate with your child's teacher, you are helping that teacher regulate your child's nervous system. And every time you set a boundary with your child or someone else, you are teaching your child what is healthy for them. There is no one path, only your child's path.

Throughout this book, you have learned how to view your child as having a nervous system in need of nurturing rather than a brokenness in need of repair. You have learned that children don't always recognize when they are overwhelmed, so we pull back, lower demands, and add support until they return to their window of tolerance. We have sorted through stressors like homework, testing, and feeling left out. You have learned that you are not the only one who receives calls from school. Beyond the topic of learning in school, we took a journey through the emotionally regulating benefits of animals, nature, movement, music, and art. And you learned how to nurture your child's autonomy in self-care, find allies, and embrace their neurodivergence.

While each neurodivergent learner's nervous system is different, you can prepare them by finding the environment and relationships where they feel safest and empower them through incorporating interests and encouraging autonomy, all while supporting their emotional regulation and executive functioning skills.

This is the dance—and you have an amazing dance partner.

Acknowledgments

This book would not exist without the numerous people who have shaped my life, gently nudging me to share my experience at the intersection of clinician and parent. First and foremost, I am indebted to all of the children, teens, and parents who have trusted me with their care over the last twenty years. We have spent countless hours looking for patterns, problem-solving solutions, and celebrating every version of success. I have learned so much from you as we navigated the complexities of growing up in a world not built for neurodivergent learners.

There are so many colleagues who have supported me as I've stretched my voice beyond the therapy office. Thank you to Dr. Mona Delahooke, Dr. Tina Payne-Bryson, Dr. Matt Zakreski, Dr. Lori Desautels, Dr. Megan Anna Neff, Debbie Reber, and Kelly Mahler for lending their voices to conversations that keep us all learning. To Penn and Kim Holderness, who called to ask me some questions about kids and anxiety back in 2018 and trusted me to keep sharing my expertise with their audience again and again. I'm so grateful.

I will never be able to express how lucky I feel that my agent, Laurie Abkemeier, said "yes." Laurie, thank you for your faith in this idea, your patience as I sorted through how to share it, and your continued support as I spread my passion for nurturing neurodivergent learners in this world.

I am so grateful for my editor, Thea Diklich-Newell, and the team at Ten Speed Press, for pushing this first-time author to make this book the best it could be. You truly made me a better writer. To my first book coach, Kathleen Furin, for helping my ideas take shape and for Jess, KJ, Sabrina, and Jennie at the *#AmWriting* podcast who may not know that they taught me everything I know about book publishing.

To my former assistant, Everette, who helped this idea get off the ground by being the firm foundation of my speaking career while I was writing this book proposal. Thank you to all the schools who have invited me to share how we can better support neurodivergent learners within systems that were not designed for them.

Thank you to those who took the time to read an early version of this book and provided the most helpful feedback: Judy Williams, Dr. Jordan Wade, Dr. Emily Edlynn, Emily Kircher-Morris, Ann Ashby, Ann Bozek, Jennifer Shonkoff, and Kristen Balhoff. You made this book even better. To my sensitivity reader who helped me make compassionate and thoughtful decisions around language and contributed helpful sensory strategies. Thank you to all of the neurodivergent kids, adults, and parents who shared their lived experience to enrich the stories in this book. Your words are going to help so many.

To my wonderful friends and family who have given me balance throughout the process of writing this book. To Marriott for sending me a DM in 2021 that changed my life. To Amalyssa for always being available to discuss the tough questions ever since our school psych days. To Corey for being both my reality check and my hype girl. To Hunter, Johnny, the Kowalskis, and the rest of my extended Purvis family for continuing to check in and ask how I was doing in the midst of writing, seeing clients, speaking, and parenting. To my brothers and sisters in the OP Band for bringing me joy and friendship through music on a weekly basis. And to the Chapel Hill Ladies and my FLOW sisters, who can solve absolutely any problem via group text.

Thank you to my mom, Judy Williams, who was my first teacher, editor, and cheerleader, always available to talk through the challenges of writing, parenting, and life. To my boys, who are my best teachers and have made me a better person by challenging me in ways that allowed me to focus my energy on what matters. And, finally, to my husband, Scott, who is my steady partner in life supporting all my crazy ideas. You are my sounding board, my reality check, and my safety.

Notes

Introduction: Connect First, Then Teach

1. S. Luterman and K. Sosin, "Who Coined the Term 'Neurodiversity'? It Wasn't Judy Singer, Some Autistic Academics Say," *19th,* April 23, 2024, https://19thnews.org/2024/04/neurodiversity-term-judy-singer-autistic-advocates.
2. N. Walker, *Neuroqueer Heresies* (Autonomous Press, 2021).
3. E. Thomas, "Why Critical Psychology and the Neurodiversity Movement Need Each Other," *Frontiers of Psychology* 15 (January 17, 2024): 1149743, https://doi.org/10.3389/fpsyg.2024.1149743.
4. "Students with Disabilities," https://nces.ed.gov/programs/coe/pdf/2024/CGG_508c.pdf.
5. "Person-First and Destigmatizing Language," National Institutes of Health, June 13, 2025, https://www.nih.gov/nih-style-guide/person-first-destigmatizing-language.
6. A. Taboas, K. Doepke, and C. Zimmerman, "Preferences for Identity-First Versus Person-First Language in a US Sample of Autism Stakeholders," *Autism* 27, no. 2 (2023): 565–70, https://doi.org/10.1177/13623613221130845.
7. L. B. Grech, D. Koller, and A. Olley, "Person-First and Identity-First Disability Language: Informing Client Centered Care," *Social Science and Medicine* 362 (December 2024): 117444, https://doi.org/10.1016/j.socscimed.2024.117444.

Chapter 1: School Readiness and Fit

1. D. Siegel, *The Developing Mind,* 3rd ed. (Guilford, 2020).
2. M. H. Neff, "Understanding the Autistic and ADHD Nervous System," *Neurodivergent Insights,* November 15, 2022, https://neurodivergentinsights.com/autistic-adhd-nervous-system.
3. C. Mills et al., "Children's Sensory Processing in the Classroom: A Cross-Sectional Study Using Teacher Rating," *Psychology in the Schools* 62 (June 21, 2025): 4080–91, https://doi.org/10.1002/pits.23598.
4. E. Vasseleu, C. Neilsen-Hewett, K. Cliff, and S. J. Howard, "How Educators in High-Quality Preschool Services Understand and Support Early Self-Regulation: A Qualitative Study of Knowledge and Practice," *Australian Educational Researcher* 49, no. 5 (2022): 915–41, https://doi.org/10.1007/s13384-021-00466-4.
5. D. Sood, G. LoCure, C. Schranz, and C. Morrison, "Supporting Participation for Children with Sensory Processing Differences in an Early Childhood Center," *OT Practice* 23, no. 12 (2018): 23–25, https://doi.org/10.7138/otp.2018.2312.center.
6. "Sensory Processing in Autism," Autism Research Institute, https://autism.org/brain-sensory-processing-differences/#:~:text=Sensory%20processing%20difficulties%20are%20a,youth%20(4:30); L. Jurek et al., "Sensory Processing in Individuals with Attention-Deficit/Hyperactivity Disorder Compared with Control Populations: A Systematic Review and Meta-Analysis," *Journal of the American Academy of Child and Adolescent Psychiatry* 64, no. 10 (2025): 1132–47, https://doi.org/10.1016/j.jaac.2025.02.019.
7. R. Aldabas, "Effectiveness of Social Stories for Children with Autism: A Comprehensive Review," *Technology and Disability* 31, nos. 1–2 (2019): 1–13, https://doi.org/10.3233/TAD-180218.

Chapter 2: Building a School Family

1. I. Bretherton, "The Origins of Attachment Theory: John Bowlby and Mary Ainsworth," *Developmental Psychology* 28, no. 5 (1992): 759–75, https://doi.org/10.1037/0012-1649.28.5.759.
2. L. Fegran, S. Helseth, and M. S. Fagermoen, "A Comparison of Mothers' and Fathers' Experiences of the Attachment Process in a Neonatal Intensive Care Unit," *Journal of Clinical Nursing* 17, no. 6 (2008): 810–16, https://doi.org/10.1111/j.1365-2702.2007.02125.x.
3. J. Belsky and R. M. Fearon, "Infant-Mother Attachment Security, Contextual Risk, and Early Development: A Moderational Analysis," *Development*

and Psychopathology 14, no. 2 (2002): 293–310, https://doi.org/10.1017/s0954579402002067.

4. M. Delahooke, *Social and Emotional Development in Early Intervention: A Skill Guide for Working with Children* (PESI Publishing & Media, 2017).
5. Delahooke, *Social and Emotional Development.*
6. S. Porges, *The Pocket Guide to the Polyvagal Theory: The Transformative Power of Feeling Safe* (W.W. Norton, 2017).
7. D. Restoy et al., "Emotion Regulation and Emotion Dysregulation in Children and Adolescents with Autism Spectrum Disorder: A Meta-Analysis of Evaluation and Intervention Studies," *Clinical Psychiatry Review* 109 (April 2024), https://doi.org/10.1016/j.cpr.2024.102410; R. G. McDonald, M. I. Cargill, S. Khawar, and E. Kang, "Emotion Dysregulation in Autism: A Meta-Analysis," *Autism* 28, no. 12 (2024): 2986–3001, https://doi.org/10.1177/13623613241257605.
8. J. B. Northrup, H. J. Nuske, A. E. Hipwell, and C. A. Mazefsky, "Review and Developmental Model: Early Childhood Emotion Regulation and Co-Regulation in Autism," *Journal of the American Academy of Child and Adolescent Psychiatry* 65, no. 4 (2025), https://doi.org/10.1016/j.jaac.2025.07.1063.
9. F. M. Lobo and E. Lunkenheimer, "Understanding the Parent-Child Coregulation Patterns Shaping Child Self-Regulation," *Developmental Psychology* 56, no. 6 (2020): 1121–34, https://doi.org/10.1037/dev0000926.

Chapter 3: Managing Your Child's Energy

1. L. F. Barrett, *How Emotions Are Made: The Secret Life of the Brain* (Houghton Mifflin Harcourt, 2017).
2. M. A. Neff, *The Neurodivergent Nervous System,* https://neurodivergentinsights.com/autism/the-neurodivergent-nervous-system.
3. M. Delahooke, *Brain-Body Parenting: How to Stop Managing Behavior and Start Raising Joyful, Resilient Kids* (Harper Wave, 2022).
4. L. F. Barrett, *How Emotions Are Made: The Secret Life of the Brain* (Houghton Mifflin Harcourt, 2017).
5. H. X. Yang et al., "Decreased Interoceptive Accuracy in Children with Autism Spectrum Disorder and with Comorbid Attention Deficit/Hyperactivity Disorder," *Autism Research* 15, no. 4 (2022): 729–39, https://doi.org/10.1002/aur.2679; S. Bonete, C. Molinero, and D. Ruisanchez, "Emotional Dysfunction and Interoceptive Challenges in Adults with Autism Spectrum Disorders," *Behavioral Sciences* (Basel) 13, no. 4 (2023): 312, https://doi.org/10.3390/bs13040312.
6. M. Madra, R. Ringel, and K. G. Margolis, "Gastrointestinal Issues and Autism

Spectrum Disorder," *Child and Adolescent Psychiatric Clinics of North America* 29, no. 3 (2020): 501–13, https://doi.org/10.1016/j.chc.2020.02.005.

7. K. Mahler, "Interoception and Alexithymia," August 25, 2022, https://www.kelly-mahler.com/resources/blog/interoception-and-alexithymia.
8. R. A. Barkley, "ADHD and Time Blindness" (video), YouTube, posted by R. Barkley, https://www.youtube.com/watch?v=IHgbNGPZphc.
9. Y. Granader et al., "Characterizing the Factor Structure of Parent Reported Executive Function in Autism Spectrum Disorders: The Impact of Cognitive Inflexibility," *Journal of Autism and Developmental Disorders* 44 (June 28, 2014): 3056–62, https://doi.org/10.1007/s10803-014-2169-8; C. Boulter et al., "Intolerance of Uncertainty as a Framework for Understanding Anxiety in Children and Adolescents with Autism Spectrum Disorders," *Journal of Autism and Developmental Disorders* 44 (November 24, 2013): 1391–402, https://doi.org/10.1007/s10803-013-2001-x.
10. Council on School Health et al., "The Crucial Role of Recess in School," *Pediatrics* 131, no. 2 (2013): 183–88, https://doi.org/10.1542/peds.2012-2993.
11. B. Hoza et al., "A Randomized Trial Examining the Effects of Aerobic Physical Activity on Attention-Deficit/Hyperactivity Disorder Symptoms in Young Children," *Journal of Abnormal Child Psychology* 43, no. 4 (2015): 655–67, https://doi.org/10.1007/s10802-014-9929-y.
12. D. J. Rhea et al., "The Impact of Recess on Chronic Stress Levels in Elementary School Children," *Children* (Basel) 12, no. 7 (2025): 865, https://doi.org/10.3390/children12070865.

Chapter 4: Motivation to Learn

1. A. J. Elliot, "Approach and Avoidance Motivation," from Handbook of Approach and Avoidance Motivation (Routledge, May 20, 2008), accessed on October 1, 2017, https://www.routledgehandbooks.com/doi/10.4324/9780203888148.ch1.
2. "InBrief: Understanding the Science of Motivation," Center on the Developing Child, Harvard University, January 20, 2021, https://developingchild.harvard.edu/resources/inbriefs/inbrief-understanding-the-science-of-motivation.
3. E. H. Simpson and P. D. Balsam, "The Behavioral Neuroscience of Motivation: An Overview of Concepts, Measures, and Translational Applications," *Current Topics in Behavioral Neuroscience* 27 (November 25, 2016): 1–12, https://doi.org/10.1007/7854_2015_402.
4. "InBrief: Understanding the Science of Motivation," Center on the Developing Child, Harvard University, January 20, 2021, https://

developingchild.harvard.edu/resources/inbriefs/inbrief-understanding-the-science-of-motivation.

5. E. Kircher-Morris and A. Morin, *Neurodiversity-Affirming Schools: Transforming Practices So All Students Feel Accepted and Supported* (Free Spirit, 2025).
6. K. P. Koenig and L. H. Williams, "Characterization and Utilization of Preferred Interests: A Survey of Adults on the Autism Spectrum," *Occupational Therapy in Mental Health* 33, no. 2 (2017): 129–40, https://doi.org/10.1080/0164212X.2016.1248877.
7. S. C. Bayoumi et al., "Promoting Classroom Engagement of Autistic Students Using Focused Interests," *Teaching Exceptional Children* 0, no. 0 (2025), https://doi.org/10.1177/00400599251346719.
8. E. O'Nions et al. "Identifying Features of 'Pathological Demand Avoidance' Using the Diagnostic Interview for Social and Communication Disorders (DISCO)," *European Child and Adolescent Psychiatry* 25, no. 4 (2016): 407–19, https://doi.org/10.1007/s00787-015-0740-2.

Chapter 5: Rethinking Homework

1. H. Cooper, *Homework* (Longman, 1989).
2. H. Cooper, J. C. Robinson, and E. A. Patall, "Does Homework Improve Academic Achievement? A Synthesis of Research, 1987–2003," *Review of Educational Research* 76, no. 2 (2006): 1–62, https://doi.org/10.3102/00346543076001001; H. Cooper, "Does Homework Improve Academic Achievement?: If So, How Much Is Best?" *SEDL Letter* 20, no. 2 (2008), https://sedl.org/pubs/sedl-letter/v20n02/homework.html#:~:text=Across%20five%20studies%2C%20the%20average,achievement%20for%20elementary%20school%20students.
3. *What Is Executive Function? and How Does It Relate to Child Development?* Center on the Developing Child, Harvard University, April 16, 2019, https://developingchild.harvard.edu/resources/what-is-executive-function-and-how-does-it-relate-to-child-development.
4. G. Leisman and R. Melillo, "Front and Center: Maturational Dysregulation of Frontal Lobe Functional Neuroanatomic Connections in Attention Deficit Hyperactivity Disorder," *Frontiers in Neuroanatomy* 16 (August 22, 2022), https://doi.org/10.3389/fnana.2022.936025; K. O'Hearn and A. Lynn, "Age Differences and Brain Maturation Provide Insight into Heterogeneous Results in Autism Spectrum Disorder," *Frontiers in Human Neuroscience* 16 (February 1, 2023), https://doi.org/10.3389/fnhum.2022.957375.
5. *What Is Executive Function? and How Does It Relate to Child Development?* Center on the Developing Child, Harvard University, April 16, 2019, https://

developingchild.harvard.edu/resources/what-is-executive-function-and-how-does-it-relate-to-child-development.

6. I. Berger et al., "Maturational Delay in ADHD: Evidence from CPT," *Frontiers in Human Neuroscience* 7 (October 24, 2013): 691, https://doi.org/10.3389/fnhum.2013.00691.

Chapter 6: Testing and Memory

1. T. P. Alloway, "Working Memory, but Not IQ, Predicts Subsequent Learning in Children with Learning Difficulties," *European Journal of Psychological Assessment* 25, no. 2 (2009): 92–98, https://doi.org/10.1027/1015-5759.25.2.92.
2. G. Schmelzer, "Understanding Learning and Memory: The Neuroscience of Repetition," January 11, 2015, https://gretchenschmelzer.com/blog-1/2015/1/11/understanding-learning-and-memory-the-neuroscience-of-repetition#:~:text=And%2C%20urgency%20also%20determines%20how,memory%20for%20an%20entire%20lifespan.

Chapter 7: Finding Friendship

1. N. Humphrey and W. Symes, "Peer Interaction Patterns Among Adolescents with Autistic Spectrum Disorders (ASDs) in Mainstream School Settings," *Autism* 15, no. 4 (2011): 397–419, https://doi.org/10.1177/1362361310387804; J. Locke, E. H. Ishijima, C. Kasari, and N. London, "Loneliness, Friendship Quality and the Social Networks of Adolescents with High-Functioning Autism in an Inclusive School Setting," *Journal of Research in Special Educational Needs* 10, no. 2 (2010): 74–81, https://doi.org/10.1111/j.1471-3802.2010.01148.x.
2. K. Spender et al., "The Friendships of Children and Youth with Attention-Deficit Hyperactivity Disorder: A Systematic Review," *PLoS One* 18, no. 8 (2023), https://doi.org/10.1371/journal.pone.0289539.
3. E. W. King, "Addressing the Social and Emotional Needs of Twice-Exceptional Students," *Teaching Exceptional Children* 38, no. 2 (2005): 16–21, https://doi.org/10.1177/004005990503800103; S. M. Baum, C. R. Cooper, and T. W. Neu, "Dual Differentiation: An Approach for Meeting the Curricular Needs of Gifted Students with Learning Disabilities," *Psychology in the Schools* 38, no. 5 (2001): 477–90, https://doi.org/10.1002/pits.1036.
4. J. S. House, K. R. Landis, and D. Umberson, "Social Relationships and Health," *Science* 241, no. 4865 (1988): 540–45, https://doi.org/10.1126/science.3399889.
5. "Protection Against Chronic Disease and Serious Illness," Centers for

Disease Control, n.d., https://www.cdc.gov/social-connectedness/about/index.html#:~:text=Protection%20against%20chronic%20disease%20and,Stroke.

6. T. J. Berndt, "Children's Friendships: Shifts Over a Half-Century in Perspectives on Their Development and Their Effects," *Merrill-Palmer Quarterly* 50, no. 3 (2004): 206–23, http://www.jstor.org/stable/23096162.
7. D. Premack and G. Woodruff, "Does the Chimpanzee Have a Theory of Mind?" *Behavioral and Brain Sciences* 1, no. 4 (1978): 515–26, https://doi.org/10.1017/S0140525X00076512.
8. C. Westby and L. Robinson, "A Developmental Perspective for Promoting Theory of Mind," *Top Language Disorders* 34, no. 4 (2014): 362–82, https://alliedhealth.ceconnection.com/files/ADevelopmentalPerspectiveforPromotingTheoryofMind-1415277382255.pdf.
9. J. W. Astington and M. J. Edward, "The Development of Theory of Mind in Early Childhood," *Encyclopedia on Early Childhood Development* (August 2010), https://www.child-encyclopedia.com/pdf/expert/social-cognition/according-experts/development-theory-mind-early-childhood.
10. T. Hutchins et al., "Explicit vs. Applied Theory of Mind Competence: A Comparison of Typically Developing Males, Males with ASD, and Males with ADHD," *Research in Autism Spectrum Disorders* 21 (2016): 94–108, https://doi.org/10.1016/j.rasd.2015.10.004.
11. M. Andreou and V. Skrimpa, "Theory of Mind Deficits and Neurophysiological Operations in Autism Spectrum Disorders: A Review," *Brain Science* 10, no. 6 (June 2020): 393, https://doi.org/10.3390/brainsci10060393; M. Altschuler et al., "Measuring Individual Differences in Cognitive, Affective, and Spontaneous Theory of Mind Among School-Aged Children with Autism Spectrum Disorder," *Journal of Autism and Developmental Disorders* 48 (2018): 3945–57, https://doi.org/10.1007/s10803-018-3663-1; S. Baron-Cohen, "Precursors to a Theory of Mind: Understanding Attention in Others," *Natural Theories of Mind: Evolution, Development and Simulation of Everyday Mindreading* 1 (1991): 233–51, https://api.semanticscholar.org/CorpusID:141187522.
12. D. E. M. Milton, "On the Ontological Status of Autism: The 'Double Empathy Problem,'" *Disability and Society* (August 16, 2012): 883–87, https://doi.org/10.1080/09687599.2012.710008.
13. Hutchins et al., "Explicit vs. Applied Theory of Mind."
14. B. Özbaran, T. Kalyoncu, and S. Köse, "Theory of Mind and Emotion Regulation Difficulties in Children with ADHD," *Psychiatry Research* 270 (December 2018): 117–22, https://doi.org/10.1016/j.psychres.2018.09.034.

Chapter 8: Anxiety

1. K. Supekar, C. de los Angeles, S. Ryali, K. Cao, T. Ma, and V. Menon, "Deep Learning Identifies Robust Gender Differences in Functional Brain Organization and Their Dissociable Links to Clinical Symptoms in Autism," *British Journal of Psychiatry* 220, no. 4 (2022): 202–209, https://doi.org/10.1192/bjp.2022.13.
2. Supekar et al., "Deep Learning Identifies Robust Gender Differences in Functional Brain Organization and Their Dissociable Links to Clinical Symptoms in Autism."
3. "Anxiety and Its Impact on Learning," Kennedy Krieger Institute, https://www.kennedykrieger.org/stories/making-difference/inspiring-stories/anxiety-and-its-impact-learning.
4. J. Klein et al., "Brief Report: Prevalence and Predictors of DSM-Specific and Distinct Anxiety in Cognitively Impaired Autistic Preschool Children," *Journal of Autism and Developmental Disorders* 55, no. 5 (May 2025): 1923–31, https://doi.org/10.1007/s10803-023-05978-9.
5. R. A. Vasa et al., "A Scoping Review of Anxiety in Young Children with Autism Spectrum Disorder," *Autism Research* 13, no. 12 (2020): 2038–57, https://doi.org/10.1002/aur.2395.
6. "Data and Statistics on ADHD," Centers for Disease Control, https://www.cdc.gov/adhd/data/index.html.
7. J. M. Nelson and H. Harwood, "Learning Disabilities and Anxiety: A Meta-Analysis," *Journal of Learning Disabilities* 44, no. 2 (2011): 3–17, https://doi.org/10.1177/0022219409359939.
8. G. Post, *The Gifted Parenting Journey: A Guide to Self-Discovery and Support for Families of Gifted Children* (Gifted Unlimited, 2022).
9. B. Arky, "Twice-Exceptional Kids: Both Gifted and Challenged," Child Mind Institute, n.d., https://childmind.org/article/twice-exceptional-kids-both-gifted-and-challenged.
10. D. C. Beidel and S. M. Turner, "At Risk For Anxiety: I. Psychopathology in the Offspring of Anxious Parents," *Journal of the American Academy of Child and Adolescent Psychiatry* 36, no. 7 (1997): 918–24, https://doi.org/10.1097/00004583-199707000-00013.
11. G. S. Ginsburg and M. C. Schlossberg, "Family-Based Treatment of Childhood Anxiety Disorders," *International Review of Psychiatry* 14, no. 2 (2002): 143–54, https://doi.org/10.1080/09540260220132662; S. E. Whaley, A. Pinto, and M. Sigman, "Characterizing Interactions Between Anxious Mothers and Their Children," *Journal of Consulting and Clinical Psychology* 67, no. 6 (1999): 826–36, https://doi.org/10.1037//0022-006x.67.6.826; R. M. Rapee, "Potential Role of Childrearing Practices in the Development of

Anxiety and Depression," *Clinical Psychiatry Review* 17, no. 2 (1997): 47–67, https://doi.org/10.1016/s0272-7358(96)00040-2.

12. M. Crosby Budinger, T. K. Drazdowski, and G. S. Ginsburg, "Anxiety-Promoting Parenting Behaviors: A Comparison of Anxious Parents With and Without Social Anxiety Disorder," *Child Psychiatry and Human Development* 44, no. 3 (June 2013): 412–18, https://doi.org/10.1007/s10578-012-0335-9.
13. A. Estes et al., "Parenting Stress and Psychological Functioning Among Mothers of Preschool Children with Autism and Developmental Delay," *Autism* 13, no. 4 (July 2009): 375–87, https://doi.org/10.1177/1362361309105658; C. F. Sharpley, V. Bitsika, and B. Efremidis, "Influence of Gender, Parental Health, and Perceived Expertise of Assistance upon Stress, Anxiety, and Depression Among Parents of Children with Autism," *Journal of Intellectual and Developmental Disability* 22, no. 2 (1997): 19–28, https://doi.org/10.1080/13668259700033261.
14. D. L. Rezendes and A. Scarpa, "Associations Between Parental Anxiety/Depression and Child Behavior Problems Related to Autism Spectrum Disorders: The Roles of Parenting Stress and Parenting Self-Efficacy," *Autism Research and Treatment* (2011): 395190, https://doi.org/10.1155/2011/395190.
15. A. R. Olczyk, P. J. Rosen, H. F. Alacha, and M. M. Flynn, "Indirect Effect of ADHD on Parenting Stress Through Increased Child Anxiety and Decreased Emotional Regulatory Coping," *European Child and Adolescent Psychiatry* 33, no. 5 (May 2024): 1407–17, https://doi.org/10.1007/s00787-023-02246-0; S. Leitch et al., "Experience of Stress in Parents of Children with ADHD: A Qualitative Study," *International Journal of Qualitative Studies on Health and Well-Being* 14, no. 1 (December 2019): 1690091, https://doi.org/10.1080/17482631.2019.1690091.
16. C. Wells,"The Experience of Parenting Stress in Parents of Twice-Exceptional Children," *Walden Dissertations and Doctoral Studies* (2018): 6146, https://scholarworks.waldenu.edu/dissertations/6146.
17. K. McMahon, D. Anand, M. Morris-Jones, and M. Z. Rosenthal, "A Path from Childhood Sensory Processing Disorder to Anxiety Disorders: The Mediating Role of Emotion Dysregulation and Adult Sensory Processing Disorder Symptoms," *Frontiers in Integral Neuroscience* 13, no. 22 (July 9, 2019), https://doi.org/10.3389/fnint.2019.00022.

Chapter 9: Interests and Extracurriculars

1. J. M. Harackiewicz, J. L. Smith, and S. J. Priniski, "Interest Matters: The Importance of Promoting Interest in Education," *Policy Insights from the Behavioral and Brain Sciences* 3, no. 2 (October 2016): 220–27, https://doi.org/10.1177/2372732216655542.

2. S. Hidi and K. A. Renninger, "The Four-Phase Model of Interest Development," *Educational Psychologist* 41, no. 2 (2006): 111–27, https://doi.org/10.1207/s15326985ep4102_4.

3. C. J. Dunst, C. M. Trivette, and D. W. Hamby, "Meta-analysis of Studies Incorporating the Interests of Young Children with Autism Spectrum Disorders into Early Intervention Practices," *Autism Research and Treatment* 2012 (2012): 462531, https://doi.org/10.1155/2012/462531.

4. J. Shi et al., "Sustained Attention in Intellectually Gifted Children Assessed Using a Continuous Performance Test," *PLoS One* 8, no. 2 (2013): e57417, https://doi.org/10.1371/journal.pone.0057417.

5. S. Morgan and D. A. O'Byrne, "How Autism Assistance Canines Enhance the Lives of Autistic Children," *Inquiry* 60 (January–December 2023), https://doi.org/10.1177/00469580231195029; C. Harwood, E. Kaczmarek, and D. Drake, "Parental Perceptions of the Nature of the Relationship Children with Autism Spectrum Disorders Share with Their Canine Companion," *Journal of Autism and Developmental Disorders* 49 (2019): 248–59, https://doi.org/10.1007/s10803-018-3759-7; A. Berry et al., "Use of Assistance and Therapy Dogs for Children with Autism Spectrum Disorders: A Critical Review of the Current Evidence," *Journal of Alternative and Complementary Medicine* 19, no. 2 (2013): 73–80, https://doi.org/10.1089/acm.2011.0835.

6. G. K. Carlisle et al., "Companion Animals in Families of Children with Autism Spectrum Disorder: Lessons Learned from Caregivers," *Journal of Family Social Work* 21, nos. 4–5 (2017): 294–312, https://doi.org/10.1080/10522158.2017.1394413.

7. R. L. Gabriels et al. "Randomized Controlled Trial of Therapeutic Horseback Riding in Children and Adolescents with Autism Spectrum Disorder," *Journal of the American Academy of Child and Adolescent Psychiatry* 54, no. 7 (2015): 541–49, https://doi.org/10.1016/j.jaac.2015.04.007.

8. M. E. O'Haire, S. J. McKenzie, A. M. Beck, and V. Slaughter, "Animals May Act As Social Buffers: Skin Conductance Arousal in Children with Autism Spectrum Disorder in a Social Context," *Developmental Psychobiology* 57, no. 5 (2015): 584–95, https://doi.org/10.1002/dev.21310.

9. S. E. Schuck, N. A. Emmerson, A. H. Fine, and K. D. Lakes, "Canine-Assisted Therapy for Children with ADHD: Preliminary Findings from the Positive Assertive Cooperative Kids Study," *Journal of Attention Disorders* 19, no. 2 (February 2015): 125–37, https://doi.org/10.1177/1087054713502080.

10. A. Gadomski et al., "Impact of Pet Dog or Cat Exposure During Childhood on Mental Illness During Adolescence: A Cohort Study," *BMC Pediatrics* 22, no. 2 (2022): 572, https://doi.org/10.1186/s12887-022-03636-0.

11. M. S. N. Fan, "Nature-Based Interventions for Autistic Children: A Systematic

Review and Meta-Analysis," *JAMA Network Open* 6, no. 12 (2023): e2346715, https://doi.org/10.1001/jamanetworkopen.2023.46715.

12. M. Hood and O. Baumann, "Could Nature Contribute to the Management of ADHD in Children? A Systematic Review," *International Journal of Environmental Research and Public Health* 21, no. 6 (2024): 736, https://doi.org/10.3390/ijerph21060736; "The Gifted in the Wild: The Benefits of Nature-Based Exploration for Gifted Learners," *SENG: Supporting Emotional Needs of the Gifted,* n.d., https://www.sengifted.org/post/the-gifted-in-the-wild-the-benefits-of-nature-based-exploration-for-gifted-learners.
13. "Gifted in the Wild."
14. S. Wang et al., "Effectiveness of Physical Activity Interventions for Core Symptoms of Autism Spectrum Disorder: A Systematic Review and Meta-Analysis," *Autism Research* 16, no. 9 (September 2023): 1811–24, https://doi.org/10.1002/aur.3004.
15. W. Sun, M. Yu, and X. Zhou, "Effects of Physical Exercise on Attention Deficit and Other Major Symptoms in Children with ADHD: A Meta-Analysis," *Psychiatry Research* 311 (May 2022): 114509, https://doi.org/10.1016/j.psychres.2022.114509.
16. A. N. Bhat, "Motor Impairment Increases in Children with Autism Spectrum Disorder as a Function of Social Communication, Cognitive and Functional Impairment, Repetitive Behavior Severity, and Comorbid Diagnoses: A SPARK Study Report," *Autism Research* 14, no. 2 (2021): 202–19, https://doi.org/10.1002/aur.2453.
17. H. Marzouki et al., "Effects of Aquatic Training in Children with Autism Spectrum Disorder," *Biology* (Basel) 11 no. 5 (2022): 657, https://doi.org/10.3390/biology11050657; P. van Hooft et al., "Aquatic Interventions to Improve Motor and Social Functioning in Children with ASD: A Systematic Review," *Review Journal of Autism and Developmental Disorders* (2024), https://doi.org/10.1007/s40489-024-00464-z.
18. S. Hattabi et al., "A Randomized Trial of a Swimming-Based Alternative Treatment for Children with Attention Deficit Hyperactivity Disorder," *International Journal of Environmental Research and Public Health* 19, no. 23 (2022): 16238, https://doi.org/10.3390/ijerph192316238.
19. M. Sharda et al., "Music Improves Social Communication and Auditory-Motor Connectivity in Children with Autism," *Translational Psychiatry* 8, no. 2 (2018): 231, https://doi.org/10.1038/s41398-018-0287-3.
20. P. Heaton, "Pitch Memory, Labelling and Disembedding in Autism," *Journal of Child Psychology and Psychiatry* 44, no. 4 (2003): 543–51, https://doi.org/10.1111/1469-7610.00143.
21. J. Katagiri, "The Effect of Background Music and Song Texts on the

Emotional Understanding of Children with Autism," *Journal of Music Therapy* 46, no.1 (Spring 2009): 15–31, https://doi.org/10.1093/jmt/46.1.15.

22. A. Paul et al., "The Effect of Sung Speech on Socio-Communicative Responsiveness in Children with Autism Spectrum Disorders," *Frontiers of Human Neuroscience* 9 (October 29, 2015): 555, https://doi.org/10.3389/fnhum.2015.00555; K. Simpson, D. Keen, and J. Lamb, "The Use of Music to Engage Children with Autism in a Receptive Labelling Task," *Research in Autism Spectrum Disorders* 7, no. 12 (2013): 1489–96, https://doi.org/10.1016/j.rasd.2013.08.013.
23. J. I. Park et al., "Effects of Music Therapy as an Alternative Treatment on Depression in Children and Adolescents with ADHD by Activating Serotonin and Improving Stress Coping Ability," *BMC Complementary Medicine and Therapies* 23, no. 73 (2023), https://doi.org/10.1186/s12906-022-03832-6.
24. N. Madjar, R. Gazoli, I. Manor, and G. Shoval, "Contrasting Effects of Music on Reading Comprehension in Preadolescents With and Without ADHD," *Psychiatry Research* 291 (2020): 113207, https://doi.org/10.1016/j.psychres.2020.113207.
25. M. J. Ismail and A. Farhana,"The Significance of Music to Gifted Students," *Quantum Journal of Social Sciences and Humanities* 1, no. 4 (2020), https://doi.org/10.55197/qjssh.v1i4.21.
26. C. López-Escribano and C. Orío-Aparicio, "Creative Arts Therapy for Autistic Children: A Systematic Review," *Arts in Psychotherapy* 91 (2024): 102224, https://doi.org/10.1016/j.aip.2024.102224; A. Bernier et al., "Art Interventions for Children with Autism Spectrum Disorder: A Scoping Review," *American Journal of Occupational Therapy* 76, no. 5 (September 1, 2022): 7605205030, https://doi.org/10.5014/ajot.2022.049320.
27. M. Uljarević et al., "Toward Better Characterization of Restricted and Unusual Interests in Youth with Autism," *Autism* 26, no. 5 (July 2022): 1296–304, https://doi.org/10.1177/13623613211056720.
28. E. Laber-Warren, "The Benefits of Special Interests in Autism," *Transmitter,* May 12, 2021, https://doi.org/10.53053/UVVZ8029.
29. B. K. Ashinoff and A. Abu-Akel, "Hyperfocus: The Forgotten Frontier of Attention," *Psychological Research* 85, no. 2 (2021): 1–19, https://doi.org/10.1007/s00426-019-01245-8.
30. https://www.davidsongifted.org/prospective-families/gifted-traits-and-characteristics.
31. E. M. L. Juul, O. Hjemdal, and T. Aune, "Prevalence of Depressive Symptoms Among Older Children and Young Adolescents: A Longitudinal Population-Based Study," *Scandinavian Journal of Child Adolescent Psychiatry and*

Psychology 9 (April 23, 2021): 64–72, https://doi.org/10.21307/sjcapp-2021-008.

32. C. C. Hudson, L. Hall, and K. L. Harkness, "Prevalence of Depressive Disorders in Individuals with Autism Spectrum Disorder: A Meta-Analysis," *Journal of Abnormal Child Psychology* 47, no. 2 (2019): 165–75, https://doi.org/10.1007/s10802-018-0402-1.
33. L. A. Wijnhoven et al., "Prevalence of Comorbid Depressive Symptoms and Suicidal Ideation in Children with Autism Spectrum Disorder and Elevated Anxiety Symptoms," *Journal of Child and Adolescent Mental Health* 31, no. 2 (2019): 77–84, https://doi.org/10.2989/17280583.2019.1608830.
34. "Data and Statistics on ADHD," https://www.cdc.gov/adhd/data/index.html.

Chapter 10: Supporting Self-Care

1. T. X. Yang, R. J. Allen, J. Holmes, and R. C. Chan, "Impaired Memory for Instructions in Children with Attention-Deficit Hyperactivity Disorder Is Improved by Action at Presentation and Recall," *Frontiers of Psychology* 8, no. 39 (2017), https://doi.org/10.3389/fpsyg.2017.00039.
2. L. N. Irwin et al., "Activities of Daily Living and Working Memory in Pediatric Attention-Deficit/Hyperactivity Disorder (ADHD)," *Child Neuropsychology* 27, no. 4 (2021): 468–90, https://doi.org/10.1080/09297049.2020.1866521.
3. N. Thomas and S. Karuppali, "The Efficacy of Visual Activity Schedule Intervention in Reducing Problem Behaviors in Children with Attention-Deficit/Hyperactivity Disorder Between the Age of 5 and 12 Years: A Systematic Review," *Soa Chongsonyon Chongsin Uihak* 33, no. 2 (2022): 2–15, https://doi.org/10.5765/jkacap.210021; Z. Liang, D. Lee, J. Zuo, and S. Liang, "The Use of Visual Schedules to Increase Academic-Related On-Task Behaviors of Individuals with Autism: A Literature Review," *International Journal of Developmental Disabilities* (2024): 1–14, https://doi.org/10.1080/20473869.2024.2402124.
4. N. E. Fears, S. A. Palmer, and H. L. Miller, "Motor Skills Predict Adaptive Behavior in Autistic Children and Adolescents," *Autism Research* 15 (2022): 1083–89, https://doi.org/10.1002/aur.2708.
5. H. L. Miller et al., "Motor Problems in Autism: Co-Occurrence or Feature?" *Developmental Medicine and Child Neurology* 66, no. 2 (2024): 16–22, https://doi.org/10.1111/dmcn.15674.
6. E. J. Meachon, J. P. Schaider, and G.W. Alpers, "Motor Skills in Children with ADHD: Overlap with Developmental Coordination Disorder," *BMC Psychology* 13, no. 53 (2025), https://doi.org/10.1186/s40359-024-02282-8.
7. M. Mokobane, B. J. Pillay, and A. Meyer, "Fine Motor Deficits and Attention

Deficit Hyperactivity Disorder in Primary School Children," *South African Journal of Psychiatry* 25 (January 22, 2019): 1232, https://doi.org/10.4102/sajpsychiatry.v25i0.1232.

8. S. Sivapalan, B. Sivayokan, K. Raveenthiran, and S. Sivayokan, "Sensory Issues and Their Impact Among Autistic Children: A Cross-Sectional Study in Northern Sri Lanka," *Cureus* 16, no. 10 (2024): e72130, https://doi.org/10.7759/cureus.72130; A. Ghanizadeh, "Sensory Processing Problems in Children with ADHD, A Systematic Review," *Psychiatry Investigation* 8, no. 2 (2011): 89–94, https://doi.org/10.4306/pi.2011.8.2.89; S. A. Green and A. Ben-Sasson, "Anxiety Disorders and Sensory Over-Responsivity in Children with Autism Spectrum Disorders: Is There a Causal Relationship?" *Journal of Autism and Developmental Disorders* 40, no. 12 (2010): 1495–504, https://doi.org/10.1007/s10803-010-1007-x.
9. D. Smirni et al., "Noli Me Tangere: Social Touch, Tactile Defensiveness, and Communication in Neurodevelopmental Disorders," *Brain Science* 9, no. 12 (2019): 368, https://doi.org/10.3390/brainsci9120368.
10. W. G. Sharp et al., "Feeding Problems and Nutrient Intake in Children with Autism Spectrum Disorders: A Meta-analysis and Comprehensive Review of the Literature," *Journal of Autism and Developmental Disorders* 43 (2013): 2159–73, https://doi.org/10.1007/s10803-013-1771-5.
11. N. K. O. Fonseca et al., "Avoidant Restrictive Food Intake Disorder: Recent Advances in Neurobiology and Treatment," *Journal of Eating Disorders* 12, no. 74 (2024), https://doi.org/10.1186/s40337-024-01021-z.
12. E. V. Larsson and S. Wright, "O. Ivar Lovaas (1927–2010)," *Journal of Applied Behavior Analysis* 34, no. 1 (2011): 111–14; T. Smith and S. Eikeseth, "O. Ivar Lovaas: Pioneer of Applied Behavior Analysis and Intervention for Children with Autism," *Journal of Autism and Developmental Disorders* 41, no. 3 (2010): 375–78, https://doi.org/10.1007/s10803-010-1162-0.
13. J. B. Leaf, "Concerns About ABA-Based Intervention: An Evaluation and Recommendations," *Journal of Autism and Developmental Disorders* 52, no. 6 (2022): 2838–53, https://doi.org/10.1007/s10803-021-05137-y. Erratum in *Journal of Autism and Developmental Disorders* 52, no. 6 (2022): 2854, https://doi.org/10.1007/s10803-021-05200-8.
14. O. I. Lovaas, "Behavioral Treatment and Normal Educational and Intellectual Functioning in Young Autistic Children," *Journal of Consulting and Clinical Psychology* 55, no. 2 (1987): 3–9, https://doi.org/10.1037//0022-006x.55.1.3; J. J. McEachin, T. Smith, and O. I. Lovaas, "Long-Term Outcome for Children with Autism Who Received Early Intensive Behavioral Treatment," *American Journal of Mental Retardation* 97, no. 4 (1993): 359–72; discussion 373–91.
15. H. Cohen, M. Amerine-Dickens, and T. Smith, "Early Intensive Behavioral

Treatment: Replication of the UCLA Model in a Community Setting," *Journal of Developmental and Behavioral Pediatrics* 27 (2 suppl.) (2006): S145—S155, https://doi.org/10.1097/00004703-200604002-00013; J. S. Howard et al., "A Comparison of Intensive Behavior Analytic and Eclectic Treatments for Young Children with Autism," *Research in Devopmental Disabilities* 26 (2005): 359–83, https://doi.org/10.1016/j.ridd.2004.09.005; S. Eikeseth, T. Smith, E. Jahr, and S. Eldevik, "Intensive Behavioral Treatment at School for 4- to 7-Year-Old Children with Autism: A 1-Year Comparison Controlled Study," *Behavior Modification* 26 (2002): 49–68, https://doi.org/10.1177/0145445502026001004.

16. S. M. Myers, C. P. Johnson, and Council on Children with Disabilities, "Management of Children with Autism Spectrum Disorders," *Pediatrics* 120, no. 5 (2007): 1162–82, https://doi.org/10.1542/peds.2007-2362.
17. "The Lovaas Approach," https://lovaas.com/lovaas-method.
18. S. L. Hyman et al., "Identification, Evaluation, and Management of Children with Autism Spectrum Disorder," *Pediatrics* 145, no. 2 (2020), https://doi.org/10.1542/peds.2019-3447.
19. W. F. Bower et al., "The Epidemiology of Childhood Enuresis in Australia," *British Journal of Urology* 78 (1996): 602–6, https://doi.org/10.1046/j.1464-410x.1996.13618.x; S. Shreeram et al., "Prevalence of Enuresis and Its Association with Attention-Deficit/Hyperactivity Disorder Among U.S. Children: Results from a Nationally Representative Study," *Journal of the American Academy of Child and Adolescent Psychiatry* 48, no. 2 (2009): 35–41, https://doi.org/10.1097/CHI.0b013e318190045c.
20. A. von Gontard, M. Pirrung, J. Niemczyk, and M. Equit, "Incontinence in Children with Autism Spectrum Disorder," *Journal of Pediatric Urology* 11, no. 5 (2015), https://doi.org/10.1016/j.jpurol.2015.04.015.

Chapter 11: Finding Allies

1. T. Long and J. Guo, "Moving Beyond Inclusion to Belonging," *International Journal of Environmental Research and Public Health* 20, no. 20 (2023): 6907, https://doi.org/10.3390/ijerph20206907.
2. H. M. S. Dodur and Y. Yüzbaşioğlu. "Parental Influence on Preschoolers' Acceptance of Peers with Special Needs: The Mediating Role of Inclusion Attitudes," *Children and Youth Services Review* 170 (March 2025): 108139, https://doi.org/10.1016/j.childyouth.2025.108139.
3. F. Guillemot, F. Lacroix, and I. Nocus, "Teachers' Attitude Towards Inclusive Education from 2000 to 2020: An Extended Meta-Analysis," *International Journal of Educational Research Open* 3 (2022): 100175, https://doi.org/10.1016/j.ijedro.2022.100175.

4. J. Galaterou and A.-S. Antoniou, "Teachers' Attitudes Towards Inclusive Education: The Role of Job Stressors and Demographic Parameters," *International Journal of Special Education* 32, no. 4 (2017), https://files.eric.ed.gov/fulltext/EJ1184123.pdf.
5. A. Heyder, A. Südkamp, and R. Steinmayr, "How Are Teachers' Attitudes Toward Inclusion Related to the Social-Emotional School Experiences of Students With and Without Special Educational Needs?" *Learning and Individual Differences* 77 (January 2020): 101776, https://doi.org/10.1016/j.lindif.2019.101776.
6. F. Heidi and U. Eran, "Determinants of Teachers' Attitudes Toward Inclusion of Pupils with Attention Deficit Hyperactivity Disorder: The Role of Teacher Education," *Frontiers in Education* 7 (September 1, 2022), https://doi.org/10.3389/feduc.2022.941699.
7. N. Libster et al., "Personal Victimization Experiences of Autistic and Non-Autistic Children," *Molecular Autism* 13, no. 2 (2022): 51, https://doi.org/10.1186/s13229-022-00531-4; C. Maïano et al., "Prevalence of School Bullying Among Youth with Autism Spectrum Disorders: A Systematic Review and Meta-Analysis," *Autism Research* 9 (October 9, 2016): 601–15, https://doi.org/10.1002/aur.1568.
8. N. Granata and J. D. Lane, "Children's Developing Disability Concepts: A Review and Recommendations For Continued Research," *Cognitive Development* 74 (April–June 2025): 101566, https://doi.org/10.1016/j.cogdev.2025.101566.

Chapter 12: Embracing Neurodivergence

1. E. Edlynn, *Autonomy-Supportive Parenting: Reduce Parental Burnout and Raise Competent, Confident Children* (Familius, 2023).
2. B. French, D. Daley, M. Groom, and S. Cassidy, "Risks Associated with Undiagnosed ADHD and/or Autism: A Mixed-Method Systematic Review," *Journal of Attention Disorders* 27, no. 12 (2023): 1393–410, https://doi.org/10.1177/10870547231176862.
3. M. H. Black et al., "Resilience in the Face of Neurodivergence: A Scoping Review of Resilience and Factors Promoting Positive Outcomes," *Clinical Psychology Review* 113 (2024): 102487, https://doi.org/10.1016/j.cpr.2024.102487.
4. E. H. Erikson, *Childhood and Society* (W. W. Norton, 1950).
5. G. A. Orenstein and L. Lewis, "Erikson's Stages of Psychosocial Development," Updated November 7, 2022, *StatPearls* (StatPearls Publishing, 2025), https://www.ncbi.nlm.nih.gov/books/NBK556096.
6. L. Fan et al., "The Influence of Disclosure of an Autism Diagnosis on Peer

Engagement and Interactions for a Child with Autism in Summer Camps: A Case Study," *Disability and Rehabilitation* 44, no. 16 (2022): 4519–30, https://doi.org/10.1080/09638288.2021.1904012.

7. N. Almog, N. Bar, and S. Barkai, "Narratives of Inclusion and Exclusion: Families Between the Medical, Social and Affirmative Models of Disability," in *To Be a Parent of a Child with a Disability: Family as an Active Agent for Social Change in Community and Society,* ed. P. Shavit and O. Gilor, 29–64 (Ach, 2019).
8. I. Singh, "A Disorder of Anger and Aggression: Children's Perspectives on Attention Deficit/Hyperactivity Disorder in the UK," *Social Science and Medicine* 73, no. 6 (2011): 889–96, https://doi.org/10.1016/j.socscimed.2011.03.049.
9. N. Almog, O. Kassel, N. Levy, and T. Gabai, "Mapping the Dilemmas Parents Face with Disclosing Autism Diagnosis to their Child," *Journal of Autism and Developmental Disorders* 53, no. 10 (2023): 4060–75, https://doi.org/10.1007/s10803-022-05711-y; J. Davidson and V. L. Henderson, "'Coming Out' on the Spectrum: Autism, Identity and Disclosure," *Social and Cultural Geography* 11, no. 2 (2010): 155–70, https://doi.org/10.1080/14649360903525240.
10. A. Riccio et al., "How Is Autistic Identity in Adolescence Influenced by Parental Disclosure Decisions and Perceptions of Autism?" *Autism* 25, no. 2 (2020): 374–88, https://doi.org/10.1177/1362361320958214.
11. Arlan Hamilton is a speaker who mainly says this phrase in talks and online. See https://www.instagram.com/reel/DJziCe5ybkv.
12. A. L. Accardo, N. M. H. Pontes, and M. C. F. Pontes, "Heightened Anxiety and Depression Among Autistic Adolescents with ADHD: Findings from the National Survey of Children's Health 2016–2019," *Journal of Autism and Developmental Disorders* 54, no. 2 (2024): 563–76, https://doi.org/10.1007/s10803-022-05803-9.
13. Cleveland Clinic, "Rejection Sensitive Dysphoria (RSD)," https://my.clevelandclinic.org/health/diseases/24099-rejection-sensitive-dysphoria-rsd.

Index

ABOUT THE AUTHOR

EMILY W. KING, PhD, is a licensed child psychologist, speaker, and parent educator with a doctorate in school psychology and more than twenty years of experience working with neurodivergent children and teens. She is the founder of the *Learn with Dr. Emily* Substack and creator of The Neurodiverse Classroom professional development curriculum for K–12 educators. A graduate of the University of North Carolina at Chapel Hill, Dr. King keynotes conferences; conducts workshops for parents, educators, and clinicians; and consults with schools across the country. She was cited in Penn and Kim Holderness's *New York Times* bestseller *ADHD Is Awesome* and has been published in *Child Today, Journal of Applied Psychology,* and *Exceptional Children.* She lives with her family in Raleigh, North Carolina.